THE GOD WHO IS FOR US

PROCEEDINGS OF THE SCOTTISH DOGMATICS CONFERENCE

This is the first volume in a new series published by Zondervan Academic. It contains the proceedings of the inaugural Scottish Dogmatics Conference (SDC) held under the auspices of the Department of Divinity at the University of Aberdeen in May 2024. The SDC was conceived as a sister conference to the Los Angeles Theology Conference (LATC), yet with its own identity and rooted in a European context. Like the LATC, the SDC seeks to fructify contemporary systematic and constructive theology by showcasing new work in the field from a range of scholars representing different communions of the Christian faith and different geographical contexts. It is hoped that this will complement other theological conferences (including the LATC) and continue the historic Scottish tradition of work in Christian dogmatics.

OLIVER D. CRISP AND
PAUL T. NIMMO, EDITORS

THE GOD WHO IS FOR US

Explorations in Constructive Dogmatics

CONTRIBUTORS

John Behr • Bruce L. McCormack • Amy Peeler • Fred Sanders • Judith Wolfe

To the memory of Prof. Dr. Jürgen Moltmann,
theologian of the God who is for us

ZONDERVAN ACADEMIC

The God Who Is for Us

Published by Zondervan, 3950 Sparks Drive SE, Suite 101, Grand Rapids, MI 49546, USA. Zondervan is a registered trademark of The Zondervan Corporation, L.L.C., a wholly owned subsidiary of HarperCollins Christian Publishing, Inc.

Requests for information should be addressed to customercare@harpercollins.com.

Zondervan titles may be purchased in bulk for educational, business, fundraising, or sales promotional use. For information, please email SpecialMarkets@Zondervan.com.

ISBN 978-0-310-17390-8 (softcover)
ISBN 978-0-310-17391-5 (ebook)

HarperCollins Publishers, Macken House, 39/40 Mayor Street Upper, Dublin 1, D01 C9W8, Ireland (https://www.harpercollins.com)

Cover design: LUCAS Art & Design
Cover image: © Grant Faint / Getty Images
Interior design: Kait Lamphere

Printed in the United States of America

25 26 27 28 29 30 31 32 33 34 35 /TRM/ 15 14 13 12 11 10 9 8 7 6 5 4 3 2 1

CONTENTS

ACKNOWLEDGMENTS

The editors would like to thank Paula Duncan, a PhD candidate in divinity at the University of Aberdeen, without whom the running of the inaugural SDC would have been much more arduous and much less smooth. Harvey Cawdron provided additional administrative support in St. Mary's College, University of St. Andrews—our thanks also to him. The Zondervan Academic team (Z-team) were a joy to work with: Katya Covrett as publisher and David McNutt as senior acquisitions editor were as much a part of this project as the editors, and we are immensely grateful for their help, support, and advice along the way. Matt Estel has been an exemplary copyeditor; our work would have been much more tedious without his assistance. We would also like to thank the Department of Divinity and the University of Aberdeen for hosting the conference in May 2024, in the beautiful surroundings of King's College, and the Hope Trust for their gracious support. We expect the next conference in 2026 to be in St. Mary's College, University of St. Andrews.

We dedicate this inaugural volume of the proceedings of the Scottish Dogmatics Conference to the recently passed Prof. Dr. Jürgen Moltmann. We recall with appreciation and admiration his timely and inspiring contributions to the work of Christian dogmatics over several decades and his prophetic voice not only in the academy but also in the church.

LIST OF CONTRIBUTORS

John Behr—is Regius Professor of Humanity in the University of Aberdeen. He holds a BA from the University of Greenwich, an MPhil and DPhil from the University of Oxford, and a DD, h.c., from the University of Melbourne.

Oliver D. Crisp—is Professor of Analytic Theology and codirector of the Logos Institute in the University of St. Andrews. He received his BD, MTh, LLM, and DLitt degrees from the University of Aberdeen, and a PhD from the University of London.

Preston McDaniel Hill—is assistant professor of integrative theology and director of the doctor of ministry program at Richmont Graduate University. He completed an MLitt in analytic and exegetical theology from the University of St. Andrews where he also did his PhD in divinity.

Danielle W. Jansen—is a postdoctoral fellow at the University of St. Andrews. She earned a BS in political science at the University of Oregon, a ThM at Dallas Theological Seminary, and a PhD in divinity at the University of St. Andrews.

Mark R. Lindsay—is Joan F. W. Munro Professor of Historical Theology at Trinity College Theological School in the University of Divinity, Australia. He received his BA, graduate diploma in theology, master of Christian doctrine, and PhD from the University of Western Australia.

Sara Mannen—is the McDonald-Agape Research Fellow in Systematic Theology at the University of Aberdeen. She earned a BS in biblical studies and an MA in theological studies both from Multnomah University, and a PhD in divinity from the University of Aberdeen.

Bruce L. McCormack—holds the Chair in Modern Theology in the University of Aberdeen and is Charles Hodge Professor of Theology Emeritus, Princeton Theological Seminary, where he taught for many years. He received his BA from Point Loma Nazarene University, his MDiv from Nazarene Theological Seminary, his PhD from Princeton

Theological Seminary, and a DTheol h.c., from the Friedrich-Schiller University of Jena in Germany.

Dolores G. Morris—is associate professor of instruction in the Department of Philosophy, University of South Florida. She received a BA in English and a BA in philosophy from Franklin and Marshall College and a PhD in philosophy from the University of Notre Dame.

Paul T. Nimmo—holds the King's Chair of Systematic Theology at the University of Aberdeen. He holds an MA from the University of Cambridge, an MTh from Princeton Theological Seminary, and a BD and PhD from New College, University of Edinburgh.

Amy Peeler—is the Kenneth T. Wessner Professor of New Testament at Wheaton College. She received a BA in biblical languages from Oklahoma Baptist University and an MDiv and PhD from Princeton Theological Seminary in biblical studies.

Lucy Peppiatt—is president of Westminster Theological Centre, where she also teaches systematic theology. She earned a BA in English literature at the University of Birmingham, a BD from the University of London, an MA in systematic theology from King's College, London, and a PhD in theology from the University of Otago.

Fred Sanders—is professor of theology in the Torrey Honors College, Biola University. He earned a BA in fine arts from Murray State University, an MDiv from Asbury Theological Seminary, and a PhD from the Graduate Theological Union, Berkeley.

Sarah Shin—is part-time lecturer at Westminster Theological Centre. She holds a BS and a master's in city planning from the Massachusetts Institute of Technology, an MA in theology from Gordon-Conwell Theological Seminary, an MLitt in analytic and exegetical theology from the University of St. Andrews, and a PhD in divinity from the University of Aberdeen.

John Swinton—is professor of practical theology at the University of Aberdeen. He holds a BD and PhD in divinity from Aberdeen, is a registered mental nurse (RMN) and a registered nurse for people with learning disabilities (RNMD) in the Scottish National Health Service, and is a Fellow of the Royal Society of Edinburgh (FRSE) as well as a Fellow of the British Academy (FBA).

Judith Wolfe—is professor of philosophical theology at the University of St. Andrews. She holds a BA from the Hebrew University in Jerusalem as well as an MPhil in English literature and an MA and DPhil in theology from the University of Oxford.

INTRODUCTION

OLIVER D. CRISP AND PAUL T. NIMMO

In Romans 8, Paul famously remarks, "If God is for us, who is against us?" (Rom 8:31).[1] At the close of this passage, and in response to his own question, he concludes: "For I am convinced that neither death, nor life, nor angels, nor rulers, nor things present, nor things to come, nor powers, nor height, nor depth, nor anything else in all creation will be able to separate us from the love of God in Christ Jesus our Lord" (Rom 8:38–39). The connection between divine intention and accomplishment in salvation in this passage could hardly be clearer. The God who saves is the God who is *for us*—supremely demonstrated in the person and work of Jesus Christ.

The Christian confession that "God is for us" is a simple one, but one which nevertheless—as this volume demonstrates—touches upon a whole host of theological questions, with particular purchase upon issues in theology proper, Christology and soteriology, and anthropology. Central to these questions are issues of identity and agency. First, who is the "God" who is for us? To speak of the God of Israel or the God who raised Jesus from the dead is a welcome start. But theological issues arise directly downstream of such identification. On the one hand, there is a prominent dogmatic concern to ensure that God's being for us is no arbitrary or capricious decision of the divine, one that might easily have been otherwise. On the other hand, there is also a frequent doctrinal desire, albeit one increasingly questioned, to affirm that God's freedom and aseity are not jeopardized in being irrevocably for us. In the theological terrain around these complexities range a whole host of enquiries into the attributes or perfections of this God who is for us. Second, who is the "us" whom God is for? Again, straightforward answers seem to lie close at hand in the tradition: the church, the communion of saints. Yet this question has taken on additional resonance in recent theological work, where there

1. Unless otherwise noted, Bible quotations from this introduction come from the NRSVue.

is a growing discomfort regarding the practice of drawing lines of inclusion and exclusion, as well as a growing awareness of the ways Christian assurance can be rendered problematic by the shock of traumatic events or by the experience of divine absence. And third, how is the God who is for us *actually* for us? Certainly, one can reach swiftly for the answer of incarnation. Yet how to conceive the incarnation within the divine economy, how to parse its embodied and gendered nature, how to conceive its efficacy and its consequences—all these further questions continue to occupy theologians.

This symposium of new essays on Christian dogmatics takes up Paul's theme of God for us and, in service of further consideration of precisely questions such as these, presses it in new directions. It does so from a range of confessional perspectives and through a variety of diverse voices, brought together by the seriousness with which they seek to take the witness of Scripture and the respect with which they—albeit sometimes in critical vein—approach the tradition passed on within the communion of saints that is the church. In the process, they seek not only to offer answers to some of these perennial questions of theology but also to pose new ones: the work of Christian dogmatics is never finished—at least, not this side of eternity.

Overview of the Chapters

In the first chapter, Fred Sanders focuses on how God is God *for God*. This is a matter of the immanent or ontological life of God as it were, or God in Godself. Before we can ask questions about how God may be for us as creatures, it is important to consider the relation of God to Godself. Traditionally, this has been cast in terms of divine qualities or attributes such as divine aseity, inseity, and proseity. These are the focus of Sanders's attention, who provides an evangelical perspective on these vital aspects or perfections of the divine nature and distinguishes as conceptually primary this approach to the divine nature over those approaches that assimilate divine aseity to "pronobeity," that is, to the idea that God is for us.

In chapter 2, Judith Wolfe considers how it is that creatures, especially human creatures, have been fashioned for communion and union with Godself. The title of her essay, "Thou Hast Made Us for Thyself," intimates this. And throughout the essay Augustine's remark in his *Confessions* serves as a kind of leitmotif. Human lives are made up of desires. The right ordering of such desire must mean setting in the appropriate context, which Wolfe takes to be the divine life. Our earthly desires make sense and are achievable only as they are part of some greater desire to which they point, namely, communion and union with God. This entails an account of what it means for us to be made for God and for union and communion with God in this life as well as more perfectly in the world to come. If the first chapter is really about matters touching the divine nature in abstraction from the question of creation, this chapter is concerned with the outworking of God's creative initiative in the lives of those created and fashioned for life everlasting.

In the third chapter, "The God Who Is for Us as God with Us," Lucy Peppiatt explores the theme of God for us as God with us through the Trinitarian lens of Romans 8:14–17. She pays particular attention to the idea that the Spirit cowitnesses (συμμαρτυρεῖ) with our spirits that we are children of God. Peppiatt proposes that Paul's use of the concept of cowitness alongside the prevalence of the *syn-* compounds in these four verses indicates that bearing witness is more than merely a verbal affirmation of a particular truth. Here Paul describes the *establishment* of a truth within the believer's spirit such that the believer themselves is then empowered to witness to the same truth about themselves. In light of this, Peppiatt contends that the witness of the Spirit is not merely an extrinsic declaration of the new status of the follower of Christ as a child of God but is a work of God that establishes a corresponding knowledge within the believer's own spirit that they are children and heirs of their heavenly Father. She goes on to argue that Paul sees precisely this work of the Spirit as the foundation of the Christian life in that it empowers the believer to participate in the divine life in and through Christ.

In chapter 4, Dolores Morris considers the relation of the God who is for us to the question of divine hiddenness—a hot topic in recent philosophical theology, indebted to the seminal work of philosopher J. L. Schellenberg. She explores what she characterizes as the tension between the God who is for us and suffered alongside us and the God who sometimes seems to hide from us in the midst of our suffering. Christian philosophers sometimes treat suffering and hiddenness as objections to be overcome. But Morris favors a different approach. Defending the rationality of theism is an admirable philosophical task, but it is not an *end point*; it is a beginning. Any Christian philosophical account of who God is and who we are must be reconcilable with the following facts: we suffer, and God knows; we feel abandoned, and God knows; we long for answers that we often do not receive, and the God who has those answers knows.

Scripture affirms this; we should too. Drawing on the work of several recent scholars concerned with this apparent conflict between a hidden and revealed deity (such as Charity Anderson and Michael Rea), Morris sketches a plan for a philosophically rich theology of tension.

Chapter 5, written by Sara Mannen, is focused on divine knowledge and, specifically, how the question of divine omniscience fares in our modern age of surveillance capitalism. The age we live in is marked by constant and unavoidable surveillance, either through corporate digital surveillance or the increasing surveillance programs of our governments. The algorithms of Amazon, Google, and Facebook function as a faux-capitalistic omniscience that knows far more about us than we would care to admit. Mannen's chapter seeks to rethink the doctrine of God's omniscience *for us* in a world shaped by surveillance that benefits from knowledge of us while mimicking omniscience. She builds on the work of Katherine Sonderegger and Karl Barth to construct a theology of divine omniscience rooted in God's personal nature as *Deus pro nobis*. Sonderegger provocatively claims that God "*respects* us and our inner life, our privacy."[2] While such claims might be contentious, her emphasis that omniscience is *personal* provides the vital first step in a constructive doctrine of divine knowledge. Based on Barth's theology of the doctrine of God, Mannen considers God's being and omniscience as radically for us and our benefit to counter the world's narrative of an "omniscient corporation" that benefits itself to our detriment.

In the sixth chapter, Danielle W. Jansen considers the paradoxical idea of God as both impassible and yet personal. In much of the Christian tradition, it has been argued that God is both immutable or unchanging, as well as impassible, that is, incapable of suffering. Yet, it is said, God is personal. Recent systematic theology has tended to go in a rather different direction, arguing that God is both changeable and has an emotional life that enables God to be responsive to the creature—indeed this is now a kind of orthodoxy in much contemporary theology. In this chapter, Jansen sets out and defends an alternative to these accounts. She argues for two major claims. First, she affirms that God is without emotions *altogether*—it is a category mistake to impute an emotional life to God. Using recent work in cognitive psychology, Jansen argues that emotions are an entirely human experience and process, whereas the divine has no need for such

2. Katherine Sonderegger, *Systematic Theology*, vol. 1, *The Doctrine of God* (Minneapolis: Fortress, 2015), 362.

processes. Second, she shows that this does not mean God is *im*personal. In fact, God can and does relate to the creature through the use of psychological language that communicates divine values and judgments, reflecting God's commitment and personal involvement in the lives of humankind. Thus, although God has no emotions, the Deity is still personal; God is still *for us*.

Chapter 7 turns from matters pertaining to the divine nature and God's relation to the created order in general to the more particular questions surrounding the action of God in the incarnation and work of Christ. The first chapter in this section is by Bruce McCormack, on God as kenotic love—a matter that is central to his own constructive theological project, the first volume of which recently appeared with Cambridge University Press.[3] His chapter is a kind of thought experiment, as he puts it, which sets out in an exploratory way some of the ideas he is developing in the second volume of his trilogy. This second installment will be concerned principally with the doctrine of the Trinity. It is the divine life, understood through a christological lens and articulated in dialogue with Karl Barth, Eberhard Jüngel, and Alexandra Pârvan, that McCormack unfolds in this fascinating, constructive, and post-Chalcedonian account of theology proper.

Chapter 8 concerns modern predicaments and ancient paradigms for thinking and speaking about the doctrine of the incarnation—the supreme instance of God being "for us." John Behr considers these matters in the context of patristic theology, especially the work of Athanasius, which he places in conversation with the recent proposal of Ingolf Dalferth that involves a "restructuring" of the grammar of Christology. Behr's contention is that, despite some differences, there is a deep resonance between Athanasius and Dalferth in that both theologians paint a picture of the person and work of Christ wherein the "Son of God, Word, Lord and Savior is always already the one who was crucified and raised from the dead by God." It is the crucified and risen Christ, not the Jesus of history, that is the subject of christological statements. What is more, Behr contends, the Greek Fathers tended to think that the "birth" of Christian martyrs was to be marked by the day of their death, when they are "born" into everlasting life. Similarly, Christ is "born" through his death by means of which he is the "firstborn from the dead." This connection

3. See Bruce Lindley McCormack, *The Humility of the Eternal Son: Reformed Kenoticism and the Repair of Chalcedon,* Current Issues in Theology (Cambridge: Cambridge University Press, 2021).

between the passion and birth of Christ presents quite a different picture of the incarnation than that often thought to be the upshot of classical Christology.

In chapter 9, Amy Peeler takes up the question of incarnation from a different perspective, focusing on the epistle to the Galatians, and drawing on feminist biblical interpretation.[4] This time the doctrine is considered in terms of God being "labored." That is, God in becoming flesh is brought into the world to bring about human salvation that yields freedom and discipleship. God's freedom in Galatians is expressed in terms of a freedom to serve, which is just what the incarnation is about. It is not that God acts in redemption from compulsion or obligation; rather, God acts in gracious freedom and according to the divine good pleasure to bring about salvation through Christ. God chooses that Christ be "born of a woman," thereby partnering with that woman to bring about the incarnation. What is more, Peeler notes the trope of pregnancy features elsewhere in the epistle, with the apostle himself taking on the role of birthing Christ in the lives of the Galatians. Gender language is used in complex ways to indicate the manner in which all are included within the ambit of Christ's saving work, both literally and figuratively. This inclusion of Jew, gentile, slave, free, men, and women (Gal 3:28–29) yields an opportunity for discipleship within which Christ may be birthed in others too. Thus, in Galatians, the God who is for us is also "freely for *all* of us."

The tenth chapter is also concerned with Christology, specifically with how it may help us to think about the difficult question of trauma, which has been an important topic of recent theological scrutiny. Preston McDaniel Hill and John Swinton together tackle these matters by means of the lens of what they describe as *promeitic Christology*. Christological promeity—Christ being "for me"—signals a specific type of divine proseity stemming from Protestant theologies of salvation that calls for subjective value judgments and contextual appropriations in the retrieval and construction of Christian doctrine. This chapter explores trauma as an emblematic modern context and undertakes a theological retrieval of dogmatic resources from Protestant soteriologies to articulate a posttraumatic promeitic Christology. Who is Jesus Christ for us today in trauma? Reformation interpretations of Christ's descent into hell are identified as promising dogmatic sources from which to resource a modern promeitic Christology for contexts of trauma and spiritual struggles. In particular,

4. See also Amy Peeler, *Women and the Gender of God* (Grand Rapids: Eerdmans, 2022).

the chapter explores the cry of dereliction (drawing from Calvin and Moltmann) as an experience of traumatic disbelief in divine goodness to suggest a generative tension between faith and doubt that falls within the purview of normative human experience in the economy of salvation. If God is for us in Christ, and Christ experienced disbelief in divine goodness, then traumatic experiences of divine hiddenness or disbelief are not necessarily evidence of an absence of saving faith in the life of survivors.

Chapter 11 moves from Christology to soteriology. Sarah Shin returns to the work of the influential twentieth-century Scandinavian Lutheran bishop Gustaf Aulén to consider whether and to what extent his account of the atonement, presented in the classic text *Christus Victor* (1931), may still be a resource for constructive theology today. Although Aulén is widely known for his proposal of the *Christus victor* idea of atonement, less well-known is his claim that atonement is not only a once-and-for-all accomplished work but also *ongoing* through the Spirit. This chapter summarizes Aulén's account of atonement as both accomplished in the one-time act of Christ's redemptive work and ongoing in God's dramatic battle and victory over evil; it also suggests that this view yields fruitful possibilities for eschatology and ethics. Shin demonstrates how Aulén locates the believer's contemporaneity with Christ in atonement—the ongoing work of the Spirit through the church. She addresses how Aulén presents the reality of ongoing sin and evil, in *this* time and *this* place, and proposes that Aulén's account possesses at least two valuable elements for constructive theology. First, Aulén's creative rendering of atonement as ongoing offers an account of God's activity for us, here and now, as the believer faces suffering, evil, and challenges. Second, ongoing atonement helps to make room for a view of human participation in God's delivering activity for us today and orients that participation towards an eschatological horizon and ethic that robustly resist evil in the present.

In the twelfth and final chapter, Mark Lindsay tackles the difficult question of the scope of God's work for creatures. The claim that God is "for us" has typically been understood to offer a description of the divine nature. Controversies, when they have arisen, have largely focused on the question of whether God's "for-us-ness" is an eternally constitutive determination of God's being or a logically subsequent and therefore secondary aspect of God's aseity. What has been less intensely examined is the constitution of the "us" who is in this phrase envisioned. Who precisely is the *us* for whom God *is*? Whether one answers this from the perspective of particularist atonement theories or from a confessional ecclesiology, the oft-unstated consequence is that the "us" obscures but also implies an equally necessary "them" for whom God is logically *not.* As Gil Anidjar, Edward Said, and others have shown, "the enemy"—the "them" in this case—resides as a perpetually necessary figure in the Christian imaginary of the "us." Indeed, the history of the Christian churches has demonstrated that this enemy is reified not simply as those outside the ecclesial boundaries but frequently also as those *within.* Critically engaging this motif of necessary enmity, the chapter explores the constitution of the "them" and asks what the dogmatic consequence of this might be for contemporary ecclesiology.

As the essays in this volume demonstrate, lively and constructive work in dogmatics that makes responsible use of the Christian tradition while pursuing new avenues of research and reflection is alive and well—in Europe as much as in North America or Australasia. We send these essays out into the world in the hope that they may enrich discussion of these important topics in the academy and in the churches and do so in the Anselmian spirit of *fides quaerens intellectum*, "faith seeking understanding."

Prof. Oliver D. Crisp, St. Mary's College, University of St. Andrews
Prof. Paul T. Nimmo, King's College, University of Aberdeen
September 2024

CHAPTER 1

GOD IS GOD FOR GOD

Aseity, Inseity, and Proseity in Evangelical Perspective

FRED SANDERS

Christian theology has a primary commission, which is to clarify and elaborate the truth that God is for us (Rom 8:31). As for what we traditionally call dogmatic theology, or dogmatics, its commission is to test the content of the church's message by continuously examining it according to the criterion of Scripture.[1] This is a mildly Barthian way of describing the old traditional meaning of the word *dogmatics*, as deployed in a particular academic tradition, a tradition which picks up from ancient Greek the word *dogma*, or judgements held to be true and confessionally binding, then transforms it through the Latin and later Germanic trick of turning words into subject headings for university study by adding plural *-ics* to the ending: ethics, homiletics, dogmatics. Those of us who continue to use the word *dogmatic* in this venerable sense are well advised to bear in mind that to all the rest of our contemporaries, *dogmatic* now simply means hard-headed, bellicose, unpersuadable, and authoritarian. A word that once picked out something doctrinal now flags the speaker as doctrinaire. So a little extra work of paraphrase or translation may be necessary to ensure clear communication. But also, as we undertake the theological ministry of testing the church's message by the criterion of Scripture, we should make it our business not to further cloud the etymology by being ourselves hard-headed, bellicose, unpersuadable, and authoritarian. We ought to do dogmatics (old denotation) without being dogmatic (new connotation).

These remarks are partly an apologetic for contributing what must read as a rather strident chapter title to this volume. A book on "the God

1. "As a theological discipline, dogmatics is the scientific test to which the Christian Church puts herself regarding the language about God which is peculiar to her." Karl Barth, *Church Dogmatics*, 1/1, 2nd ed., trans. G. W. Bromiley (Edinburgh: T&T Clark, 1975), 3.

who is for us" now includes the insistence that, on the other hand, God is in fact God for God. It may read as if I am offering a counterslogan provoked by the proposed slogan, with an intention to protest or contradict. But fear not. The present chapter is not a slogan versus a slogan because the goal of our instruction is not to force an exclusive choice between alternatives. Rather, the goal is to guide us toward a deeper understanding and a right ordering of these two necessary confessions, both strongly urged upon Christian theology by God's self-revelation: God is for us, and God is God for God.

The dogmatic assertion that God is God for God is a doubly recursive statement, conspicuously self-referential. By triply repeating the divine monosyllable in the most cramped quarters possible, it risks the logical offense of mere tautology. But it also risks inducing semantic satiation, that repetitive stress injury of the ear and mind caused by hearing the same word too many times in a row. Under pressure of repetition, in semantic satiation sound and sense dissociate and refuse to keep keeping company; you wonder where the word went.

We will accept the risk of semantic satiation, because in order to say what needs to be said about God and salvation, we must use the word *God* quite a bit, but not in vain. I could state my basic thesis with maximal compression: The God who is for us is God for God; or, God is God for us for God. This has the virtue of being concise, but it has almost no other virtue. Instead of proceeding further down that line, let us sneak up on the key insight, using a strategy of synonyms, conceptual paraphrases, and fruitful redescriptions.

This chapter has three main movements. First, we will describe the particular kind of self-referentiality that is appropriate for responsible speech about God, a self-referentiality that I call *auto*-discourse. From this perspective, second, we will engage the modern retrieval of the doctrine of divine aseity and will do so by invoking the less familiar terms inseity and proseity. And third, against this necessary background, we will consider the soteriological vision of the God who is for us.

I. GODSELF: HOW *AUTO*-DISCOURSE FUNCTIONS IN THE DOCTRINE OF GOD

Verbal repetition is not the only conceptual option in the doctrinal toolkit for theologians seeking to speak well of God, nor even the most basic. Another important strategy is what we might call *auto*-discourse, or any form of speech that fills out the doctrine of God by directing our attention back to the subject itself. *Auto*-discourse makes constant use of locutions about God in himself, or Godself. God is goodness itself, truth itself, beauty itself, and so on. Because it often proceeds by taking up a series of words (goodness, truth, beauty, and so on), *auto*-discourse is a form of speech that can dramatically multiply the categories of discourse, for example by enumerating the attributes of God. There is no end to the number of divine perfections that can all be identified in this way, and here dogmatics joins with Charles Wesley in saying to God: "Glad thine attributes [we] confess, glorious all and numberless."[2] In so doing, the opening move of *auto*-discourse can expand the conceptual range of topics being contemplated. Nevertheless, *auto*-discourse's recursive return to God himself means that the expanded conceptual range is always expansion in service of reference back to the singular one about whom we are speaking. God has power, but that power by which God is strong is not some other power, but is God himself. God has wisdom, but is himself the wisdom with which he is wise, and so on.[3] *Auto*-discourse is recognizably a pattern of speech governed by divine simplicity. But since the doctrine of divine simplicity has become the subject of considerable dispute and elaborate distinctions in recent decades,[4] it may be helpful to recognize that the linguistic and conceptual strategy of *auto*-discourse is built into the grammar of the doctrine of God at an utterly primal level. It would be misleading to think of *auto*-discourse as being one grammatical application of a doctrine of divine simplicity; it is more nearly the case that a doctrine of divine simplicity is one of the ways of drawing out and focusing on the implications of the movement of thought expressed by *auto*-discourse.

As an extended example, we can consider a passage from the work of John of Damascus. John serves well both as a classic voice of the Greek patristic tradition, intentionally summarizing what has gone before,[5] and as a highly influential source in turn for later theology, east and west.[6]

---

2. John and Charles Wesley, *Hymns and Sacred Poems* (London: William Strahan, 1739), 129.

3. A classic treatment of this is book 5 of Augustine's *De Trinitate.* Augustine, *The Trinity*, trans. Stephen McKenna (Washington, DC: Catholic University of America Press, 1963), 175–98.

4. Steven J. Duby reviews modern criticisms of the doctrine in his *Divine Simplicity: A Dogmatic Account* (London: Bloomsbury, 2015), 34–53.

5. See Andrew Louth, *St. John Damascene: Tradition and Originality in Byzantine Theology* (Oxford: Oxford University Press, 2002), 16.

6. In addition to John's influence in later Greek theology, his work via Latin translation was important for the Western tradition. Corey Stephan, "Catechisms, Communion, and Latin Scholastic Reception of Byzantine Thought: St. John Damascene's De fide orthodoxa in St. Bonaventure's Breviloquium," *Nova et Vetera* 19, no. 4 (2021): 1215–35.

All roads lead to and from John of Damascus's *On the Orthodox Faith.*[7] This work includes a few long passages on the doctrine of God which are given in the form of lists, and these lists are practically lexicons of all the most important biblical, philosophical, and doctrinal terms that have come to be ingredient to the doctrine of God.[8] In the longest of these passages, John employs four different categories of speech about God and even organizes his list broadly according to them. The four categories are negation, completeness, transcendence, and self-reference. Each is theologically significant and is marked by a characteristic lexical structure.

The negations say what God is not, and they are formed by alpha privatives: *anarchos* for unbeginning; *aktistos* for uncreated; *asuntheton* for uncomposed; *asōmaton* for nonphysical; and so on.[9] Second, the statements of completeness say what God comprehensively is, and they are formed by connection with the prefix *pan-*, for all: filling all things, having power over all things, and so on. Third, the statements of transcendence declare what God exceeds, and they are characteristically formed as *huper-* compounds. Drawing on the Dionysian tradition, John describes God as "superessential and beyond beings, beyond the divine, beyond the good, beyond fullness (*huperousion, hupertheon, huperagathon, huperplērē*) . . . more than essence, life, word, and concept."[10] These *huper*-compounds certainly signal a flying leap into the conceptual beyond. You cannot say much more about God than "beyond the divine . . . more than essence."

But there is another step. Finally, after the alpha privatives, the *pan-* discourse, and the *huper-* prefixes, John turns to a set of self-reference terms, formed by *auto*-compounds: the divine nature is "light itself, goodness itself, life itself, essence itself" (*autophōs, autoagathotēta, autozōēn, autoousion*). What are these *auto*-compounds doing? In part, they follow the path of the knowledge of God by completing the movement upward from created things: God does not have life but is life—life itself. So the relation of God to the notion of life is that he is deathless (alpha privative, *athanaton*), he lacks no life (*pan*-compound, all life), he exceeds the notion

7. John of Damascus, *On the Orthodox Faith: A New Translation of An Exact Exposition of the Orthodox Faith*, trans. Norman Russell (New York: St. Vladimir's Seminary Press, 2022).

8. The two lists occur in sections 2 and 8; see pages 61 and 70–71 of Russell's translation. Russell's bilingual edition makes it much easier to trace John's terminological maneuvers with alpha privatives and *auto-* compounds, which cannot always be translated consistently.

9. Russell points out, in a footnote to the first list, that it "begins with fifteen negative attributes (all beginning in Greek with the privative alpha)." He goes on to identify these as belonging to "the province of apophatic theology," in contrast to the kataphatic elements later in the list, "revealed through the divine economy." Russell, trans., *On the Orthodox Faith*, 61n3. The second list, which we are examining, follows a similar logic but is more complex.

10. John of Damascus, *On the Orthodox Faith*, 71.

of life (*huper*-compound, *hyperzōēn*, more than life), and finally, that he does not just have, but simply is, life itself (*auto*-compound, *autozōēn*).

In this final step,[11] introducing self-reference by way of *auto*-discourse, something new breaks through the veil of conceptual elaboration.[12] To call God "life itself," "goodness itself," and so on is to move on from noting how God relates to each proposed category via negation, perfection, and transcendence, by changing the subject, as it were, back to God himself. We have here the recursive move that settles back into divine identity because there is finally no other referent, no other home. Self-reference is an admission that there really is no other reference point adequate for the task.

By introducing this final, looping movement, John confesses that the knowledge of God returns to its own divine resources because no other resources are adequate to bear witness to God. If the theological question is, "What is God like?" the ultimate answer, when all else is said and done, is simply "God." John expands on this by introducing the notion of measurement, or *metron*. By what standard is God to be measured, known, or evaluated? The answer is either nothing—there is no measure—or else the answer is God: God is his own measure. Accordingly, John calls God "a power unknowable by any standard of measurement, but measured only by his own will—for he can do anything that he wishes—a single principle productive of all created things both visible and invisible."[13]

If God is his own measure, and we are emphatically back where we started and measuring God by God, what have we gained by indulging in this tradition of theological *auto*-discourse? Two things: First, we have gained the conceptual amplitude of touring through all these other categories, and second, we have gained a certain noteworthy density of reference to the divine subject. Recall that *auto*-discourse functions to fill out the doctrine of God by directing our attention back to the subject itself, but with the gain of greater concentration. That concentration or density has the character of an achieved return to God, perhaps with a felt sense of knowing more fully what it means to say God. To say God means to say

---

11. The *auto*- step is final for our purposes, but John's list actually goes on to a series of statements about oneness ("one essence, one divinity, one power," and so on). The immediate reason for this is that the section is about the Trinity, and John is concerned to begin and end with an affirmation of the single principle of deity.

12. See Robert Grant, "The Prefix *Auto*- in Early Christian Theology," in *The Impact of the Church upon Its Culture: Reappraisals of the History of Christianity*, ed. Jerald Brauer (Chicago: Chicago University Press, 1968), 5–16.

13. John of Damascus, *On the Orthodox Faith*, 71.

God is God: Godself, *Idipsum*, the Selfsame.[14] The God who declares himself to be incomparably unique must be spoken of in ways that echo that uniqueness.

The dogmatic rehearsal of the dynamic of divine self-reference is a fruitful and resonant study. Herman Bavinck treated it under the heading of the doctrine of divine independence. What drew his attention to the phenomenon was the way the *auto-* prefix anchored the word *autarkeia* or self-sufficiency. Following this lead, Bavinck noted that "in the East, a number of terms were used" with the same overall thrust. He lists *autoousios* (self-existent), *autotheos* (self-divine), *autophōs* (self-luminous), *autosōphia* (self-wise), *autoarētē* (self-virtuous), and *autoagathos* (self-excellent).[15] Bavinck cites this rich list and draws from the *auto*-phenomenon the main point that "all that God is, he is of himself. By virtue of himself he is goodness, holiness, wisdom, life, light, truth, and so on."[16] Bavinck's list is fuller than any that can be found in any one Greek patristic source, even the encyclopedic sources such as John of Damascus or the patristic catenae. He is in fact drawing from a seventeenth-century reference work, the *Thesaurus Ecclesiasticus* of Johann Caspar Suicer.[17] Suicer devotes sixteen columns to an impressive range of *auto-* compound words gathered from Greek patristic texts, providing running references to the sources: Athanasius, Dionysius, Gregory Nazianzen, Chrysostom, and more. His standard way of rendering the Greek compounds in Latin is with the reflexive words *per se* or *ipsa*: *autohagiotes* is *per se sanctitas*, holiness per se; *autoadamas* is *ipssissimus adamas*, actually invincible; *autoalētheia* is *ipsa veritas*, truth itself. The point is that the early Christian traditions represented in this lexical survey considered all divine perfections, and indeed all good things, to be ways of referring back to God as the one source, measure, and meaning of

---

14. For stimulating analysis of idipsum (self-same, identical), see Jean-Luc Marion, "Idipsum: The Name of God According to Augustine," in *Orthodox Readings of Augustine*, ed. George Demacopoulos and Aristotle Papanikolaou (Crestwood, NY: St. Vladimir's Seminary Press, 2008), 167–89, and, disagreeing with Marion on some crucial metaphysical judgements, Lewis Ayres, *Augustine and the Trinity* (Oxford: Oxford University Press, 2010), 196–203.

15. Herman Bavinck, *Reformed Dogmatics*, four volumes, ed. John Bolt, trans. John Vriend (Grand Rapids: Baker Academic, 2003–2008), volume II, 151. In the Dutch original, Bavinck gives only the Greek words without translation. It is the English editors who provide the translations that take on the form "self-wise" and "self-luminous," whereas Bavinck may well have thought constructions like "wisdom itself" or "light itself" were equally appropriate. The next sentences show how Bavinck paraphrases in Dutch and in Latin the intent of the self-referential phenomenon of the Greek words: "God is al wat Hij is door zichzelf. Hij is ipsa per se bonitas, sanctitas, sapiential, vita, lux, veritas, etc." Bavinck, *Gereformeerde Dogmatiek*, 4 vols., 3rd ed. (Kampen: Kok, 1918), 2:117.

16. Bavinck, *Reformed Dogmatics*, 2:151.

17. Suicer's German name is Schweizer, which yields the Latin Suicerus (1620–1684). *Tesaurus ecclesiasticus, e patribus Græcis ordine alphabetico exhibens*, 2nd ed., vol. 1 (Amsterdam: Wetstonios and Smith, 1728), s.v. *autarkeia*.

them all. The cultivation of the *auto*-compound strategy not only serves to provide a few linguistic tools for echoing divine self-referentiality but actually makes it possible to requisition the entire vocabulary of meaningful nouns as redirections toward God's unique identity. The unique goal of *auto*- compounds is not to compare God with other things directly but to use other things to compare God with God.

When we call *auto*-discourse a linguistic tool for echoing divine self-referentiality, we are skirting one of the possible implications of God's self-naming in Exodus 3:14: Whatever else is involved in the locution "I am that I am," there is at least a repetition that indicates self-reference. The God who cannot be successfully compared to or comprehended by other things identifies himself by verbally placing himself in correspondence with himself. The metaphysical interpretation of this revealed name has had a dominant role in its theological understanding: "I am" refers to he who is. But whatever we decide about the being verbs (their tense, their translation, their possible ontological thickness or metaphysical entailments), the repetition and correspondence itself establishes some kind of metaphysic. It is an expression of the being and identity of God made known by first-person recursive self-reference: I am that I am. *Auto*-discourse echoes that self-reference in the indicative mode, within a kind of metaphysical frame.[18] Indeed, the prefix *auto*- has often been translated as the adjective *absolute*, so that *autoagathos* means that God is goodness absolute, or absolute goodness. The justification for this translation is that it draws a distinction between things which are only relatively good, strong, or wise, and the one reality which is all of these things not with reference to anything outside of it that would render it relative but with reference to itself alone: absolutely.

Making explicit this notion of absoluteness is what pushes *auto*-discourse into the realm of metaphysics. The term *metaphysics* raises a number of issues, so I hasten to point out that there is no particular package of school-metaphysics that I am linking up with. Readers familiar with the recent discussion of "prepositional metaphysics" in the intellectual milieu of the New Testament may well note some similarities to the way *auto*-discourse participates in an ancient metaphysical tradition according

18. We could say something here about how the Euthyphro problem yields to the dynamic of divine self-correspondence, which is also part of the puzzle of worship: What is the meaning of calling God good? The English word *worship* is etymologically descended from "worth," or ascribing value to God as judging him in comparison to some other standard. But that is impossible. True worship has a transcendent meaning that is non-trivially tautological.

to its own idiom.[19] In Greco-Roman antiquity there was an intellectual tradition of speaking of the ultimate nature of reality using an integrated series of prepositions: all things are from something, by something, through something, and for something. A philosophically alert ancient writer could discourse about ultimate issues by means of a recognizable pattern of calling out those humble little words, the prepositions, without necessarily deploying any of the more obviously technical terminology of Platonic, Aristotelian, or Stoic philosophical schools. If this line of argument is correct, then we can recognize prepositional metaphysics in key New Testament passages such as John 1:3, 10; 1 Corinthians 8:6; Colossians 1:15–20; and Hebrews 1:2. *Auto*-discourse is metaphysical in a sense very much like that, staking its claims by pressing a relation of identity to the absolute.

We have mainly surfaced *auto*-discourse to think more comprehensively about aseity. Before turning from *auto*-discourse to aseity proper, two further implications of *auto*- discourse are worth noting more explicitly. The first is christological; the second is Trinitarian. The christological point is as follows: Origen of Alexandria pioneered the use of auto- compounds for articulating the deity of Christ. In his commentary on Matthew 18, while grappling with the parable that says the kingdom of heaven is "like a certain man who is a king," Origen asserts that it is obviously the Son of God incarnate who is this king, or rather, who is the kingdom itself. To make the point about Christ as the kingdom itself, Origen coins the word *autobasileia*: the absolute kingdom, or the kingdom in person.[20] Furthermore, Origen seeks to persuade his reader to recognize Christ as *autobasileia* by multiplying *auto*- terms: Christ is *autosōphia* and *autodikaiosune*, absolute wisdom and absolute righteousness, so therefore "is he not also *autobasileia*?" Origen obviously expects to increase the plausibility of calling Christ the kingdom itself, the absolute kingdom, or himself the kingdom, by situating the claim within the context of Christ as the one about whom *auto*-discourse can rightly take place.[21] Whether Origen is directly thinking of the Johannine Christ's "I am" statements as

19. Chris Kugler, "Judaism/Hellenism in Early Christology: Prepositional Metaphysics and Middle Platonic Intermediary Doctrine," *Journal for the Study of the New Testament* 43, no. 2 (2020), 214–25. Kugler provides helpful bibliography on previous treatments.

20. *Origen on the Gospel of Matthew*, trans. Ronald E. Heine (Oxford: Oxford University Press, 2018), sec. 14:7; 432.

21. For the more complicated issues that emerge in Origen's widespread use of *auto*- compounds in Trinitarian discourse, see Micah M. Miller, "The *Auto*-X Attributes of the Father and the Son in Origen," *Journal of Theological Studies* 73, no. 1 (2022): 132–66.

he makes this argument in his Matthew commentary may or may not be demonstrable, [22] but we do know he had an imagination powerfully alert to such ontological resonances.[23]

Once we are alert to this christological use of *auto*-discourse and are appropriately sensitized to the powerful implications of the word root *auto-* when used in christological contexts, we will detect it elsewhere. Consider Colossians and Chalcedon. In Colossians 1:18–20, Paul evokes a cosmic Christology precisely by way of the repetition of *autos* as a pronoun. He (*autos*) is the head of the body; he (*autos*) is preeminent in all things; in *autō* the fullness was pleased to dwell, and by *autou* to reconcile all things through the blood of the cross of *autou*. Of course all reputable translations render this close-recurring masculine personal pronoun as simply "he;" he is preeminent, and in him the fullness was pleased to dwell. That is no doubt the sober judgment and the readable option. Sometimes *auto* just means *auto*. But even at the level of rhetorical force, the sheer repetition could be captured by translating it "the same [one]." He is the head; the same is preeminent; in the same the fullness was pleased to dwell. This pattern of rapidly repeated *auto*-references to Christ occurs at the heart of the Chalcedonian definition. Ten times the word *auto* occurs as the document traces its single-subject Christology through the several things that need to be affirmed about this same one: "We teach that Christ is one and the same Son (*hena kai ton auton*), the same perfect in deity, the same perfect in humanity, the same born of the virgin, the same Christ, Son, Lord, Only-begotten," and so on. Indeed, one nineteenth-century translation renders each of these *auto*-occurrences emphatically as "the Self-Same."[24] A simple *he* might carry most of the weight, if Chalcedon were only undertaking to follow the thread of personal continuity from eternity through the life of Jesus. But there may also be a higher continuity to be secured by this *auto* usage. If texts like Colossians and Chalcedon are engaging in *auto*-discourse, then we can almost hear "the Same" as a christological title, and a title that is especially, even uniquely exalted. "Thou art the

22. Interpreters who have wondered about the gap between the Synoptic theology of the kingdom of God and Johannine "I am" theology should consider how this gap is bridged by the notion of *autobasileia*.

23. See Origen on Ephesians 1:1, where he notes that some manuscripts omit "in Ephesus" and simply greet the saints "who are." Encountering this verb of being, he instantly takes up an edifying discourse on these saints who serve "He who is," thereby themselves coming to be truly "those who are." *The Commentaries of Origen and Jerome on St. Paul's Epistle to the Ephesians*, trans. Ronald E. Heine (Oxford: Oxford University Press, 2003), 78.

24. *The Oecumenical Documents of the Faith*, ed. T. Herbert Bindley (London: Methuen, 1899), 297. In this volume, Bindley also uses "Self-Same" in his translation of Cyril's letters and Leo's *Tome*.

same," *su de ho autos ei* (Psalm 102:27 as used christologically in Hebrews 1:12). This is the christological implication of *auto*-discourse.

The Trinitarian implication of *auto*-discourse follows in turn. In the thought-world of Greek patristic theology, it would be uncharacteristic or even unseemly to assert the deity of the Son and the Holy Spirit in isolation. While a theologian might sometimes pick out the Son or the Holy Spirit and then demonstrate their deity by canvassing divine prerogatives, actions, or titles, such a form of argument was never decisive and was rarely used by itself. The more characteristic proof of the deity of the Son and the Holy Spirit pointed not so much toward the things that are beneath these persons in the order of being (the world and everything in it, visible and invisible) but to that which is above all. Consider the Nicene Creed. It certainly asserts the deity of the Son, but it does so precisely by affiliating the Son with the Father: he is *monogenēs* of the Father and of one substance with the Father. The key conceptual move, in other words, is not to look down on all creation and identify the Son as divine by contrast to it, but to look up to the Father and confess that the Son is proper to him. The word *autos* is not used. But the recursive, self-referential movement of thought is there. A judgement has been made that in coming to terms with the Son, we must confess him to be the kind of person who cannot be measured by any measure except the divine measure itself. He is *homoousios*; he is *monogenēs*; this is the measure of this one. Parallel conceptual moves are made in respect of the Holy Spirit, after which the doctrine of God, as Athanasius says, is made perfect in a triad.[25] It is a triad that exceeds every possible measure except itself; this is the Trinitarian application of the claim that God is God.

II. The Province of Aseity, Inseity, and Proseity

As we turn from *auto*-discourse to the doctrine of divine aseity, we trade Greek terms for Latin and move from patristic dialogue partners to later scholasticism, especially Protestant scholasticism. The move involves trade-offs. Though there is a gain in precision and clarity, there is perhaps a loss in power, allusiveness, and resonance. In fact, the reason to have lingered so long over *auto*-discourse is to consolidate as much heft and

25. Athanasius, *Orations Against the Arians* 1:18, in *A Select Library of Nicene and Post-Nicene Fathers*, 2nd series, vol. 4 (New York: Christian Literature Company, 1890), 317.

evocative range as possible in describing God's Godness, before picking up the comparatively sterile tools of more analytic work. *Auto*-discourse is the broad, underexplored field out of which the more focused doctrine of aseity arises.

We can also make one brief remark about terminology: Aseity comes from the Latin roots *a* (from or of) and *se* (self). Aseity is, etymologically, from-self-itude. From-self-itude is not a proper word at all, but even *aseity* remains an unlovely word, never quite fully at home in English and always wearing its scholastic Latin word-origin on its sleeve. But those who use it do so partly because it provides a linguistic tool for pointing recursively to God, to God *a se*. So far this chapter has avoided using *aseity*, so several of its sentences have had to make this recursive gesture using terms like *God in himself*, *God himself*, or *Godself*. We can thank feminist theology for having provided incisive critiques of the *him* in *God himself*. Nobody can read the feminist theological critiques of the twentieth century and continue saying "him" naively or uncritically.[26] Even those of us who maintain the traditional usage on principle do so with less temptation to using the terms literally or univocally. But even more distracting than the *him*- in *himself* is the *-self*. The English word *self* has had, and continues to have, a thriving career that simply bristles with psychological, cultural, and social-scientific presuppositions and implications that are by turns underexamined and overtheorized. When we speak of God himself, do we mean God is, or has, a self? Is the divine self substantial or hypostatic? Does the Trinity have one self or three? And so on! Imagine someone who first encounters these theological discussions about God and salvation, complete with statements about God in himself, and tried to make progress by analyzing the noun *self* along any currently available lines. To this inquirer we would have to explain that we are not using *self* in that manner. We only wanted a word or root that would allow us to point recursively back to the one with whom we have to do. In one sense, we can say that the term *aseity* comes to the rescue: its linguistic coldness gives us another way to point back without conjuring the sources of the self.

Aseity is a doctrine that confesses God's self-existence by denying that God exists from another. If we emphasize this negative aspect of the doctrine, we might well prefer to confess that God is *non ab alio*, not from another. Of course, we would not want to coin or circulate the resulting

26. For a recent survey of some of the issues involved, see Amy Peeler, *Women and the Gender of God* (Grand Rapids: Eerdmans, 2022).

word *nonabaleity*! But that absolute denial of dependence on anything prior is the kernel of aseity. Richard Muller traces in the post-Reformation Reformed scholastics the connection between God having aseity and God being autotheos.[27]

John Webster undertook a spirited retrieval and rehabilitation of the doctrine of aseity in recent decades. Webster appealed to aseity as part of his programmatic resistance to the historicist tendencies of modern thought, which seemed to threaten to naturalize the doctrine of God, bringing theology without remainder into alignment with an exaggerated sense of the immanent dynamics of world process. In a series of essays over several years, Webster sought to rehabilitate doctrines that would give theology the conceptual leverage to confess God transcending those reductions. His studies of several divine perfections (immensity, holiness, eternal generation) contributed to this project, and in due course the notion of divine perfection itself emerged as a master organizing category for his project.[28] But aseity occupied a special place of prominence in his thought[29] because it served as the vantage point for his key insight into confessing a God whose "being is self-originating, self-moving, self-explicating, self-fulfilling."[30] You can sense the full tide of *auto*-discourse turning and flowing into Webster's theology through his retrieval of aseity.

But even as Webster publicly educated himself in how to employ the neglected category of divine aseity for the correction of persistent errors in contemporary theology, he had one eye on a dangerous tendency lurking in the category itself. In modern theology, he noticed, aseity had shown a tendency to drift from its proper place as a statement about God's own perfect life (which Webster characteristically calls "the doctrine of the immanent Trinity and of the triune God's economy of nature and grace"[31])

---

27. Richard A. Muller, *Dictionary of Latin and Greek Theological Terms Drawn Principally from Protestant Scholastic Theology* (Grand Rapids: Baker, 1985), 47.

28. See John Webster, "God's Perfect Life," in *God's Life in Trinity*, ed. Miroslav Volf and Michael Welker (Minneapolis: Fortress, 2006), 143–52, and "Perfection and Participation," in *The Analogy of Being: Invention of the Antichrist or the Wisdom of God?*, ed. Thomas Joseph White (Grand Rapids: Eerdmans, 2011), 379–94.

29. John Webster, "Life in and of Himself," *God Without Measure*, vol. 1, *God and the Works of God* (T&T Clark, 2015), originally published in 2007, with a few differences, as "God's Aseity," in *Realism and Religion: Philosophical and Theological Perspectives*, ed. Michael Scott and Andrew Moore (Aldershot: Ashgate, 2007), 147–62. The best published study of Webster on aseity is Brent Rempel, "'God corresponds to Godself': John Webster's doctrine of God 'after' Karl Barth," *Scottish Journal of Theology* (2023): 164–77. See also the unpublished dissertation of Mark Adams, "The Use of Aseity in the Theology of John Webster" (PhD diss., Christ College, Australian College of Theology, 2022).

30. "God's Perfect Life," 143. Webster is not in fact talking about aseity directly yet in this passage from 2006.

31. Webster, "Life in and of Himself," *God Without Measure*, 1:16.

and instead to occupy a new location on the frontier of the God-world relation in general. Modern theologians (Webster especially points to Samuel Clarke's 1704 account *Demonstration of the Being and Attributes of God*) conceived of aseity as a tool for contrasting God and world, distinguishing absolute from contingent. Webster observes: "With this migration, aseity becomes a 'paired' concept, inseparably attached to and expounded in terms of the contingency of the world. In a curious irony, divine self-existence becomes a derivative concept."[32] Put another way,

> As the function of the concept shifts, its content is adapted accordingly. Aseity becomes less an affirmation of the underived beauty and goodness of God, and more a property which must be ascribed to *deitas* if it is properly to fulfil its function of supporting the contingent. The sheer originality of God's aseity, the perfection and completeness of his existence in and from himself, is in some measure eclipsed, overtaken by a kind of "finite" transcendence or aseity, comparatively rather than absolutely different.[33]

After offering this diagnosis, Webster concludes: "Such is the pathology; the corrective is trinitarian."[34]

What Webster intends by invoking the Trinity here is that the only way to free aseity from its captivity to a merely cosmological or exhaustively apologetic assignment is to redirect its attention to the richness of the inner life of God; that inner life will always be the life of the Father, Son, and Holy Spirit, "for trinitarian teaching offers a conceptual paraphrase of the life of God, both in his inner depth and in his gracious turn to that which is not God."[35] God has aseity not at the boundary between God and world but at the very center of the divine life.

Turning aseity in this direction (from outward to *auto-*, from excursion to recursion) actually entails speaking more properly of inseity rather than aseity. Webster does not make this distinction or use the terminology programmatically, but he does register it and notes in passing that a proper doctrine of aseity, "following the gospel's usage," has in view "inseity as much as aseity."[36] If aseity says that God is not from another, inseity says

---

32. Webster, "Life in and of Himself," 16.
33. Webster, "Life in and of Himself," 18.
34. Webster, "Life in and of Himself," 18.
35. Webster, "Life in and of Himself," 18–19.
36. Webster, "Life in and of Himself," 27. See also the preface Webster added to the 2016 republication of his collection *Confessing God: Essays in Christian Dogmatics II* (London: Bloomsbury

that God is not in another, but in Godself. When Webster first published his aseity essay in 2006, he gave it the title "God's Aseity." When he lightly revised it and republished it in 2015, it bore the new title, "Life in and of Himself." The new title is highly significant. The focus of Webster's consideration of this doctrine is not just "God of himself," which would be the most direct translation of the root words of aseity: of-self-itude. Instead, Webster spoke also of God having life in himself, thereby signaling his intent to retrieve a doctrine of aseity that was materially informed by biblical truth, and even by the actions of God in the gospel. So he no longer speaks only of aseity but also of inseity, and he introduces the two themes in reverse order: "in and of himself" means inseity and then aseity. Finally, Webster indicated a more concrete and material set of considerations by introducing an actual, solid, biblical noun into the title to anchor all the prepositions and pronouns: life. "Life in and of himself" gets at the key point of the doctrine of aseity. Inseity does more positive work than aseity, and Webster fronts it in his title precisely to make the doctrine less formal, more concrete, and more intensely self-referential. Inseity is also more obviously open to Trinitarian elaboration. Conceptual analysis of aseity might involve us in making some careful distinctions about the relations of origin: The Father, as has often been noted, has also a certain hypostatic aseity along with the common essential aseity. But inseity has more to say because it naturally evokes perichoresis. For God to have life in himself points either to the divine essence and its attribute of life or to the mutual in-being and in-living of the three. In fact, a possible justification for retaining aseity as the guide word and explaining it first is that in a carefully ordered Trinitarianism clarity about the divine processions is logically prior to articulating interexistence.

Aseity and its less famous relative inseity thus stand in a certain order with regard to each other. But there is one more word in this recursive triad, and that is *proseity*.[37] The word is even more lightly attested in the theological tradition than inseity, but it is not wholly absent. Bonaventure makes some use of *pro se* formulas in the thirteenth century, but it is not

T&T Clark, 2016), where he says, "The governance of all theological topics by the confession of God's aseity and inseity does not entail the separation of God and creatures, because God's perfection is not self-enclosed, but the ground and cause of his creative, communicative, preserving, and restoring presence." These brief remarks from the new preface (pages ix–x) are important to the interpretation of Webster's work offered by Katherine Sonderegger in "The God-Intoxicated Theology of a Modern Theologian," *International Journal of Systematic Theology* 21, no. 1 (2019), 24–43 (at 36 and 43).

37. Readers who have only ever encountered the word in this chapter can rest assured that proseity is in fact listed in the Oxford English Dictionary, complete with examples.

until the pressures of German idealism begin to be felt that proseity becomes the subject of reflection.[38] Proseity, "for-self-ness," evokes the notion of purpose, of final cause, of what something is for. The Erlangen Lutheran theologian F. H. R. Frank, as part of an extended disagreement with Albrecht Ritschl, drew out the idea of God as the absolutely absolute, who is a se, in se, and pro se.[39] Proseity thus unfolds and displays itself only when certain questions arise about purposes and ends.[40] But following the prompt to take them together as a triad, we can venture to say that these three indicate the source, form, and purpose of the divine life.[41] God is from God, in God, and for God. There is obviously something peculiar about asking what God is for. Even if we are instantly ready to answer with the sharp monosyllables "God is for God," the question itself seems like a category error. But there are three angles of approach that promise some light on proseity.

First, if we glance for a moment at how the triad "from, in, for" functions for creatures, we get some light: Creatures live from, in, and for many things. Creatures flow from a diversity of proximate sources, in a multitude of settings, for a variety of reasons. Even if the chief end of man is to glorify God, humans also have proximate and subordinate ends. We are constituted, located, and intended multifariously. Praise God for dappled things! But when we turn to God, we do not find such a variety of sources, means, and ends. God is from, in, and for God. So aseity, inseity, and proseity marks the creator-creature distinction.

Second, if we expand the sense of *pro* to the full connotations of the classical notion of final causality, we can gather in some related notions. Final causality connotes fulfillment, satisfaction, completion, and perfection. What is God for, in this more capacious sense? In this context, the answer "God" returns a rich enough meditation on the fullness and fruition of divine life that we may feel more justified in having asked it in the first place. An added benefit of considering proseity under the unfurled banner of final causality is that it may be tentatively appropriated to the

38. F. H. R. Frank articulated the triad aseity, inseity, proseity as part of his idiosyncratic theological project, into which we need not investigate very far; it is enough to say that he seemed to be intentionally provoking Ritschl by speaking of the structure of the Absolute, *System der christlichen Wahrheit*, volume 1 (Erlangen: Deichert, 1878).

39. F. H. R. Frank, *Zur Theologie A. Ritschl's*, third edition (Erlangen und Leipzig: Deichert, 1891).

40. Proseity shows up in theological cultures that have developed a way of talking that has salvation history in view as well as universal history.

41. See Andrew Davison, *Participation in God: A Study in Christian Doctrine and Metaphysics* (Cambridge: Cambridge University Press, 2019) for a careful discussion of the Trinitarian appropriation of these three forms of causation.

Holy Spirit, as the one to whom consummation is appropriated due to his location in the Trinitarian taxis as third. From this vantage point, there is reason to think of efficient cause as appropriated to the Father as source (from whom), formal cause to the Son (through whom), and final cause to the Holy Spirit (in whom or to whom).

Third, there has emerged a characteristically Barthian and Bonhoefferian way of speaking about the action of God for us as being a manifestation of divine promeity, sometimes pluralized to pronobeity, God-for-us-ness. In a field where divine pronobeity has become a way of framing questions, divine proseity is also helpful as a placeholder for a contrasting emphasis or direction. God is God for us: pronobeity. But God is also already God for God: proseity.

Are pronobeity and proseity both to be reckoned among the divine perfections? If the two are mutually exclusive, we will be required by the iron laws of logic to make a choice between them. But if not, then much in theology depends on rightly ordering our understanding of them. By investing heavily in *auto*-discourse to develop out of it a confession of aseity and inseity, God's life in and of himself, I hope to have secured a place of priority for proseity. I propose that God is for God, being and living and acting for himself. In freely undertaking creation and redemption, God in his wisdom makes a way to put us and our need in between himself and himself, outflanking us and surrounding us with his own purposes. Thereby he enfolds his purposes for us within his own proseity. God defends his justice, and enacts our justification on the way. He cannot deny himself, and so he remains true to us along the way. His wisdom and glory are enacted for our instruction and glorification. Athanasius narrates the way the human project misfires and suggests the emergence of divine dilemmas, and ponders, "What is God to do?" The answer is that God successfully seeks our good along the way to maintaining his right. He enters into his rest and summons us to join him in it. Creation itself is a case of God lodging us firmly into his own best interests. In many ways and in many portions, God refers perpetually back to himself, looping us perpetually into that recursive *auto*-discourse, for God's glory and our good.

CHAPTER 2

"THOU HAST MADE US FOR THYSELF"

JUDITH WOLFE

> "You are great, Lord, and highly to be praised: great is your power and your wisdom is immeasurable." Man, a little piece of your creation, desires to praise you, a human being "bearing his mortality with him," carrying with him the witness of his sin and the witness that you "resist the proud." Nevertheless, to praise you is the desire of man, a little piece of your creation. You stir man to take pleasure in praising you, because you have made us for yourself, and our heart is restless until it rests in you.
>
> —AUGUSTINE, *CONFESSIONS* 1.1[1]

INTRODUCTION: BIBLICAL ORIENTATION

That God is for us is implied in the very first precepts of Christian theology, namely that God made us out of nothing. As John Webster has reminded us, this is an act of sheer generosity and plenitude, an act of God's loving will, for no reason other than to share life and being with creatures he had no need to make and thus makes freely but consonantly with his own being, which is itself love. Love and goodness are generous, creative, self-sharing. We creatures are both the results and the recipients of these free gifts of love and life. God is radically for us in the sense that we are both the fruit and the beneficiaries of his love: for Christian doctrine, it could be no other way.

1. Augustine of Hippo, *Confessions*, trans. Henry Chadwick (Oxford: Oxford University Press, 2008).

There are plenty of passages in the Bible that express this beautifully, including Psalm 103:

> 2 Praise the LORD, O my soul, * and forget not all his benefits:
> 3 Who forgiveth all thy sin, * and healeth all thine infirmities;
> 4 Who saveth thy life from destruction * and crowneth thee with mercy and loving-kindness;
> 5 Who satisfieth thy mouth with good things, * making thee young and lusty as an eagle.[2]

And yet in Scripture, there is also plenty of testimony to other ways of dealing with us. God is for himself rather than for us when he asks Job, "Where were you when I laid the foundation of the earth?" (Job 38:4); when he declares that "it is not for your sake, O house of Israel, that I am about to act, but for the sake of my holy name" (Ezek 36:22); or when he deals with the nations of the world, drowning the riders and horses of Egypt, declaring Moab his washpot, throwing his sandals over Edom (Ps 60:8).

In a concrete and radical way, it is in Jesus that God is the God who is for us, as reflected in the name *Immanuel*—God with us. Jesus offers salvation to all peoples, extending to and well beyond Israel's former enemies. And as Paul says, "If God is for us, who is against us? He who did not withhold his own Son but gave him up for all of us, how will he not with him also give us everything else?" (Rom 8:31–32). Yet Jesus, too, acts in some sense for himself rather than for us: "When I am lifted up, I will draw all people to myself" (John 12:32). Paul demands that the Romans "present your members as slaves to righteousness" (Rom 6:19) and reminds the Philippians that "at his name every knee shall bow" (Phil 2:10). God is for us and with us, but just as much, we are made *for* him.

How to Speak of God for Us

All of this raises the question not only of what we can say about the God who is for us but also from what position we can say it. "Are you for me?" is a fraught question, for it depends on what we count as being "for" us. What does the other party need to wish for me or affirm about me to count as being "for me"? The prosperity gospel, so influential in both the

2. Translations are taken from the Coverdale Psalms as reproduced in the Book of Common Prayer; all other biblical translations are taken from the anglicized NRSV.

United States and parts of the developing world, seems to offer a clear account: material and emotional wellbeing. That God is for us means that he provides these. But the gospel is much more demanding than that. "Deny yourselves"; "take up your cross"; "you have died with Christ." If we want to affirm that God is for us and also accept these demands—in other words, if we want to collapse neither into a simple projection of our selfish ideas of "for us" onto God nor into a self-denying asceticism that makes Christianity the playbook of a despotic God—what standpoint do we need to assume?

This may seem like an evasive question for a dogmatics conference on the doctrine of God, which should, after all, be concerned first and foremost with the character and nature of the Deity, not with our interrogative posture. However, it is a necessary question. This is one of the great things of which phenomenology and hermeneutics remind us. For phenomenology and hermeneutics, there are at least some things and realities of which we cannot speak in isolation from our experience of them. At a minimum, this is because there is always an observer effect which, when dealing with living beings or objects of our own cultural production, cannot be bypassed because these realities are shaped and changed by us. Artifacts are what they are because we make and use them. People are who they are in their interactions with others. When we speak of God, we cannot abstract from our experience of him precisely because of what this conference affirms, namely that we know God only because he is God for us.

It is important to add that in speaking of God this way—in asking what it means to say that he is "for us"—we also interrogate ourselves. As Kierkegaard showed so laboriously, humans' relations with God are necessarily subjective and personal because God defies objectification.[3] To assume an "objective," disengaged standpoint from which to investigate God's existence and character misses an essential part of what one seeks to understand, namely that there is no such standpoint. If there is a God, we are existentially dependent on him and know him only in relation to us. In other words, God is a transformative subject matter which is known partly in how it affects our vision not only of the world but also of ourselves, our modes of knowledge, and how we are to live, act, and speak in the world. This fact, in turn, does not leave phenomenology or hermeneutics untouched.

---

3. See e.g. Søren Kierkegaard, *The Concept of Anxiety*, trans. Reidar Thomte (Princeton, NJ: Princeton University Press, 1980); Søren Kierkegaard, *The Sickness unto Death*, trans. Edna H. Hong and Howard V. Hong (Princeton, NJ: Princeton University Press, 1983).

There is a hermeneutical circle at work here. On the one hand, doctrinal beliefs form the ground of our enquiry. We build on a belief received from Scripture and tradition: God is for us. He is not an indifferent god like the gods of the Stoics or Epicureans or a god to be appeased like Moloch. The entire story of creation, redemption, and consummation is a story of God for us, not directly accessible to experience but handed down in texts and creeds. On the other hand, this belief both shapes our experience of the world and is itself in need of experiential or phenomenological investigation. We can and should ask what we mean by saying "for us," what counts as an answer, and above all, how we are to relate ourselves to God in order to be able to wish and affirm his being "for us" without entangling ourselves in narcissistic fantasy. The aim of phenomenological investigation here is not to relativize the subject but to elucidate our relation to it.

Dogmatic Groundwork

First, let us consider the doctrinal ground of our enquiry. We have already said that the claim that "God is for us"—sometimes referred to as "divine promeity"—is a basic belief of Christianity. It is sometimes associated especially with Martin Luther and, in the twentieth century, Dietrich Bonhoeffer (whose translators may have coined the term).[4] Indeed, we know God *only* as God for us, in the sense that we know him as our creator, redeemer, and that towards which we strive: our origin and end.

Further, as the tradition has consistently emphasised, this divine promeity is grounded in divine aseity: God could not be radically for us if he were in any sort of competition with us or had any sort of need for us that might limit our own possibilities. As John Webster puts it, quoting Athanasius:

> God's work of creation manifests that, precisely because his perfect goodness cannot be expended, he does not begrudge other things their being, but, on the contrary, gives being to other things. "God is good—or rather the source of goodness—and the good has no envy for anything. Thus, because he envies nothing its existence, he made everything from nothing through his own Word, our Lord Jesus Christ." . . .

4. See esp. Philip Ziegler, "God," in *The Oxford Handbook of Dietrich Bonhoeffer*, ed. Philip Ziegler and Michael Mawson (Oxford: Oxford University Press, 2019), ch. 10.

> Because God is not one being and agent alongside others, and because he is in himself entirely realized and possesses perfect bliss, he has nothing to gain from creating. Precisely in the absence of divine self-interest, the creature gains everything.[5]

What does this mean concretely? At the most global level, it means that the world is a work of love; that we are not random, insignificant, or incongruous with the world, but deliberate, fashioned, loved. This fact raises the provocative and difficult questions that lie at the heart of the Christian study of ethics: How does this absolutely fundamental promeity relate to the highly contingent, highly volatile ways concrete human beings come into existence and develop? How does it relate to the processes of natural selection, of scarcity and competition, of sickness and death? These questions are difficult, but they are interesting and urgent precisely because we affirm God for us. Otherwise, they would be very different sorts of questions.

Personhood and Promeity

At a more personal level, the fact that we know God—if at all, then only as God for us—also implies that we know ourselves—if at all, then only as loved by God. To be loved by God is constitutive of our existence and should be of our self-knowledge. But what does that mean? It can*not* mean that God will provide our material needs, or even that he will necessarily support us or take our side in a fight. There are at least three reasons for this. The first is that we do not necessarily know ourselves well—we do not know whether we are in the right or in the wrong, what our needs are, and where we have to adjust them; we often cannot see beyond a selfishness that blinds us to our own good as well as that of others. The second is that God is not only for you but also for me, and him, and her. There is a requirement in making the assertion "God for us" that this "promeity" not be construed as taking a side in a zero-sum game. How God can be for all of us at the same time, when we live in a world in which different people's needs and flourishing are often in conflict with each other, is a mystery. And this mystery cannot be solved either by an individualist or by a communist reduction of what counts as flourishing. It can be solved only

5. John Webster, "'Love Is Also a Lover of Life': *Creatio ex nihilo* and Creaturely Goodness," *Modern Theology* 29, no. 2 (2013): 105, quoting Athanasius, *De Incarnatione*, in *Contra Gentes and De Incarnatione*, ed. and trans. R. W. Thomson (Oxford: Oxford University Press, 1971), §3.

by the third reason that follows. A third reason why being "for us" cannot necessarily mean that God will take our side in a fight, or provide for our material needs, is that what he reveals as "good for us"—the *substance* of God being for us—is not legible in isolation from a theological framework or from outside a particular orientation to God.

This does not mean that we should err on the other side and read Augustine in a purely Neoplatonist frame. The prayer "You have made us for yourself, and we are restless until we rest in thee" has been read in this way, in which God is the unmoved and unmoving centre to which all things strive in an unquenchable *eros*. Dante's vision of "that love which moves the sun and other stars" is a vision of such eros.[6] In the *Paradiso*, God moves us not by impulsion but by *attraction*: Love for God is the principle of motion for created things. Augustine's prayer is sometimes read as implying such a motionless God. But it should not be. The prayer, rooted in the Christian doctrine of creation, implies something more proactive on God's part: a movement of divine *agape* preceding and eliciting that of human *eros*. Augustine affirms that God has *made* us to be his own and that in this our creation also lies our vocation and thus our (rightly ordered) desire. To be well is to want to be what we are called to be, God's own. That God is for us means primarily that he has made us for himself and helps us (by grace) to become his own. There is no other principle of the substance of God's promeity, no other measure of our own wellbeing.

Restlessness and Temporal Existence

This raises two difficulties: One is that we are turned away from God by sin and want what is not good for us. But the more basic is that Augustine knows or believes that this goal will not be fulfilled until eternity, though we can already experience it proleptically. Though we are God's children now, we do not yet know what we will be, as it says in one of Augustine's favourite verses, 1 John 3:2. This means that temporal existence, even if good, is also a perpetual wound, a "*distentio* of . . . the soul itself."[7] In the *Confessions*, Augustine talks movingly of this inconsolable longing to be gathered up into divine eternity:

6. Dante Alighieri, *The Divine Comedy*, trans. C. H. Sisson (Oxford: Oxford University Press, 2008), *Paradiso* canto 33.

7. Augustine, *Confessions*, 11.26.

> But Thy mercy is better than life, and behold my life is but a stretching-out [*distentio*]. Thy right hand has held me up in my Lord, the Son of Man who is the Mediator in my things and in divers manners—that I may apprehend by Him in whom I am apprehended and may be set free from what I once was, following your Oneness: forgetting the things that are behind and not stretched out upon things to come and things that are transient, but stretching forth to those that are before (not according to distention but according to intention), I press towards the prize of the supernal vocation, where I may hear the voice of Thy praise and contemplate Thy delight which neither comes nor passes away. But now my years are wasted sighs, and Thou, O Lord, my eternal Father, art my only solace; but I am scattered in time, whose order I do not know, and my thoughts and the deepest places of my soul are torn with every kind of tumult until the day when I shall be purified and melted by the fire of Thy love and wholly joined to Thee.[8]

To explore the God who is for us is also to explore this condition of distention in time: of the relationship of earthly and heavenly desire, and of an experience of "God for us" that is *legible* to us as humans without reducing the measure of our vocation.

Augustine's confessions and prayers relate to the paradoxical human experience of at-homeness and not-at-homeness in the world; the strength and importance of the human desire for joy in this ordinary life; and the sense of the brittleness, precarity, and transience of such desire and joy. For Augustine, it is futile to associate God's promeity only with a safeguarding of earthly joys, but it is equally futile to dissociate it from them so entirely that they become meaningless.

Neither is it an option simply to turn away from earthly joys and towards God, for he is not necessarily bearable in this life either. There is powerful witness to the devastation of human safety and assurance by the divine. Abraham, Moses, and Job; Dostoevsky's holy men maddened by God; the opening of R. M. Rilke's *Duino Elegies* and his poem "The Seer"; and above all Friedrich Hölderlin's hymns and elegies—all testify to the near-unbearableness of the divine and of the human vocation in its light ("beneath God's thunderstorms," as Hölderlin puts it[9]). There is no

8. Augustine, *Confessions*, 11.29.
9. Friedrich Hölderlin, *Sämtliche Werke*, ed. Friedrich Beissner (Stuttgart: Cotta, 1953), 2:122–24.

guarantee that our vocation is humanly bearable, though we trust that it will not utterly destroy us.

Yet to make the substance of God being "for us" merely antithetical or perpendicular to ordinary notions of being cared for—an ordinary sense of the promeity of those who love us or an ordinary sense of fulfilment that might be vouchsafed by God—seems to me to risk being impaled on either horn of a Nietzschean dilemma. On Nietzsche's critique, the Christian imposition of a morality of self-abnegation on oneself and others is merely an underhanded bid to attain, as the *reward* of self-denial in the next life, the self-realization that is explicitly condemned in the present. A modern Protestant response (inspired by Kierkegaard) to this Nietzschean threat is to insist that Christian faith be lived as a radical self-abnegation that does not feed a clandestine ambition for self-gratification after death. This might take the form of suggesting a different joy or serenity found in the work itself. The proverbial Protestant work ethic is sometimes associated with this response, and Karen Blixen's short story *Babette's Feast* shows characters initially clinging to such a dedication to serenity in work.[10] It might also take the more radical form (as it does in Simone Weil and Stephen Mulhall) of a resolute rejection of any notion of God as an "object" of loving faith or eschatological hope which would provide a surrogate or *Sicherung* (safeguard) within the attempt to detach ourselves from our hubristic desires.

But *Babette's Feast* shows a different path. The community's ascetic life is not itself enough: They need to receive beneficence as gift. In some ways, their life has taught them to *resist* rather than receive goodness (out of excessive fear of luxuriance or idolatry); on the other hand, they are well-prepared to receive the gift in the way worldly gifts ought to be received, not as a good in itself (an idol) but as something that *transports* to the joy of community and well-being.

Desire and Fulfilment

And this brings me to the main point of this essay. There are many directions that one could take the observations I have offered so far. But one of the most interesting sits at the intersection of the contributions to this symposium by John Behr and Amy Peeler: the curious interplay between death and embodied life in Christian existence, the fact that we seem

10. Karen Blixen [Isak Dinesen, pseud.], *Babette's Feast* (McLean, VA: Trinity Forum, 2010).

at once called to flourish in this life—to understand the fulfilment of our earthly needs and desires as at least analogically revelatory of God's promeity—and to be radically oriented towards a kind of flourishing that from the vantage point of this life shows up only as death, because its substance is so far removed from ours.

This gets us right to the heart of human existence and experience. I take human lives to be made up above all of desires: individually, interpersonally, and communally. Desires shape and motivate our lives. Sometimes the Christian path can seem like a choice between gratifying desires that arise in and for things in this life and the desire that Augustine expresses so eloquently, of being assumed into eternity. But in fact, I think it is often not so at all. On the contrary, we often find that this-worldly desires are just as elusive as heavenly ones, and often we either achieve our desires at a considerable cost to ourselves and others or give them up in a sort of stoical apathy. I would go so far as to say that one of the enduring curses of humans is that we pursue our desires almost invariably in such a way as to destroy either their subjects or their objects. It may be only God who creates the space in which this is not so.

In other words, earthly desires may be achievable, often, only as a sort of by-product of greater desires. This is true even on a purely immanent level. If we want the help and succour of a friend, we can only get it as a by-product of friendship: It will not do to be friends with someone purely for the help they can give us. If we want good marks at university, (in theory) we can only get them as a by-product of a love for learning or for the subject. If we want the admiration of others, (in theory) we can only get it as a by-product of wanting other things, including their good. The challenge of human life is that the things we want most deeply may only be available as by-products of a love not of them but of something greater—"and that, all people call God."

Anselm and Aquinas

We can parse this dynamic in terms of Anselm's theory of the will, which posits two fundamental "affections," desires or impulses: the desire for fulfilment (*affectio commodi*) and the desire for justice (*affectio iustitiae*).[11] Although these impulses often strain apart, they need to be held together

11. See Anselm of Canterbury, *On the Fall of the Devil*, 12–14, in *Anselm of Canterbury: The Major Works*, ed. Brian Davies and G. R. Evans (Oxford: Oxford University Press, 2008).

to achieve genuine happiness. The *affectio commodi* alone is not enough; it must be counterbalanced by the *affectio iustitiae* to achieve even its own aims. For example, we may wish to win a competition. But we cannot coherently, or for long, wish to win it without also wishing for justice—that is, that the best should win, no matter who it is—because otherwise, the very condition of the joy of winning would be undermined. (That is the problem with the Mock Turtle's prizes for everyone, or the ubiquitous A's in today's higher education). By pursuing our desire for success without also honouring justice or our desire for closeness without also honouring a beloved's good, we are pursuing our desire at the cost of its object, and there is no hope of satisfaction, not of more than a brief illusory satisfaction. That is one simple phenomenological meaning of Christ's injunction that if you will to save your life, you must lose it (Matt 16:25).

This double movement also lies at the heart of Aquinas's definition of love, which is the greatest form of willing. To love, for Aquinas, is both to wish to be *with* the beloved and to wish them *well*. Love, in other words, is a double movement of desire for *union* and for the beloved's *good*.[12] Similarly to Anselm's will, which comprises a desire for fulfilment and a desire for justice, love on Aquinas's account therefore spans two impulses that belong together yet often strain apart. Indeed, love often places us in situations where we have to choose the wish for the good over the wish for union: when our children leave home or when we have to let go of someone for their own good. This is because in pursuing our desire for union otherwise than by choosing to prioritize the beloved's good, we would pursue it in such a way as to thwart its object: there is, in fact, ultimately no way of being with someone we love healthily except by willing the good for them because the person will no longer be themselves otherwise. And the very *pathos* of our choice for the good of those we love, when it means letting them go, arises from a contrasting wish for closeness, which is present even, and perhaps especially poignantly, in its renunciation.

The flipside of this claim is that the wish for the good is not divorced from the wish for union. This second claim is less intuitive and less easily defensible than the first, both for theological and for experiential reasons. Anders Nygren influentially argued that God's love is entirely self-giving—a single-minded wish for the good of the beloved—and that our love, at its purest, should similarly be a form of *agape* unvitiated by

12. Thomas Aquinas, *Summa Theologica*, trans. Fathers of the English Dominican Province (New York: Benziger Brothers, 1947), I.20; I-II.28.

eros.[13] This reading seems, at first glance, dogmatically required by God's aseity, historically evinced by Christ's sacrifice on the cross, and necessary for making sense of the dominical command to "love your enemies" (Matt 5:44; Luke 6:27), which is more easily understood as a wish for their good than as a wish for closeness. However, I think that Nygren's account is distorting. God lacks nothing and has no need for union with humans. But the Bible suggests that he nevertheless wishes such union. The human experience of desire is necessarily and indelibly marked by finitude: by incompleteness and limitation. Nevertheless, the desire for union—unmarked by such forms of lack—may not be foreign to the divine life. Even if God does not experience desire for union in the way humans do (because he does not lack it), it may be that such desire is the only *image* through which we can see God's eternal joy in union, both within the Trinity and in the consummation of creation. (This principle of analogy is present in many domains: time itself, as Boethius and C. S. Lewis suggest, may be the only image through which we can see divine eternity in its dynamism and freedom.[14]) If Jesus gave his life on the cross, it was not out of sheer disinterested good will but to gain us for himself. And even our love for our enemies, I believe, should in part be a desire that each should become such a one as we would like to be closer to.

Desire, in other words, is not a linear movement. To think that it *is*—to think, say, that fulfilment can be achieved *purely* by pursuing an object or, in Aquinas's terminology, union with a beloved—is to undermine oneself. And yet merely to disavow that desire for union is to make oneself inhuman. C. S. Lewis expresses this powerfully in *The Four Loves*:

> Love anything and your heart will be wrung and possibly broken. If you want to make sure of keeping it intact you must give it to no one. Wrap it carefully round with hobbies and little luxuries; lock it up safe in the casket of your selfishness. But in that casket, it will change into something unbreakable, impenetrable, irredeemable. The alternative to tragedy, or at least to the risk of tragedy, is damnation.[15]

We are, it seems, caught between the threats of destroying what we desire by pursuing it single-mindedly and losing a vital part of our

13. See Anders Nygren, *Agape and Eros: A Study of the Christian Idea of Love*, trans. Philip S. Watson (London: SPCK, 1953).

14. See C. S. Lewis, *The Great Divorce* (London: Geoffrey Bles, 1945), ch. 13.

15. C. S. Lewis, *The Four Loves* (London: Geoffrey Bles, 1960), ch. 6.

humanity by simply denying the desire. Human love, as well as life more generally, is a balancing act between these, and one of the questions that theology raises to psychology is where we find the resources to walk the tightrope.

Conclusion: Love, Faith, and Hope

This brings us back to Augustine's prayer that "thou hast made us for thyself." In relation to God, the conflicting impulses that make up our earthly acts of desiring and loving—the *affectio commodi* and the *affectio iustitiae*, the desire for union with and for the good of the beloved—are not opposed but at one, because in God fulfilment and justice are one and the same. If we cannot ultimately be with others without wishing their good, this is because those we love have their deepest identity only in and in relation to God, the source of all goodness. If we know ourselves at all, we know ourselves only as loved by God; and so we must also know each other. Without a shared orientation towards that source, we can ultimately neither know nor be with them.

God makes the double movement of love intelligible and sufferable. After all, as I have just said, in a sense it is easy for God and with God because in him there is no conflict between justice and fulfilment or between the good of those he loves and union with them: To be well and good is to be in right relationship with God. And for those who believe that in God good and union are *one*, the balancing act of love is fuelled by a confidence that, ultimately, these two impulses tend towards the same, even if they are divided in this life. In a version of Kant's *summum bonum*, we hope that goodness and union will ultimately converge in God.

This is not simply a hope for earthly fulfilment—for a God who is for us by supplying our material needs or always supporting our ambitions. But neither is it a hope only for a heavenly destination in anticipation of which we should renounce all earthly desires and attachments. That "our heart is restless until it rests in thee" does not mean taking an ambivalent or lukewarm attitude to the world, maintaining a safe distance from it. Rather, it means holding our desires loosely, hoping that all that is good in them will find fulfilment in our eternal life with God. Such hope is well-grounded in the Christian belief that we know God only because he is always already a God for us. If he created us, he will also raise us, and "when Christ our life appears, we shall be like him, for we shall see him as he is" (1 John 3:3).

CHAPTER 3

THE GOD WHO IS FOR US AS GOD WITH US

LUCY PEPPIATT

When reflecting upon the theme of the God who is for us, it seems natural to turn to Romans 8, not least of all because it is here that Paul proclaims, "If God is for us, then who can be against us" (Rom 8:31). In this chapter, I focus on a couple of verses in the pivotal point in the chapter, verses 14–17. As Mike Bird writes, Romans 8:14–17 is

> a transitional passage that uses the theme of adoption to move between the Spirit/flesh contrast of vv.1–13 to the following section on the future dimension of Christian hope in vv.18–39. The substance of vv.14–17 is that those led by the Spirit are adopted as children of God. Such adoption brings a new status, it provides an intimate relationship with God, and it secures a glorious future as co-heirs with Christ in glory.[1]

In the middle of this transitional passage, in verse 16, Paul writes, "The Spirit cowitnesses (*summarturei*) with our spirit that we are children of God."

Although verses 14–17 are rich in meaning and give rise to much debate on a number of issues, here I simply focus on Paul's claim that the Holy Spirit "cowitnesses" with the human spirit, exploring various perspectives on how we might understand this claim as well as what this might mean for a life of faith.[2] In the course of the discussion, I attend

1. Michael F. Bird, *Romans* (Grand Rapids: Zondervan, 2016), 265.

2. Most of these discussions are beyond the scope of this short chapter, such as debates over what precisely a believer inherits, the place of Israel in Paul's narrative, and the question of what Paul means by the spirit of slavery or bondage over against the spirit of sonship. There are different views on what constitutes the inheritance: God himself, divinization, immortality, glory, eternal life, heaven, the kingdom, the earth, dominion and rulership, or all of the above.

to three main questions: (1) how we might understand Paul's claim that there is a cowitness of the human spirit with the Holy Spirit; (2) whether there are *signs* of the cowitness of the Spirit with our spirit; and (3) what the cowitness of the Spirit with the human spirit means for the life of faith. In sum, I explore the questions of who is testifying, to whom are they testifying, and to what purpose. My proposal is that Romans 8:14–17 is best understood as prophetic rather than paraenetic discourse. Paul is not really instructing the churches in Rome here on Trinitarian doctrine or even telling them *how* to relate to the Father through Christ in the power of the Spirit. Instead, he is speaking of a mystery that has been revealed, what he calls in 1 Corinthians the "deep things of God," things we only have access to through the Spirit.

Translating verses 15b–16 is not straightforward. James Dunn writes, "The most obvious way to take the force of the συν- compound is that 'the Spirit bears testimony along with our spirit,' . . . but the lack of a connection leaves it unclear how Paul relates this witness-bearing to the 'Abba, Father' cry."[3] Thus there are two options for translation:

Option A

> You have received the spirit of sonship in whom we call, "Abba, Father." The Spirit bears witness with our spirit (that we are children of God).

Option B

> You have received the spirit of sonship. When we call, "Abba, Father," the Spirit is bearing witness with our spirit (that we are children of God).

In this chapter, I follow option B, seeing a causal link between the Spirit bearing witness with our spirit and the cry to our Abba, Father, although as Dunn points out the precise nature of the connection is unclear.

In my opinion, these verses are best understood through John Wesley's phrase a "joint testimony," which nicely captures the intention of the expression to cowitness. Furthermore, it appears this work of the Spirit, this witness, has a particular significance in the face of suffering for the sake of Christ. As Ben Blackwell notes in relation to these verses

3. James D. G. Dunn, *Romans 1–8* (Grand Rapids: Zondervan, 2015), 454. Here Dunn cites the NJB, "The spirit of adoption enabling us to cry out, 'Abba! Father!'" as well as the NIV, "The Spirit himself . . . ," the NEB, and the RSV.

> Paul has not yet introduced suffering into his argument in chapter 8, though of course it does arise in the immediately following verses. However, the intersection of the theme of suffering and the Spirit's inward work in 5:1–5 already establishes this importance. Thus, when we encounter this here, the interconnection is just deepened.[4]

As Blackwell notes, the theme of suffering arises in the verses following. It should be noted that the section headings in many translations serve to obscure this connection as verse 17 becomes disconnected from what follows in verse 18, "I consider that our present sufferings are not worth comparing with the glory that will be revealed in us."[5]

Thus, in the instance of suffering for Christ, the joint testimony in question is evidenced primarily through the cry, "Abba, Father." This particular sign may or may not be evidenced by further outward signs, but that is not the point that Paul is making. Here he is speaking of the knowledge of "sonship" and thus heirship that is given by the Holy Spirit to reside in the human spirit but which will inevitably be tested through times of suffering when to all intents and purposes it may feel as though the Father has abandoned the child.

The cowitness of the Spirit as the gift of grace specifically comes to the fore in the face of apparent abandonment and desolation because in these times only the witness of the Spirit is able to establish a corresponding witness in the human spirit that a person is, nevertheless, a beloved child of God. This is true first of Christ himself in his earthly life and then of those who are in him. Thus, I propose that this revelation resides in the spirit as spirit-knowledge that lies at the heart of a life lived by faith and not by sight.

A Trinitarian Gospel

The context for Romans 8:15–16 is the believer's participation in the filial relation of the Son through the work of the Spirit who himself is God. Whether we call the theology in verses 14–17 proto-Trinitarian or simply Trinitarian, I see this section, and indeed the entire chapter, as markedly Trinitarian in its intention. Throughout the chapter, Paul refers to the relations of God, the Son/Christ, and the Spirit with reference to the work of the Godhead in both the creature and the cosmos and with specific

4. This was a comment added by Ben Blackwell when reading through my work.
5. This section break occurs in the NIV, ESV, MSG, and NRSVue, but not in the NASB.

reference to the taking up of the creaturely into the life of God, Father, Son, and Spirit.[6] God is the one who embraces humanity as his children through the Son and the Spirit. Thus, although Paul only uses the term *Father* once in chapter 8 (v. 15), the import of the entire chapter is that those who are "in Christ" and "led by the Spirit" are the "sons" and the "children" of God. Verses 15–16b, therefore, are pivotal in both senses of the word; they are of crucial importance with regard to the theology of the whole chapter, which centres around adoption, and the moment upon which Paul pivots to explain what life in the Spirit holds for those who suffer this earthly life in Christ.

The gospel here is expounded in terms of freedom from condemnation, the theme which bookends the whole chapter. This freedom is comprised of a rescue from the deathly life of the flesh for eternal life in Christ Jesus which, through the Spirit of life, brings the creature into the Father/child relation which is the ground of their inheritance.[7] Leaving aside what precisely the children of God inherit, the logic of Paul's argument—as Richard Longenecker points out—is "*if* sons, *then* heirs, and *if* heirs, *then* co-heirs with Christ."[8] Romans 8, therefore, is an uncompromisingly pneumatological account of the Trinitarian gospel where the Holy Spirit plays what Fred Sanders calls a "connective" role.[9]

The Spirit's role is connective but also personal. As Gilles Emery writes, "By his action, the Holy Spirit is revealed as a *person*, because he accomplishes the actions that are properly the actions of a person—even as the Holy Spirit reveals himself as God by accomplishing actions that belong exclusively to *God*."[10] In one sense then, the Spirit is the one who is God *for us* in this life, indwelling the believer and uniting them with Christ. Thus, the Spirit reveals the truth of this new relationship of God with humanity and makes plain that the God who is for us, even in the face of all or any evidence to the contrary, is the God who is eternally with us. There is *now*, therefore, no condemnation. The echo of the human spirit to this truth is given voice in the human cry, the cry of a child to a father which *is* itself the witness, to those watching and listening, that nothing can separate us from the love of God.

---

6. Cyril writes, "All God-befitting actions are carried out by the Father through the Son in the Spirit," *Commentary on the Epistle to the Romans*, 8.11 in *Commentaries on Romans, 1–2 Corinthians, and Hebrews*, ed. Joel C. Elowsky, trans. David R. Maxwell (Downers Grove [IL]: IVP Academic, 2022).

7. The central focus of Romans 8:1–13 is the movement from death to life.

8. Richard N. Longenecker, *The Epistle to the Romans* (Grand Rapids: Eerdmans, 2016), 268.

9. Fred Sanders, *The Holy Spirit: An Introduction* (Wheaton: Crossway, 2023), 4.

10. Gilles Emery, OP, "The Holy Spirit in Aquinas's Commentary on Romans," in *Reading Romans with St. Thomas Aquinas*, ed. Matthew Levering and Michael Dauphinais (Washington, DC: Catholic University America, 2012), 134.

The Meaning of *Summarturei*

Not all commentators emphasize the joint testimony. Augustine, in relation to the Romans verse, writes, "The Spirit itself bears witness to our spirit that we are children of God."[11] This appears to be more descriptive of Galatians 4:6, where Paul writes that it is the Spirit within our hearts who calls out, "Abba, Father." Furthermore, Augustine interprets this cry as purely internal, a "cry of the heart, not of the mouth, not of the lips," which is not how I read Paul's intent in Romans.[12] Ambrosiaster similarly places the emphasis on the Spirit's work in and through us but not on the creature's response, apart from a reference to the ethical conditions attached to the indwelling of the Spirit. He writes: "When we do what is right the Spirit of God dwells in us, and for this reason he becomes our voice and our mind, by which we cry in prayer: Abba, that is, Father."[13] Note Ambrosiaster's preference for the idea that the Spirit *becomes* our voice and our mind, losing the notion of a corresponding cry. Again, this latter view appears to be closer to what Paul is describing in Galatians 4:6 rather than the text here in Romans.

Aquinas identifies three ways in which those who receive the Holy Spirit are sons of God. There is, first, the gifts of the Holy Spirit; second, "our own testimony, *at whereby we cry*; and third, . . . the testimony of the Spirit, *at for the Spirit himself*."[14] Wesley, as we have seen, uses the term joint testimony and speaks of "two witnesses," observing that "there is, in every believer, both the testimony of God's Spirit, and the testimony of his own, that he is a child of God."[15] The idea of two witnesses is picked up by Dunn, who believes that two witnesses giving testimony to the same truth would have been significant for Paul in the light of Deuteronomy 19:15.[16] Thus, he avers, the "inward conviction" of the believer is her own and "not simply the presence of the Spirit" in her. He continues:

---

11. Augustine, *Sermons*, vol. 5, *Sermons 148–183*, ed. John E. Rotelle, OSA, trans. Edmund Hill, OP (New Rochelle, NY: New City, 1992), sermon 156.16.

12. Augustine, *Sermons*, vol. 5, sermon 156.16. In sermon 156.15, he writes, "This is a cry of the heart, not of the mouth, not of the lips; it makes itself heard inside, it makes itself heard in God's ears."

13. Ambrosiaster, *Commentaries on Romans and 1–2 Corinthians*, ed. and trans. Gerald L. Bray (Downers Grove, IL: IVP Academic, 2009), 66.

14. Thomas Aquinas, *Commentary on Romans*, trans. Fabian R. Larcher, OP (Steubenville, OH: Emmaus Academic, 2020), lect 3, §637, 247.

15. John Wesley, "The Witness of the Spirit," sermon 10, 1. Also see sermon 2, 3.1 and 4.8 where he speaks of two witnesses. https://www.resourceumc.org/en/content/sermon-10-the-witness-of-the-spirit.

16. Paul echoes Deuteronomy 19:15 in 2 Corinthians 13:1, where he writes, "Every matter must be established by the testimony of two or three witnesses."

> [Paul] evidently has in mind two sides of the same experience (we cry; the Spirit bears witness), he neither reduces the Spirit to a feeling of sonship, nor absorbs the concept of God's Spirit within his anthropology. This human assent to divine grace is itself an expression of the renewal of "the inner man" (7:22; 2 Cor 4:16).[17]

Hendrikus Berkhof summarises as follows: "The verb *summarturein* means that God's Spirit bears witness to our self in such a way that this self can no longer remain merely passive, but feels urged to support and transmit this witness."[18]

What is of note here is that the Spirit bears witness with our *spirit* and not to or with our minds. I would not wish to press this distinction too far, as Berkhof rightly makes the point that the reference to the human "spirit" in Paul's epistles is not in contradistinction to the mind or the heart.[19] However, Paul does highlight the role of the human spirit in 1 Corinthians, drawing an analogy between the Spirit of God within God and the spirit of a person within them and the communication that passes between the two. "The Spirit searches all things, even the deep things of God," and communicates those things to the human spirit "so that we may understand the gifts bestowed on us by God" (1 Cor 2:10, 12). Longenecker sees the human spirit as "the activating or essential principle influencing a person" which has its own energy.[20] Dunn describes the human spirit as that dimension of being to which and through which God's Spirit is able to "communicate its revelatory and redemptive power."[21] Both these insights seem apposite here.

In Romans 11:33–34, Paul writes of the depths (*bathos*) of the riches of the wisdom and knowledge of God as unsearchable (*anexeraunēta*). However, in 1 Corinthians, he claims the Holy Spirit is given to us so we *can* discover the depths (*bathos*) of God and his ways because the Holy Spirit searches (*ereunaō*) all things, even the depths (*bathos*) of God and communicates them to the human spirit. The Spirit does this in order that we may understand "what God has prepared for those who love him" (1 Cor 2:9–10).

The revelation of the riches of God's wisdom and knowledge can be apprehended neither by our rational sense perception (in the sense of our

---

17. Dunn, *Romans 1–8*, 454.
18. Hendrikus Berkhof, *The Doctrine of the Holy Spirit* (London: Epworth, 1965), 98.
19. Berkhof, *The Doctrine of the Holy Spirit*, 97.
20. Longenecker, *Romans*, 703.
21. Dunn, *Romans 1–8*, 454.

powers of deduction) nor via our physical senses (what we see and hear in a concrete form). We cannot think our way to apprehending God's wisdom, and neither can our own eyes and ears see and hear what God has prepared for those who love him. However, the eyes of our hearts (to which Paul refers in Ephesians 1:18) and our spirits are able to perceive such things. The Spirit not only reveals the riches of God's wisdom and knowledge but also makes known his judgements and his paths. And yet we only have access to this knowledge by faith and not by sight.[22] What then are the signs of this impartation of spiritual knowledge, this witness of the Spirit with our spirit?

Signs of the Witness of the Spirit

There is a notable trend in the history of commentary on this passage in which scholars go on to discuss the signs of the witness of the Spirit that go beyond the initial sign of the cry of the child to their Abba, Father. Some are concerned to see further outward evidence for the authenticity of this cry, as if the cry itself is not enough to witness to the filial relation. As I mentioned above, Ambrosiaster avers there is an ethical imperative to the cry to our Abba, Father, whereby the children of God must then "live a life worthy of this cry." The witness of children is thus to "bear the sign of the Father," which for Ambrosiaster means we "must govern our life with great care."[23] In a sense, he reads the cry as less of a prayer and more of a sign of discipleship. In a similar vein, Wesley demonstrates some considerable anxiety regarding the need to authenticate the cry by insisting that the fruit of the Spirit and a godly character must also be evident as the "marks" of the testimony of the Spirit.[24] Berkhof insists this cry should manifest in the outward mission of the church, the witness to the world.[25]

---

22. Gilles Emery, writing on the work of Aquinas on Romans, highlights this supernatural means of knowing: "By natural reason, philosophers could know only the essential attributes that belong to God insofar as God is the transcendent principle of the world: they have not been able to recognize the divine persons, because the properties that constitute and distinguish these persons are not accessible to us by way of causality." "The Holy Spirit," 135.

23. Ambrosiaster, *Commentaries on Romans*, 66.

24. Wesley, "The Witness of the Spirit," sermon 11, 7. Wesley's reason for this concern is his suspicion of the behaviour of the enthusiasts and his belief, interestingly, that there can be a false witness in the cry. For this reason, he suggests there might be a need for further authentication of a believer's true sonship, namely obedience. https://www.resourceumc.org/en/content/sermon-11-the-witness-of-the-spirit-ii.

25. Berkhof, *The Holy Spirit*, 89, 98.

Susan Eastman rightly brings out the address of Paul not to the individual but to the community. In her view, the cry to "Abba, Father" is a public event referring to "communal, shared acclamation or prayer. So if the cry itself is the Spirit testifying 'with our spirit' that we have status and inheritance as children of God, then the testimony also is a public, shared event."[26] This last point resonates with Beverly Gaventa's emphasis that at the heart of the cry "Abba, Father" is worship.[27] Eastman further brings out the deeply affective nature of the cry; *kradzomen* "occurs frequently in prayer, it can also refer to the screaming of infants, weeping, shrieking, and even Jesus' cry from the cross (Matt 27:50)."[28] The cry represents "primitive and powerful emotions, here in the most primal of human relationships."[29]

Against Augustine then, there is no doubt Paul is describing a strong crying out here, something more than an internalized voice or a whispered prayer. Some draw a direct connection between the emotional language described here and assurance or inner, affective conviction. Douglas Moo, who holds to the joint testimony view, writes, "Paul stresses that our awareness of God as Father comes not from rational consideration nor from external testimony alone but from a truth deeply felt and intensely experienced."[30] He goes on to say that the witness of the Spirit to the human spirit "about our adoption as sons affects the deepest and innermost part of our beings. It is because of this that we cry so sincerely and spontaneously, 'Abba, Father!'"[31] Dunn writes, "It is presumably this same intense consciousness of sonship expressed in the cry 'Abba, Father' which Paul still has in mind—a sense that it is not just himself praying but his inner being enabled to pray by the enabling of God. Here beyond dispute it is an inner confirmation or assurance that Paul has in mind."[32]

---

26. Eastman, "Oneself in Another: Participation and the Spirit in Romans 8," in *"In Christ" in Paul: Explorations in Paul's Theology of Union and Participation*, ed. Michael J. Thate, Kevin J. Vanhoozer, and Constantine R. Campbell (Grand Rapids: Eerdmans, 2014), 103–25, 114.

27. Gaventa writes, "Yet Paul's language is not simply about *knowing* that God is creator or *assenting* to certain propositions about God. His language concerns rendering praise and thanksgiving, actions that are fundamentally actions of worship." Beverly Roberts Gaventa, *When in Romans: An Invitation to Linger with the Gospel According to Paul* (Grand Rapids: Baker Academic, 2016), 89–90.

28. Eastman, "Oneself in Another," 117.

29. Eastman, "Oneself in Another," 117.

30. Douglas J. Moo, *The Letter to the Romans* (Grand Rapids: Eerdmans, 2018), 524–25. Moo writes, "Indeed, taking the verb Paul uses here to mean 'bear witness with,' Paul involves our own spirit in the very process of testifying to us that we are 'children of God.'" 526.

31. Moo, *Romans*, 526.

32. Dunn, *Romans 1–8*, 462.

The Cry Itself

There is a value in all these perspectives as each brings out some aspect or implication of the richness of the notion of cowitness. I see the main emphasis in the text, however, as the simple but profound ability to cry to God as our Abba, Father in the face of suffering, which, by necessity, is a cry of faith. It is in this context that Paul explicitly highlights the Spirit-led and prophetic nature of the cry. There are four *sun-* compounds in two verses (*symmartyrei*, *synklēronomoi*, *sympaschomen*, and *syndoxasthōmen*) which are all connected in the flow of the argument. In verse 16b, the Spirit cowitnesses with our spirit that we are children of God. As we saw, the logic is that if children, then heirs, and if heirs, then coheirs with Christ. The *if* (*ei*) at the beginning of verse 17 denotes a simple logical and causal connection between Paul's assumptions regarding children as coheirs.

This is followed, however, by *if-then* (*eiper*) in relation to cosuffering. The term *eiper* denotes "if indeed, if after all, since," signalling a slightly different causal connection. The suffering is not the requisite cause of the glorification, but if (and when) suffering comes to pass or rather in the event of suffering for Christ, the suffering of the coheirs will be a cosuffering because it will be "in Christ." Those who suffer in Christ, then, will also be glorified with him. They cannot not be. Thus, the logic of the passage is that the Spirit first establishes that the believer is a coheir with Christ—they have inherited every blessing in the heavenly realms, which is received and testified to by the human spirit. This joint testimony, which can only be known in and by the Spirit and only resides in the human spirit by faith, serves as the foundation for trusting that suffering with Christ will lead to being glorified with him.[33]

The Life of Faith in Christ

I have discussed the question of whether Jesus exercised faith elsewhere, but to summarize in brief, I hold to the view of Aquinas and later John Owen, that Jesus in his humanity was in need of habitual grace.[34] For Owen, not Aquinas, this forms the foundation for his assertion that Christ exercised faith in the promises of God in his humanity.[35] Owen argues

33. Cyril writes, "They are promised no earthly reward, but eternal glory and participation in realities beyond thought and understanding," *Commentary on the Epistle to the Romans*, 8.17.

34. See Lucy Peppiatt, "Life in the Spirit: Christ's and Ours," in *The Christian Doctrine of Humanity*, ed. Oliver D. Crisp and Fred Sanders (Grand Rapids: Zondervan, 2018), 171–73.

35. Thomas Aquinas describes the object of faith as "a Divine thing not seen" and writes, "Now from the first moment of His conception Christ saw God's Essence fully, as will be made clear.

that Jesus's knowledge of the promises of God is communicated to his human mind through the Spirit (which is his own Spirit) and received by Christ in a creaturely mode.[36] Thus, when we see Jesus cry to his Abba, Father in Mark 14:36, we are witnessing a cry of faith from Jesus in his humanity. The cry to the Father by Jesus is uttered in confidence of what is hoped for and assurance of things yet unseen (Heb 11:1), rooted in the spirit-knowledge that what lies ahead is suffering but that glorification will follow.[37] Owen, as a scholar of the epistle to the Hebrews, takes seriously the fully human life of Christ, "who through the eternal Spirit offered himself unblemished to God," (Heb 9:14), and who goes to the cross "for the joy set before him" (Heb 12:2). This has many implications for Christ's life as a prototype of those who follow him.[38]

Owen's Christology lays the foundation for seeing Jesus's prayers to the Father in the Spirit as analogous to our own prayers offered to the Father in faith in the power of the Spirit.[39] Those in Christ participate by grace in the filial relationship which, to be sure, will be a shadowy reflection of the relationship the Son has with the Father by nature; nevertheless, the gifts of grace given to the Son in his earthly life are then bestowed upon his coheirs. Emery notes this analogy when he writes, "This interior testimony of the Holy Spirit in the children of God is compared to the voice of the Father declaring of Christ: 'This is my beloved Son, in whom I am well pleased.'"[40] For the child of grace, then, the Spirit's testimony is the countertestimony to the testimony of our sins which we read, in Isaiah, "testify against us" (Isa 59:12). If our sins are able to testify against us, their testimony will condemn us as those who are lost and blind children of wrath,

---

Hence there could be no faith in him." Aquinas, *Summa Theologica*, trans. Fathers of the English Dominican Province (New York: Benziger Brothers, 1947), 3.7.3, ans. Aquinas subsequently connects Christ's knowledge to his sanctification: "For it has been shown above that in the first instant of conception, Christ's body was both animated and assumed by the Word of God. Consequently, in the first instant of His conception, Christ had the fulness of grace sanctifying His body and His soul," Aquinas, *Summa Theologica*, 3.34.1, ans. John Owen would be in complete agreement with the sanctification of Christ's body and soul, but held to the idea that Jesus was not in receipt of the beatific vision in his earthly life apart from what he received by faith in God's promises.

36. John Owen, *The Works of John Owen*, vol. 3, *Pneumatologia*, ed. William H. Goold (Carlisle, PA: Banner of Truth, 1972), 162.

37. John Owen, *The Works of John Owen*, vol. 20, *Epistle to the Hebrews with Preliminary Exercitations* (volume IV), ed. William H. Goold (Edinburgh: Banner of Truth, 1991), 513.

38. For a further helpful explanation of the life of faith in Christ construed in this way, see Steven J. Duby, *Jesus and the God of Classical Theism: Biblical Christology in Light of the Doctrine of God* (Grand Rapids: Baker Academic, 2022), 193–242.

39. Owen writes, "for although believers are so, as to measure and degree, unspeakably beneath what Christ was, who received not the Spirit by measure, yet as he is the head and they are the members of the same mystical body, their unction by the Spirit is of the same kind." *Pneumatologia*, 61.

40. Emery, "The Holy Spirit," 147.

thus keeping us under condemnation. The Spirit's testimony not only nullifies the testimony of our sins, witnessing to the freedom won through the cross from the slavery of and to sin, but also enables the human creature to join in the declaration that this freedom has been established in the heart of the child.

The Power of the Joint Testimony

Obscuring the reality of the joint testimony loses the force of what Paul intends here as the cowitness. The Spirit is the source of the testimony, but the responsive testimony of the human spirit is crucial in establishing the knowledge of sonship.[41] Khaled Anatolios writes,

> Our response to God's grace both is and is not our own. It is not our own insofar as even this response derives from God's grace and is "received." And yet it is our own precisely because we do actually receive it: "those things which you give Me are yours, as having received them from Me." Moreover, it is precisely their becoming "our own" through our having received them which makes it possible for us to "give" them back to God. If they do not become our own, we would not be able to give them back to God; neither would God be able to require them back of us.[42]

The focus of Romans 8 is the revelation that no created thing has the ability to separate God's children from God's love however much those things are experienced as profound opposition to life. The human cry as a response to the cry of the Spirit first demonstrates that the testimony of the Spirit has been received and can be trusted and then, by echoing the same, establishes that testimony before those forces of opposition both without and within. I do not purport to know what precisely Paul has in mind with regard to those to whom this witness is declared, but Luke 12 comes to mind. Jesus warns his disciples not to fear those who "kill the body and after can do no more." Instead, he tells them they are to fear

---

41. N. T. Wright writes this on receiving the Spirit: "The cry of 'Abba, father' is the sure sign that we have received the spirit of sonship—otherwise why would we find ourselves calling God father in this familiar way? *And* he wants to say that this is the sign, more specifically, that the holy spirit is getting together with our spirit, fusing with our own deepest inwardness, to say, Yes, we really are God's children." *Into the Heart of Romans: A Deep Dive into Paul's Greatest Letter* (Grand Rapids: Zondervan, 2023), 105.

42. Khaled Anatolios, *Athanasius: The Coherence of His Thought* (New York: Routledge, 1998), 174–75, cited in Gary A. Anderson, *Christian Doctrine and the Old Testament: Theology in the Service of Biblical Exegesis* (Grand Rapids: Baker Academic, 2017), 52.

God and to remember that the very hairs of their head are numbered as they are of great worth. He concludes that in these times of persecution, "do not worry about how you will defend yourselves or what you will say, for the Holy Spirit will teach you at that time what you should say" (Luke 12:11–12).

It also appears there is an overlap between the witness or testimony of the Spirit to the human spirit and the intercession of the Spirit which Paul comes to in 8:26–7. This is further developed in verse 34, where Paul adds that Christ is "at the right hand of the God and is also interceding for us." This intercession for God's children is explicitly for them in their weakness and when "trouble, hardship, persecution, famine, nakedness, danger, and sword" is coming against them. At those times, the Spirit and Christ are able to persuade us that "nothing will be able to separate us from the love of God that is in Christ Jesus our Lord" (Rom 8:39).

Thus, the cowitness or joint testimony establishes and secures the truth of the claim as is spoken of in Deuteronomy 19:15 and 2 Corinthians 13:1. The human spirit repeating the words it has been taught by the Holy Spirit is the sign in itself of the trust within, and the power of the cry is that this is cried out in the face of suffering. The witness of the Spirit to the human spirit means the believer is able to echo the truth that they too are the beloved child come what may. Not only is the cry of faith to the Father in the face of suffering a prophetic cry in and of the knowledge of the love of God the Father for his children, but it is a prophetic witness to those watching and listening of the certain hope of future glorification.

CHAPTER 4

THE GOD WHO IS FOR US IS HIDDEN FROM US

DOLORES G. MORRIS

The God of the Jewish and Christian Scriptures is, or seems to be, a God who hides. In some instances, we are given a measure of divine explanation. In Micah 3:4, for instance, the prophet warns of those who "love evil and hate good":

> Then they will cry out to the LORD,
> But He will not answer them.
> Instead, He will hide His face from them at that time
> Because they have practiced evil deeds.[1]

This kind of hiddenness is not especially difficult to understand. From those who live as if there is no God, God will sometimes "hide his face." The purpose is clear: the hidden God triumphs in time, making his presence and his power known. Thus, Isaiah 45:15–17 states:

> Truly, You are a God who hides Himself,
> God of Israel, Savior!
> They will be put to shame and even humiliated, all of them;
> The manufacturers of idols will go away together in humiliation.
> Israel has been saved by the LORD
> With an everlasting salvation;
> You will not be put to shame or humiliated
> To all eternity.

1. Unless otherwise noted, Scripture quotations in this chapter originate from the NASB translation.

By hiding for a season, God demonstrates his sovereignty and faithfulness with a dramatic, well-timed reappearance.

There is another, more troubling way the Judeo-Christian God seems hidden. David was far from blameless, yet we understand the anguish in his question, "How long, LORD? Will You forget me forever? How long will You hide Your face from me?" (Ps 13:1). More challenging still is the cry of Job, targeted precisely *because* of his faithfulness: "Oh that I knew how to find Him, That I might come to His home!" (Job 23:3). Lest we seek a neat and tidy explanation of God's hiddenness in the midst of Job's suffering, Christopher Watkin's explication does an excellent job of showing us that no simple explanation is available. Instead, Watkin locates Job at the intersection of Proverbs and Ecclesiastes. The former suggests a God who ensures that the good triumph and the wicked flounder; the latter paints a picture of a morally chaotic universe. As Watkins notes, "The genius of the book of Job is that it finds a way of holding these two radically different perspectives together without blunting either of them."[2] God is sovereign; we are powerless. God is faithful; his actions will not always look to us like the actions of a faithful God. God is for us; he is also hidden from us. This is the message throughout Scripture, up to and including Christ's own cry on the cross. We worship a hidden God.

I think it is important that Christian scholars be up front about this. In the first place, it is *true*. In the second place, I am convinced that simply acknowledging this difficult feature of reality is a good first step toward better dialogue with skeptics. Consider, for example, an excerpt from one of Alex O'Connor's online debates. Visibly moved by the contrast of Psalm 139 with his own experience, O'Connor decries, "'Where can I go from your spirit? Where can I flee from your presence?' Where can I go, I should ask in response, to find it?"[3] I think our first response to someone like O'Connor should be to join in his lament. "It is true," we can say. "It is not always easy to find God. It is a terrible thing to seek and not find." Having done so, we can then begin to ask what this difficult aspect of reality *means*.

This last step is a crucial one, and it brings me to the third reason why I think Christian scholars ought to acknowledge divine hiddenness.

2. Christopher Watkin, *Biblical Critical Theory: How the Bible's Unfolding Story Makes Sense of Modern Life and Culture* (Grand Rapids: Zondervan Academic, 2023), 324.

3. Alex O'Connor, "Debate: Theism vs Atheism: Jonathan McLatchie vs Alex O'Connor," debate, May 16, 2022, at Sattler College in Boston, Massachusetts, posted May 25, 2022, by Alex O'Connor, https://www.youtube.com/watch?v=rnIQFI1pYLM&t=0s. (Because this quotation was transcribed from a video, the punctuation is my own.)

According to the "hiddenness argument," evidence of divine hiddenness could only mean one thing: divine *absence*. If the hiddenness argument is correct, no loving God could be hidden. If, therefore, the Christian God seems hidden, we ought to have an answer to the argument from hiddenness.

To that end, here is my plan for what follows. I want to examine the argument from divine hiddenness. I do not think that the argument succeeds, but my primary goal is constructive rather than defensive. Really, I think there is a family of arguments here—each informative and worthy of consideration. As Michael Rea wrote in his book on the subject, "The problem of divine hiddenness, like the problem of evil, is fundamentally a problem of violated expectations."[4] We should, therefore, examine those expectations. Finally, I will explore the role of religious experience in hiddenness arguments. In the process, I hope to sketch a new way forward for the theist and the agnostic alike.

The Hiddenness Argument

The hiddenness argument first rose to attention through the work of J. L. Schellenberg, most notably in a book bearing the name of the argument as its title.[5] Formally stated, Schellenberg's argument is a little unwieldy.[6] Nevertheless, the statement of the argument given in his 2015 book, *The Hiddenness Argument*, yields insight into Schellenberg's position. We ought to begin there:

1. If a perfectly loving God exists, then there exists a God who is always open to a personal relationship with any finite person.
2. If there exists a God who is always open to a personal relationship with any finite person, then no finite person is ever nonresistantly in a state of nonbelief in relation to the proposition that God exists.
3. If a perfectly loving God exists, then no finite person is ever nonresistantly in a state of nonbelief in relation to the proposition that God exists (from 1 and 2).

4. Michael C. Rea, *The Hiddenness of God* (Oxford: Oxford University Press, 2018), xvi.

5. J. L. Schellenberg, *The Hiddenness Argument: Philosophy's New Challenge to Belief in God* (Oxford: Oxford University Press, 2015), kindle edition.

6. For this reason, I will, at times, refer to Charity Anderson's concise reformulation.

4. Some finite persons are or have been nonresistantly in a state of nonbelief in relation to the proposition that God exists.
5. No perfectly loving God exists (from 3 and 4).
6. If no perfectly loving God exists, then God does not exist.
7. God does not exist (from 5 and 6).

Central to this argument is a powerful entailment claim—from a loving God to the absence of nonresistant nonbelief. Where premises 1 and 2 provide support for this crucial entailment, it is in premise 3 that the rhetorical force becomes clear. If Schellenberg is correct, then the existence of a loving God would *rule out* the possibility of sincere skepticism about that God's existence.

Anderson captures the core of the argument by condensing this central claim:

1. If a loving God exists, then there are no nonresistant nonbelievers.
2. There are nonresistant nonbelievers.
3. No loving God exists.[7]

Despite their differences, each of these statements shares the same central idea: A loving God would have to be *epistemically accessible* to everyone who wished to find him, at least in the minimal sense of *obviously existing*.[8] Such a God need not be transparent in motives; some degree of transcendence would be fine. The one scenario ruled out, on pain of contradiction, is this: A loving God exists and a person who is open to his existence remains unconvinced of it.

I say "on pain of contradiction" because this is not an inductive argument. Strikingly, Schellenberg does not claim that theism is unlikely given the presence of certain hiddenness facts.[9] Instead, he takes the existence of a certain class of persons—nonresistant nonbelievers, or what we might call *sincere agnostics*—as incontrovertible evidence against theism. He emphasizes the benefits of this deductive structure, writing:

---

7. Charity Anderson, "Divine Hiddenness, Defeated Evidence," *Royal Institute of Philosophy Supplements* 81 (2017): 120.

8. To get a sense of the epistemic bar being set here, it may help to note Schellenberg's clarification: "The argument nowhere states nor implies that God's presence would be *felt* by all, let alone felt overwhelmingly, but only that all who are nonresistant will believe that God exists." *The Hiddenness Argument*, 106.

9. I believe the use of the term *hiddenness facts* originates with Charity Anderson, "Divine Hiddenness: An Evidential Argument," *Philosophical Perspectives* 35 (2021): 5–22.

> There's an important structural point here. . . . This is that no similarly deductive argument for the existence of God is even being defended these days. . . . Even if completely successful, such a case [for an inductive argument] is going to be outweighed by a deductive argument for atheism with premises that seem clearly true even after objections have been considered, and with conclusions that clearly follow with necessity.[10]

According to the hiddenness argument, a hidden God would be *no God at all.* The very idea of a perfectly loving, perfectly just, eternal being whose existence is up for debate is, on this view, internally incoherent. "In other words," he writes, "there's no logical room for agnosticism; seeing what makes her agnostic, the agnostic should be led by it straight past agnosticism to atheism."[11] To say that the existence of God might be hidden is, therefore, akin to saying that a triangle might be round—the former as much a contradiction as the latter.[12]

Doubt as Incoherence

Suppose that Schellenberg is correct about this. What follows? Every major religion ascribes some degree of transcendence to God; every Abrahamic religion acknowledges the human experience of feeling, at times, that God has abandoned his post. I am not sure that anyone has captured this experience as well as Elie Wiesel. In the introduction to Wiesel's *Five Biblical Portraits*, Ariel Burger offers the following exemplification of Wiesel's "*wounded faith*":

> In Auschwitz, he witnessed a rabbinical court hold a trial of God. . . . As Wiesel recounts in his memoirs and elsewhere, after several days of deliberation, the head rabbinic judge announced the court's verdict: "In the matter of omnipotent God allowing His children to be oppressed, attacked, and destroyed *en masse*, our verdict is: *guilty*." The rabbi paused, then continued: "Now it is time for the evening prayer: let us pray."

---

10. Schellenberg, *The Hiddenness Argument*, 112–13.

11. Schellenberg, *The Hiddenness Argument*, 25.

12. In chapter 1 of her forthcoming book on the subject, Anderson notes that Schellenberg's argument is akin to Mackie's logical argument from evil. That is, it is not merely structured in a deductive form, but the premises are intended as conceptual truths. Anderson, *Divine Hiddenness and Evidence for God* (forthcoming).

> This scene, the basis for Wiesel's play *The Trial of God*, remained with him all his life. It perfectly captured a seemingly paradoxical Jewish ethos of arguing *against* God *within* a faith context—the essence of what would become Wiesel's wounded faith.[13]

If Schellenberg is correct, then this Jewish ethos is not merely paradoxical; it is nonsensical. More broadly, if sincere agnosticism is logically incompatible with the existence of God, then every major religion is internally incoherent. Insofar as they leave room for doubt, they are all—every one of them—intellectual nonstarters. This is, I think, a claim so bold as to demand scrutiny.

Schellenberg does not dispute the possibility of a loving God whose *ways* are, in some respects, beyond our comprehension. He acknowledges that "there are all kinds of ways in which facts about God might be hidden from us even if God's existence—with which the argument is alone concerned—were not hidden."[14] The only thing he deems impossible is for there to be a God whose *existence* is hidden. I suppose there is a way of reading Wiesel's account on which every member of the rabbinic court remained steadfast in his belief in the existence of a loving God. This is, I submit, not the most plausible of readings. Instead, I am inclined to leave room for the possibility of serious doubt about the existence of the very God to whom they prayed.

The line between grappling with God and doubting that God exists is a fine one. I am not confident that we can always rightly discern which of the two we ourselves are engaged in. I will return to this point towards the end of the paper, for I think there is much to be said about the role of interpretation in introspection. For now, I offer the following illustration. Both Flannery O'Connor and Mother Teresa lived lives of public faith. Both also struggled with private doubts, revealed by their posthumously published correspondence. Mother Teresa's letters mostly display a profound perseverance of faith through the unfathomable suffering she witnessed in her ministry. Still, it cannot be denied that her despair, at times, clearly manifested as doubts about the existence of God:

> Where is my faith?—even deep down, right in, there is nothing but emptiness & darkness.—My God—how painful is this unknown pain.

13. Elie Wiesel, *Five Biblical Portraits* (Notre Dame, IN: University of Notre Dame Press, 1981; 2023), xii–xiii.
14. Schellenberg, *The Hiddenness Argument*, 17.

> It pains without ceasing.—I have no faith . . . If there be God,—please forgive me.[15]

Likewise, Flannery O'Connor wrote:

> I think there is no suffering greater than what is caused by the doubts of those who want to believe. I know what torment this is, but I can only see it, in myself anyway, as the process by which faith is deepened.[16]

If O'Connor and Mother Teresa are any indication, then doubt can be transformative; it can be sanctifying. Moreover, if Christianity is right about who God is, then God allows his creatures to *wonder* about his existence. He leaves room for doubt. He knows this. He is able to prevent it—though, presumably, not without cost. He does not prevent it. This much, I am convinced, is a straightforward Christian commitment.

We are now in a position to see the scope of the consequences of Schellenberg's central claim. If he is correct, then the moment lament begins to include sincere doubt about the existence of God, it becomes self-contradictory. There is some tension in the act of despairing *to God* such that you are beginning to wonder whether God even exists. This much is obvious; tension, alone, is not the claim here. Instead, on Schellenberg's view, crying out to God while doubting his existence becomes *rationally impossible*; to do so would be to cry out to a God who *cannot*, on pain of contradiction, exist. Your own sincere doubt refutes the possibility. You are, in your *nonresistant nonbelief*, incontrovertible evidence of atheism.[17] To reiterate Schellenberg's succinct conclusion, "there's no logical room for agnosticism."[18]

Situating the Hiddenness Argument

This conclusion would come as a shock to the great wealth of historical philosophers and religious scholars. How should we explain the history of philosophical and theological reasoning about a topic that is, at the end

---

15. Mother Teresa and Brian Kolodiejchuk, *Come Be My Light: The Private Writings of the "Saint of Calcutta"* (New York: Doubleday, 2007), 187.

16. Flannery O'Connor, *The Habit of Being: Letters of Flannery O'Connor* (New York: Farrar, Straus and Giroux, 1988).

17. It is worth noting, here, that *nonbelief* is carefully chosen terminology. The bar here is not atheism; one need only be "nonresistantly in a state of nonbelief."

18. Schellenberg, *The Hiddenness Argument*, 25.

of the day, literal nonsense? Schellenberg considers this question, asking, "But why did it take so long for such a thing to occur? Where was the hiddenness argument during all of philosophy's history?"[19] Ultimately, he settles on this answer: The hiddenness argument was waiting for conditions to be right. I don't think conditions were right for this challenge to theistic belief to be taken seriously until fairly recently. Several interwoven sorts of cultural evolution had to take place before it could be.[20] What kinds of *cultural evolution*? Schellenberg details three broad categories of evolution: social/psychological, moral, and theological/philosophical.

All three categories of cultural evolution have significant implications for the idea of a loving God. Schellenberg writes,

> Not so very long ago, no one thought anything of it if a father was absent from the lives of his children for considerable stretches of time, or if he had some trouble relating with them amiably. Indeed, any male who absented himself from ordinary contexts of social interaction to carry out admirable feats on behalf of the "common good" was especially praised.[21]

In contrast, loving fathers today can be found "summoning the strength required to be a stay-at-home dad."[22] On the whole, we are increasingly inclined to value emotional intimacy over what Schellenberg calls the "benevolence from a distance" approach to love. Finally, we have grown suspicious of viewing God as *masculine* and the world as *sinful.*[23]

As a result of these changes, we are better able to see certain features necessary for a loving relationship that were, prior to this cultural evolution, unclear to us. "And in these altered circumstances," he writes, "the flourishing in philosophy of a new argument against the existence of God focused on divine hiddenness has become possible."[24] More directly, we are finally able to *see* the logical tension—further, the *outright incompatibility*—that arises from considering the existence of a loving, hidden God.

Schellenberg's conception of a loving God is incompatible with the God of every Abrahamic religion. The two cannot be reconciled. If, as Schellenberg claims, this incompatibility is a matter of logical deduction

19. Schellenberg, *The Hiddenness Argument*, 23–24.
20. Schellenberg, *The Hiddenness Argument*, 31–32.
21. Schellenberg, *The Hiddenness Argument*, 32.
22. Schellenberg, *The Hiddenness Argument*, 33.
23. Schellenberg, *The Hiddenness Argument*, 33.
24. Schellenberg, *The Hiddenness Argument*, 33.

from purely rational concepts, then the hiddenness argument is a powerful argument indeed. For this reason, I will now turn my attention to this crucial concept—that of a *perfectly loving* God. Insofar as Schellenberg's *perfect love* stands opposed to the divine love depicted in Scripture, Christians have some reason to oppose it. Even so, we should take care to avoid circularity. Rather than argue from the biblical God to a conception of divine love that allows for skepticism, it would be better to show that Schellenberg's love fails for independent reasons. This is a straightforwardly attainable task. Where Schellenberg sees *cultural evolution*, I think we should be wary of going so far. In claiming that some concept has evolved, we are saying two distinct things: There has been a *change*, and the change is for the *better*. I will argue, in response, that we have reason to reject both claims.

In an interesting aside, Schellenberg explicitly rejects the link between evolution and improvement. Although he takes these cultural changes to be for the good, he also writes that "evolution does not necessarily signal improvement."[25] I am including this fact because, *contra* his attempt to distance the success of the argument from the goodness of these changes, no such distance is possible. By his own admission, the argument depends upon these areas of cultural evolution. If they have not been improvements, then we have reason to be wary of the argument they engendered. Divine love was not formerly taken to entail what Schellenberg calls *openness*. If we are to accept the argument today, we must therefore agree that the former conception of divine love was in error.

Love and Openness: Human and Divine

The central claim of Schellenberg's argument is the incompatibility of a loving creator God with a creation that includes sincere (nonresistant) skeptics. Hence, his first three premises run:

1. If a perfectly loving God exists, then there exists a God who is always open to a personal relationship with any finite person.
2. If there exists a God who is always open to a personal relationship with any finite person, then no finite person is ever nonresistantly in a state of nonbelief in relation to the proposition that God exists.

25. Schellenberg, *The Hiddenness Argument*, 33.

3. If a perfectly loving God exists, then no finite person is ever nonresistantly in a state of nonbelief in relation to the proposition that God exists (from 1 and 2).

Perfect divine love entails perfect openness, which entails a degree of self-revelation sufficient to ensure theism among all but those who are resistant to God. This is the crux of Schellenberg's argument.

The theist who rejects this line of reasoning has two options: She can reject the move from *love* to *openness* (premise 1), or the claim that *openness* entails the kind of evidence that Schellenberg takes it to require (premise 2). Unlike the general category of love, Schellenberg explicitly defines *openness*, and he does so in a way that guarantees the truth of the second premise. Holding constant what he means by this term, I will therefore focus on the first of these entailments. As I hope to show, divine love and Schellenberg's *openness* come apart. There is no straightforward entailment from the former to the latter.

To see why, consider Schellenberg's initial definition. He writes, "Being open in the relevant sense at a certain time simply means not (then) being closed. It means not through one's own actions or omissions making it impossible for the other, whom one loves, to participate in personal relationship with one at that time should the other wish to do so."[26] So understood, the connection between love and openness seems to be a modest assumption. In the general case, when a person loves another, she works to avoid preventing the other from being in a relationship with herself. Of course, as Schellenberg notes, finite humans are not always able to prevent some degree of distance. From the practical limitations of daily living to the extreme cases of war or serious illness, loving human relationships are often subject to periods of painful separation. Sometimes, the *closed* periods are even necessary for the good of the beloved. We are finite beings. We can only do so much.

In contrast, Schellenberg notes, God faces no such limitations. Unlike us, "God has the resources to accommodate the possible consequences of openness to relationship with finite persons, making them compatible with the flourishing of all concerned, and of any relationship that may come to exist between them."[27] In other words, God has the ability to be *maximally* open. There could be no conflict between his openness to us and

26. Schellenberg, *The Hiddenness Argument*, 41.
27. Schellenberg, *The Hiddenness Argument*, 45.

our flourishing, for he is the source of all flourishing and the origin of all possible conflicts. Remember, "God gets to set everything up in the first place."[28] Schellenberg thus concludes that a loving God would be open to all finite creatures, at all times, without exception.

In the case of God, a failure to be open would be, according to Schellenberg, a failure to be loving. Not so for finite creatures. Ordinary loving people often face circumstances which prevent them from being open in the way they might otherwise be. Neither is it merely a matter of possibility; they sometimes have to weigh competing goods. Thus, Schellenberg issues this final clarification. We can, he says, expect love to yield openness reliably "wherever the lover has the resources to accommodate the possible consequences of such openness, making them compatible with the flourishing of both parties and of any relationship that may come to exist between them."[29] The love of a finite creature tends towards openness. It does not entail openness. If it did, then the person who was closed would no longer count as loving—even if their reasons were quite good and the period of separation quite short. When love is understood as entailing openness, then the person who is closed must, for as long as she is closed, fail to love. This is a bar too high for human love. Schellenberg admits as much, and he is right to do so.

Better, still, would be to see that this is a bar too high even for divine love. If not *too high*, then certainly *wrongly placed*. If finite love tends, on balance, to yield openness, and if that balance concerns competing goods, then we might say that love is *all things considered open*. When being open is compatible with the flourishing of the lover and the beloved, then love yields openness. Why, then, should perfect love not include perfect consideration of competing goods? Schellenberg addresses this, of course. He rejects the possibility of there being any competing goods for God to consider. What is notable, however, is that this claim makes no real appearance in the argument.

This subtle shift from finite to divine openness is significant. Where the argument appears to proceed on the basis of divine love alone, the meaning of divine openness relies upon this implicit, substantial philosophical claim. By collapsing the latter into the former, by explicitly referencing only love and openness, Schellenberg masks a significant assumption: There could be no competing, greater goods at stake; maximal love would

28. Schellenberg, *The Hiddenness Argument*, 45.
29. Schellenberg, *The Hiddenness Argument*, 44–45.

be maximally open, no matter the consequences. It is, of course, precisely this assumption that the standard theistic responses to the problems of evil and hiddenness reject; this is where theodicies, defenses, and skeptical theism all have something to say.

The theist should reject the second premise of Schellenberg's argument.[30] In its place, we might instead propose:

> If there exists a God who is always open to a personal relationship with any finite person, then [God desires, all things considered, that] no finite person is ever nonresistantly in a state of nonbelief in relation to the proposition that God exists.

In this way, we can affirm that God is *all things considered* open, without thereby eliminating the possibility of a loving God who permits hiddenness for the sake of some greater good. To move from here to the atheistic conclusion, one would have to include a premise about overriding goods. At this point, Schellenberg's deductive argument would become something like an evidential argument.[31]

An Argument from Hiddenness Amidst Suffering

In a number of significant ways, Schellenberg's argument reminds me of another recent argument from (a kind of) hiddenness. In "The Parent-Child Analogy and the Limits of Skeptical Theism," Erik Wielenberg argues against the existence of the Christian God on the basis of divine hiddenness in the midst of suffering.[32] His argument proceeds as follows:

1. A loving parent would never permit her children to experience prolonged, intense, and apparently gratuitous suffering together

30. In her 2023 keynote address at a Society of Christian Philosophers conference, Charity Anderson noted that Schellenberg's argument uses a "Mackie-style" structure. (In her forthcoming manuscript, she affirms the same, *Divine Hiddenness and Evidence for God.*) It is perhaps unsurprising, then, to find that there is a strong similarity between this weakness in Schellenberg's argument and Plantinga's response to Mackie's logical argument from evil. Both arguments assume the compossibility of the goods that God would value. Unlike Mackie's argument, Schellenberg builds the assumption into a single entailment claim, thereby preserving a valid structure. Even so, the truth of the premise depends upon the assumption shared by Mackie and Schellenberg.

31. In her forthcoming book, Anderson suggests precisely this—that the hiddenness argument is an evidential argument. See Anderson, *Divine Hiddenness and Evidence for God.*

32. Erik J. Wielenberg, "The Parent–Child Analogy and the Limits of Skeptical Theism," *International Journal for Philosophy of Religion* 78 (2015), 301–14.

with a sense she has abandoned them or never existed in the first place if she could avoid doing so.

2. If the Christian God exists, then the God-human relationship is relevantly like the parent-child relationship.
3. So, if the Christian God exists, then He never permits humans to experience apparently gratuitous suffering and abandonment if He can avoid doing so (from 1 and 2).
4. But if the Christian God exists, then He does permit His children to experience apparently gratuitous suffering and abandonment when He could avoid doing so.
5. Therefore, the Christian God does not exist (from 3 and 4).[33]

This argument is notable in two respects: it targets the Christian God in particular, and it avoids the "noseeum inference" so often featured in evidential arguments from evil.[34] At no point does Wielenberg explicitly appeal to God's possible reasons for acting. Instead, he attempts to describe a scenario that would never—for *any* reason—occur in a loving parental relationship.

I have already claimed that the Christian God permits us to experience divine hiddenness. I will now go further: In response to Wielenberg, I grant that our God allows his creatures to feel abandoned even in the midst of what feels to them like terrible suffering. Not only does God allow this kind of suffering, but loving human parents do, as well. This is why, in a response to Wielenberg's argument, I have argued that his first premise is demonstrably false. At first glance, I grant that this is an unpalatable premise to reject:

1. A loving parent would never permit her children to experience prolonged, intense, and apparently gratuitous suffering together with a sense she has abandoned them or never existed in the first place if she could avoid doing so.

With reflection, ordinary, mundane counterexamples abound. (Just how mundane? My response is titled "Sleep Training, Day Care, and Swim

---

33. Wielenberg, "The Parent–Child Analogy," 307.

34. Briefly, a "noseeum inference" makes the following claim: "I cannot see reasons why a good God would allow so much suffering, so there must not be any such reasons." See Steve Wykstra, "Rowe's Noseeum Arguments from Evil," in *The Evidential Argument from Evil*, ed. D. Howard-Snyder (Bloomington: Indiana University Press, 1996), 126–50.

Lessons.")[35] It is, of course, true that no loving parent would allow her child to feel abandoned in the midst of great suffering *without good reason*. This is not the same as saying that she would never do so *if it could, in any way, be avoided*.

In addition to my mundane counterexamples, we can add the following devastating realities faced by loving parents: those in war-time London who sent their terrified children away to strangers while their homes were bombed; parents of children who, for reasons of disability or age, could not understand the extended isolation of their Covid-era hospital stay; every parent who, in desperation, sends their infant away *forever*, knowing that an international adoption is their child's best chance of survival. In each of these cases, the action could have been avoided. The costs would have been high, but—crucially—a *justifiable* decision is not an *unavoidable* one. The premise is false. Loving parents make hard choices. What love *looks like* to the beloved is so much more complicated than we would like it to be.

What does this have to do with Schellenberg? Structurally, Wielenberg's argument shares the deductive force prized by Schellenberg. More strikingly, in both Wielenberg's and Schellenberg's arguments we find a reliance on a conception of love that is highly culturally embedded. Schellenberg writes:

> If it is hard to see why consistent openness should be built into our idea of God's unsurpassable love, then it may be worthwhile contemplating a bit the most obviously loving people in our experience. For such people—loving parents, siblings, friends, teachers—consistent openness is taken quite for granted: this is where things start in the story of their interaction with us.[36]

It is a contingent fact about our culture that we expect those who love us to be available to us at all times. We should take care not to build this contingency into the very idea of love. If we do so, we run the risk of hubris. When we go further, requiring even of God that his love meet this standard, we run the risk of philosophical error.

Here, I am reminded of Amy Peeler's caution, developed in the process of making sense of what it means to say that God is our father: "The language of the Bible is language that accommodates the human experience.

---

35. Morris, "Sleep Training, Day Care, and Swim Lessons: Skeptical Theism and the Parent-Child Analogy," *Faith and Philosophy: Journal of the Society of Christian Philosophers* 40, no. 1 (2023), 10.37977/faithphil.2023.40.1.2.

36. Schellenberg, *The Hiddenness Argument*, 41.

Revelation from God can be trusted to be true of God but does not indicate that humans who use the revealed language have mastered God. For if God could be mastered, such an entity would no longer be God."[37] There are limits to how far we can stretch our concepts. We can, I think, be confident about some features of love: a desire for the wellbeing of the beloved; a desire, all things considered, for union with the beloved. We can even appeal to our culturally informed ideal to draw probabilistic conclusions about how we might expect a perfectly loving being to behave. To take this culturally embedded ideal and attempt to derive a contradiction, as Wielenberg and Schellenberg both do, is a step too far.

Revisiting Schellenberg's remarks about cultural evolution, I am now in a position to reject both aspects of his claim. In the first place, it is not clear that our idea of love has changed. If the expectation that love yields openness has always been dependent upon circumstance, then perhaps we should instead say this: our expectations have shifted in light of our privileged circumstances. We now expect those who love us to be open to us. We do so not because our conception of love has changed but because we rarely face the kinds of challenges that would justify the alternative. We are eminently reachable; technology has radically altered our expectations in this regard. We have grown used to openness. In the second place, it is equally unclear that even this change is an improvement, all things considered. It may be! But it may instead be the case that there are cultural virtues that are enhanced by self-sacrifice and impeded by individualism. This is a topic for another day. Even so, we would do well to remember how difficult it is to accurately assess the historical value of one's own cultural moment.

Returning to their arguments, at a crucial juncture both Wielenberg and Schellenberg appeal to an implicit assumption: There is nothing God could value that would justify the kind of divine hiddenness we find in our world. It is not merely that a loving God would value openness; he must value it *above all else.* This is a weighty philosophical claim. If it is to play a role in an argument, then it ought to show up, explicitly, among the premises.

The Role of Experience in Hiddenness Arguments

There is one further feature held in common by these arguments: both appeal to the experience of an individual. In Wielenberg's case, the appeal

37. Amy Peeler, *Women and the Gender of God* (Grand Rapids, Eerdmans, 2022), kindle edition, 26.

is straightforward: His premise invokes the feelings of some individuals. Schellenberg's reliance on first-person experience is less explicit but no less important. In granting that at least one person is a nonresistant nonbeliever, we must say both that a person lacks belief and is not *resistant.* The latter criterion requires an appeal to introspection and interpretation. It requires that the nonresistant nonbeliever be right about what kinds of evidence she has encountered.

I wonder, therefore, whether the right way of conceptualizing the hiddenness argument might be as an argument from religious experience. In a response to Harold Netland's book *Religious Experience and Knowledge of God*, I focused on "negative religious experience"—that is, experiences of the world *as* devoid of God.[38] William Rowe, having had a dramatic conversion experience in his youth, later shared the following account of the years that came after that conversion:

> I longed for a sense of God's presence in my life. . . . And although I spent hours in prayer and thirsted after some dim assurance that God was present, I never had any such experience. . . . So, it was the absence of religious experiences of the appropriate kind that, as I would put it now, left me free to seriously explore the grounds for disbelief.[39]

Alex O'Connor, in the debate to which I previously referred, notes:

> I was once an altar boy. . . . In the time since then, I have, to put it mildly, been looking for God. . . . Just recently I agreed to embark on a series of studies of the wisdom literature, specifically reading it again in the hopes that this time I might finally feel a divine presence seeping from between the lines. I moved into a house for a year with two devoutly Christian housemates with the express intention of seeing if the obvious truth of Christianity and theism that people like to talk about can be found in the minutia of daily life. . . . Nothing. Not once, not nearly, not ever, not even briefly have I experienced anything that speaks to the existence of a God in the universe.[40]

---

38. Dolores G. Morris, "Experiencing the World as Godless," *Philosophia Christi* 25, no. 2 (2023): 169–79.
39. Trakakis, "Interview with William Rowe," *Philosophy Now* 47 (2004): 16–18.
40. Alex O'Connor, "Debate: Theism vs Atheism."

These are, if not statements of the hiddenness argument, then something like them. They are first-person reports of nonresistant nonbelievers.

What are we to make of these claims? I want to suggest we treat them as we do all first person reports of religious experience: with sympathy, with charity, but not without scrutiny. When a person claims that she has unsuccessfully pursued a religious experience, she is making a claim that is precisely analogous to a positive religious experience. We do not treat negative religious experiences in quite the same way that we do positive ones. We ascribe a degree of *veridicality* to the former that even the most ardent of theists will typically withhold from the latter.

In a fascinating passage, Schellenberg shares his own history with religious experience, writing, "At various times early in my life I had powerful theistic religious experiences. But since leaving theistic religion—indeed, after becoming an atheist—I have also at various times had powerful and unmistakably religious experiences that had no distinctively theistic content at all."[41] Here is one way of understanding Schellenberg's experiential shift: As a young Christian, his religious framework led him to ascribe doctrinal meaning to his general religious experiences. Those interpreted experiences, in turn, generated religious beliefs. Now, he is free to have such experiences without forming any religious beliefs. This is a story of progress, a kind of liberating enlightenment. It also undermines the evidential weight of religious experience in belief formation—Schellenberg's express aim in this passage. There is another possibility, though. It may be that Schellenberg continues to experience the God of his youth but no longer recognizes him as such. We should acknowledge this possibility.

From the ordinary to the mystical, every experience can be parsed in at least two ways: What was the experience *like*? And what was it an experience *of*? Even in the most mundane cases, the two can come apart. When we introspect on our own experience, we can get the object of our experience wrong. For positive religious experiences, we accept this.

I submit that this reveals a significant asymmetry in our treatment of negative religious experiences. We commonly remain agnostic about positive religious experiences. "I met God" is not taken to constitute irrefutable evidence that a person has, in fact, met God. Why, then, are we hesitant to hold negative religious experiences to the same standard? When a person claims to have sought God without success, to have experienced the world as *godless*, on what basis do we accept this report as *true*?

---

41. Schellenberg, *The Hiddenness Argument*, 115–16.

We have all unwittingly encountered some object of experience—a book we think we have not read, a band we think we have not heard. Nor is it merely that we forget; we can miss it in the moment. As a silly example, a friend in graduate school wanted to play Poison at a party. We all objected. He insisted, swearing that we actually liked Poison. We were all quite sure that we did not. Song after song, he was vindicated. It was embarrassing to have to admit, over and over again, "Well, I never knew *this* was Poison."[42]

Poison, it goes without saying, is not God. It is one thing to unwittingly encounter a band. It is another thing entirely to encounter *God* and not know it. Surely, we might say, an experience of God would be pretty clear. Perhaps this explains our hesitation to make such a claim. If it succeeds as an explanation, it fails as a justification. Indeed, it confirms the asymmetry, for we do not say the same about those who claim to have encountered this unmistakable God.

As a final illustration, consider the following argument from religious experience. Notably, this argument satisfies the criteria for a counterargument set by Schellenberg: It is deductive, and it is an argument for "a 'person-like' God."[43]

1. If God does not exist, then every person who takes herself to have had an experience of God is wrong.
2. It is false that every person who takes herself to have had an experience of God is wrong.
3. Therefore, God exists.

The first premise of this argument is indisputable. For atheism, the person who claims to have encountered God may be right about what her experience *seemed like*, but she cannot be right about the object of that experience. No one has ever experienced that which does not exist. The second premise is a minimal empirical claim. It requires only that *one* of the countless people who have taken themselves to have experienced God be right about that. Remember, if we wish to say that an experience of God would be obvious, then we ought to be wary of rejecting every report of a purported experience of God as confused, misguided, or otherwise false.

It is not my intention to advance a new argument for theism on the

42. Ironically, there is some disagreement in my marriage as to whether this band was Poison or Rush. It is possible this even happened twice!

43. Schellenberg, *The Hiddenness Argument*, 112.

basis of religious experience. I am inclined to believe that this argument is valid and sound, but I am skeptical of its rhetorical power. My real aim is to illustrate the disparity in our treatment of positive and negative religious experiences. If my argument lacks force, it is only because premise 2 is an easy target. This is telling. When confronted with the argument from hiddenness, we are wary of telling nonbelievers that they may be missing something—evidence of or experience with God. But we are not at all wary of dismissing the claims of those who take themselves to have had such encounters.

What would it look like to *miss* an experience of God? Here, I think the case of Alex O'Connor may be especially noteworthy. By his own report, O'Connor has dedicated his life to questions about the existence of God. Having long ago ceased believing in God, he nevertheless *pursues* this belief to a nearly all-consuming degree. We should ask: Might this *be* an experience of God? Could what feels like nagging compulsion be divine invitation? I think it is a possibility worth considering—not just for O'Connor but for reports of negative religious experience in general.

My driving question is this: How confident should we be that we can tell the difference, through introspection, between a God who is *absent* and a God who is *hidden*, *silent*, or otherwise *inscrutable*? Earlier I referenced Job. Perhaps the most striking literary depiction of the God who refuses to explain himself can be found in Dostoevsky's "Grand Inquisitor." In this poem-within-a-novel, the Grand Inquisitor lays out his case against Jesus, accusing him of grossly overestimating his creatures. The inquisitor lambasts Jesus for his unwillingness to use coercive power to win more followers. Jesus responds in three ways: First, he persists in doing exactly that which he is accused of, refusing to use miracle, mystery, or authority to overpower the inquisitor. Second, he remains silent. Finally, when he does respond, he simply kisses the inquisitor. This is a God whose silence is oppressive. Even so, it is a God who loves us.

Conclusion

In the introduction, I wrote that my primary goal in this paper was constructive rather than defensive. To that end, I want to conclude by noting two things. In the first place, Schellenberg, Wielenberg, Rowe, and Alex O'Connor are right to note that the existence of God is not always obvious to everybody. It is not even obvious to everybody who wishes it were the case. If Mother Teresa and Flannery O'Connor had to navigate doubts, and if Scripture tells us that we should expect as much, then we ought to grant this point without hesitation. As Christians, we worship a hidden God.

Those same Scriptures also tell us that God is for us. How can this be? Here, I think, the point at which we break from the hiddenness argument matters. If our God is for us, then our God loves us—and *it matters* what that means. If perfect love means prioritizing our awareness of God's existence above all else, then we must admit that our God is falling short.[44] What if, instead, God values more than this? What if a loving God would value goods that might, at times, *stand in the way* of his openness to us? Even Schellenberg grants that we must distinguish love from goodness or benevolence, writing, "Love entails benevolence but goes beyond it too."[45] But so too does benevolence go beyond love. If God is perfectly good, then he is also just and righteous and worthy of all praise. When we remember this, when we remember that the God who is for us is not therefore *subject to* us, we are better able to see the astonishing love behind those actions such a God might take to reconcile us to himself: the incarnation of the second person of the Trinity and the passion and resurrection of Christ. The beauty of the Christian story is that if it is true, then the God who is hidden from us nevertheless pursues us, redeems us, and restores us.

Going forward, how should we respond to the hiddenness argument? Existentially, we can agree that hiddenness is hard. Philosophically, we should resist the tendency to assume that those who experience God as hidden are immune to introspective error. This is not to say that sincere skeptics are *secretly resistant* to God. In rejecting the claim that a loving God would be maximally open in the way Schellenberg describes, I absolutely affirm the possibility of nonresistant nonbelievers in a theistic world. Crucially, there are so many alternatives to resistance. When we encounter evidence of something, we do not always rightly interpret it *as* evidence. On matters other than God, we all know this. With respect to purported experiences of God, we grant this as well. We ought, therefore, to do the same for those to whom God seems especially absent. We should ask how much emphasis we ought to place on introspection. Could we justifiably conclude an *absent* God, as opposed to a *hidden* or *silent* one? If not, then perhaps part of what is needed is further reflection—about love, about goodness, and about our experiences of this world.

---

44. Rea goes further, arguing that an all-consuming attention to our wellbeing would undermine God's personhood and be something akin to the improper worship of humans, *The Hiddenness of God*, chapter 5.

45. Schellenberg, *The Hiddenness Argument*, 43.

CHAPTER 5

RETHINKING OMNISCIENCE IN AN AGE OF SURVEILLANCE CAPITALISM

God's Knowledge for Us

SARA MANNEN

Every day we are under nearly constant surveillance. Most of us have probably made a joke about Facebook, Amazon, or Google watching us—no doubt in response to our deep-seated fear and discomfort with the, at times, unnerving accuracy of their advertising algorithms. At each one of our waking moments, we are being surveilled as we read the news online, drive on roads covered in CCTV cameras, use a rewards card to purchase lunch, tap a debit card, and post on social media. At these points and countless others, information about us is extracted and collated to create a data profile that is sold to countless companies. We are rarely aware of the extent of the surveillance we are under, nor do we know how the data about us is used.[1] Others have observed that the digital age's information or "knowledge" gained through corporate surveillance mimics the doctrine of divine omniscience.[2] Hanna Reichel states, "[I]t is not

1. For more on this, see Hanna Reichel, "Worldmaking Knowledge: What the Doctrine of Omniscience Can Help Us Understand about Digitization (Part II)," *Zeitschrift für Explorative Theologie* (2019): 1–14; Shoshana Zuboff, *The Age of Surveillance Capitalism: The Fight for a Human Future at the New Frontier of Power* (New York: Public Affairs, 2019); Wolfie Christl, "Corporate Surveillance in Everyday Life: How Companies Collect, Combine, Analyze, Trade, and Use Personal Data on Billions," Cracked Labs: Institute for Critical Digital Culture, June 2017, 79–81, https://crackedlabs.org/en/corporate-surveillance; Finn Brunton and Helen Nissenbaum, *Obfuscation: A User's Guide for Privacy and Protest* (London: MIT Press, 2015), 49–51.

2. This paper focuses on the issue of privacy, surveillance, and omniscience; therefore, it will not address the distinctions between data, information, and knowledge. There is no consensus among those in information science regarding the definition and relation between data, information, and knowledge. However, research has found that those in informational science generally take

farfetched to postulate the digital age is an age of superhuman knowledge . . . machine-learning empowered 'big data' analytics allows for both 'more' and a different kind of knowledge than could ever be accumulated (or understood) by human agents, whether individual or collective."[3] Humanity now lives in an age of surveillance capitalism and expanding superhuman knowledge that increasingly serves as an imitation of or substitution for divine omniscience. This should not be surprising given that Adam Smith explicitly understood the "invisible hand" of the market as divine providence.[4] Surveillance capitalism usurps God with its version of omniscient knowing so that it can itself become the invisible hand controlling the market.

While fully acknowledging that the issue of privacy does not begin to solve or adequately address the complex and numerous problems related to big data and corporate surveillance,[5] this chapter explores how big data's "omniscience" that relies on the constant invasion of privacy through digital surveillance poses challenges to the doctrine of divine omniscience that requires rethinking the doctrine in light of God's personal nature *for us.* This essay presupposes that privacy, when properly defined, is a good of human life *and* that we are now living in the age of surveillance capitalism. The questions to be further explored are how divine omniscience differs from big data's "omniscience" and whether the good of privacy applies to the God-human relation.

---

a non-metaphysical, human-centred, cognitive-based, propositional approach to defining these terms. Data and information are usually viewed as external phenomena while knowledge is usually considered an internal phenomenon. Data can be thought of as representations of raw facts and material of sensible stimuli; information is generally thought in terms of the meaning of data or communication; knowledge can be thought of as the assimilation and experience of perceiving information or a construct used to organise and relate information. See Chaim Zins, "Conceptual Approaches for Defining Data, Information, and Knowledge," *Journal of the American Society for Information Science and Technology* 58, no. 4 (2007): 479–93. Regardless of whether the information of big data surveillance meets the criteria for the philosophical definition of knowledge, this is still a pressing issue since big data and its surveillance create a reality and powerful metaphor of "knowledge" and "omniscience" that significantly shapes and transforms how humanity thinks about itself and God's omniscient knowledge.

3. Hanna Reichel, "Worldmaking Knowledge: What the Doctrine of Omniscience Can Help Us Understand about Digitization (Part I)," *Zeitschrift für Explorative Theologie* (2019): 2.

4. For the explicit connection of the invisible hand to providence, see Adam Smith, *The Theory of Moral Sentiments*, 2nd ed. (Edinburgh: Kincaid and Bell, 1761), 4.1, 273. However, the underpinning of providence is evident in his later discussion in *An Inquiry into the Nature and Causes of the Wealth of Nations* (London: Electric, 2000), 4.2, 593. It is important to note that the invisible hand functions as a sort of theodicy for Smith. The invisible hand of divine providence explains how selfish local economic actors can benefit the good of the whole society.

5. The issue of privacy fails to grasp the depth of the transformation surveillance capitalism has caused in society and its structures and constructs. However, we do not currently have new vocabulary to address properly the way surveillance capitalism collectively dehumanises and extracts information from us as sources. Therefore, the language of privacy is used throughout this essay. For more on this, see Reichel, "Worldmaking Knowledge (II)," 1–3; Zuboff, *Surveillance Capitalism*, 14, 194.

First, this essay briefly examines the opaque nature of corporate digital surveillance that exists in asymmetric power relations, which seek to exploit and manipulate consumers for profit. Next, the axiological argument against theism based on the claim that divine omniscience violates one's privacy is connected to the concerns of our digital age. This essay contends that our experience of corporate digital surveillance only heightens the axiological argument against theism. The final section attends to the pressing concern that surveillance capitalism's "omniscience" harmfully shapes our thinking and conception of God and divine knowledge. The fear that divine omniscience is a form of voyeurism is addressed by examining Katherine Sonderegger's thought-provoking suggestion that God graciously grants us privacy. The argument of this essay utilises Sonderegger's insistence on the personal nature of divine omniscience to help answer the charge that God violates our privacy. The essay concludes by rejecting the notion that humans need or require privacy from God's perfect knowledge since this usually assumes a competitive model between God and the world. Instead, God's personal knowledge—the knowledge that God *is*—is christologically shaped and, therefore, always the knowledge of God's love for us. Rather than God's omniscient knowing violating our privacy, it is God's intimate knowing of us that constitutes us as persons. Divine omniscience challenges every one of the core tenets of surveillance capitalism's imitation of it. With the Christian God, instead of the opacity of big data, we have the light of God's self-revelation; instead of manipulating data subjects for profit, we recognise that God's omniscience is lovingly *for us*; and in place of asymmetric power relations, we find the divine power manifested in the love of God in Jesus Christ.

Opacity, Asymmetric Power, and Profits

The rapidly evolving and expanding digital world is nearly impossible to avoid.[6] It is precisely the inescapability of the digital that makes

6. Digitisation is becoming a worldwide phenomenon. India's use of *Aadhaars* (digital identifiers) as a prerequisite to access government services and banking has created an environment where one is essentially coerced into a system of digital financialisation and surveillance. The Philippines and Morocco have already instituted their own version of *Aadhaars* while many other countries are looking to follow India as an exemplar, including Russia, Algeria, Mexico, and Tunisia. See Sudeep Jain and Daniela Gabor, "The Rise of Digital Financialisation: The Case of India," *New Political Economy* 25, no. 5 (2020): 813–28; Dia Rekhi, "Philippines, Morocco Implemented Aadhaar-like System; More Countries to Follow Suit, Says Officials," *The Economic Times*, 22 March 2023, https://economictimes.indiatimes.com/magazines/panache/people/et-circle-the-private-equity-playbook-with-manish-kejriwaltrust-mentorship-and-intellectual-honesty-as-pivotal-pillars/articleshow/110211288.cms.

surveillance capitalism effective. Shoshana Zuboff, the pioneer of academic work on surveillance capitalism, defines it thus:

> Surveillance capitalism unilaterally claims human experience as free raw material for translation into behavioral data. Although some of these data are applied to product or service improvement, the rest are declared as proprietary *behavioral surplus*, fed into advanced manufacturing processes known as "machine intelligence," and fabricated into *prediction products* that anticipate what you will do now, soon, and later. Finally, these prediction products are traded in a new kind of marketplace for behavioral predictions that I call *behavioral futures markets*. Surveillance capitalists have grown immensely wealthy from these trading operations, for many companies are eager to lay bets on our future behavior.[7]

This section highlights how surveillance capitalism's "omniscience" relies on opacity, asymmetric power relations, and the objectification of humans as data sources for the increase of corporate profits.

First, there is a complete lack of transparency and honesty regarding how and for what purposes our data is collected and used. The "omniscience" of big data relies on conglomerating data from various unrelated sources to create as detailed and accurate a picture possible of each data subject.[8] Through inferences made using statistical probability to predict our future behaviour, this information becomes "knowledge" that is used to make crucial decisions about our lives, including our finances, insurance, and employment.[9] However, these decisions made with algorithms based on unrelated data become the "ultimate unknowable unknown of data collection."[10] No one knows *why* a decision was made. When companies are pressed to explain their use of data, they retreat into darkness by claiming these practices constitute proprietary trade secrets that must be protected at all costs:

---

7. Zuboff, *Surveillance Capitalism*, 8. Zuboff argues that surveillance capitalism is a significant departure from market capitalism through its insistence on "the privilege of unfettered freedom *and* knowledge," the abandonment of "long-standing reciprocities with people," and the desire for a "collectivist societal vision sustained by radical indifference and its material expression in Big Other" (Zuboff, *Surveillance Capitalism*, 495; cf., 495–512).

8. Christl, "Everyday Life," 54–65; Brunton and Nissenbaum, *Obfuscation*, 49–51; Reichel, "Worldmaking Knowledge (II)," 1–14; Michael Steinmann, "Alienation in a World of Data: Toward a Materialist Interpretation of Digital Information Technologies," *Philosophy & Technology* 35, no. 4 (2022): 99:1–24.

9. Christl, "Everyday Life," 79.

10. Brunton and Nissenbaum, *Obfuscation*, 51–52. For a similar point about our data, see Reichel, "Worldmaking Knowledge (II)," 6–7.

> Perhaps more importantly, though, companies make no effort to improve transparency or understanding; on the contrary, they inform consumers incompletely, inaccurately, or not at all, often employing ambiguous, misleading, and obfuscating language. Whether in user interfaces or in contracts, the disclosures that do exist—such as privacy policies and terms of service—are difficult to understand, obscure, and use hypothetical language.[11]

Surveillance capitalism intentionally seeks to be invisible and incomprehensible so that we remain completely unaware of how and what information about our lives leads to real-world effects.[12] Companies rely on this opacity to continue the practice of data surveillance and to maintain profitability.

Second, the opacity of data surveillance extends and takes place in asymmetric power relations. While companies often claim that we freely consent to sharing our data in exchange for valuable services, the reality is that "opting out of surveillance capitalism is like opting out of electricity, or cooked foods—you are free to do it in theory. . . . The reality is . . . [it] means opting out of much of modern life."[13] Just think about what you would be required to give up to opt out of surveillance capitalism and how this might seriously affect you.[14] What "control" a person is given over her data is often illusory and granted by the system itself. Privacy agreements or the option to opt out of cookies are examples of this type of practice.[15] Additionally, we face daily surveillance and data collection for which we do not give explicit consent. Since data collection and surveillance are intertwined with the essential elements of our daily lives, this creates and further supports growing inequalities in power: "It is obvious that information collection takes place in asymmetrical power relationships: we rarely have a choice as to whether or not we are monitored, what is done with any information that is gathered, or what is done to us on the basis of

---

11. Christl, "Everyday Life," 67.
12. Zuboff, *Surveillance Capitalism*, 10–11.
13. Maciej Cegłowski, "The Moral Economy of Tech," Text version of remarks, SASE conference, Berkeley, June 26, 2016, http://idlewords.com/talks/sase_panel.htm.
14. For example, India's *Aadhaars* are a powerful example of the hold the surveillance capitalism has over humanity. Rejecting a digital identifier means rejecting all government services; see Jain and Gabor, "The Rise of Digital Financialisation," 814–7.
15. Steinmann, "Alienation in a World of Data," 10–14. Case in point, Europe's GDPR has *strengthened* Facebook and Google's hold over consumer data and advertising, see Nick Kostov and Sam Schechner, "GDPR Has Been a Boon for Google and Facebook," *Wall Street Journal*, 17 June 2019, https://www.wsj.com/articles/gdpr-has-been-a-boon-for-google-and-facebook.

conclusions drawn from that information."[16] This vast disparity in power is further reinforced through the asymmetry in knowledge created by surveillance. Zuboff states:

> Surveillance capitalism operates through unprecedented asymmetries in knowledge and the power that accrues to knowledge. Surveillance capitalism knows everything *about us*, whereas their operations are designed to be unknowable *to us*. They accumulate vast domains of new knowledge *from us*, but not *for us*. They predict our futures for the sake of others' gain, not ours.[17]

The opacity and asymmetric power relations of big data's mimicry of omniscience serve one purpose—generating and increasing profits.

Third, it is vital to recognise that the systems and technology needed to sustain data surveillance are costly. The only reason systems like this are in place is because they generate profit for the current economic system.[18] It is vital to recognise that the everyday consumer is *not* the customer in the economy created by surveillance capitalism. The everyday consumer is the data object or source of extracted surplus behavioural information for surveillance capitalism's true customers—enterprises that buy future behavioural predictions.[19] The push to digital forms of communication and commerce is primarily motivated by the vast amount of data that is generated, which allows for more precise predictions of our future behaviour.[20] The goal of a more digitised world is the ability to accurately predict behaviour, which allows "companies to not just predict customer behavior and preferences but also modify them for commercial gain."[21] The objective of surveillance capitalism is to use future

---

16. Brunton and Nissenbaum, *Obfuscation*, 49.

17. Zuboff, *Surveillance Capitalism*, 11, cf. 12, 187–90.

18. Steinmann, "Alienation in a World of Data," 6; Jain and Gabor, "The Rise of Digital Financialisation," 817–19; Christl, "Everyday Life," 67–79.

19. Zuboff, *Surveillance Capitalism*, 10. According to Zuboff, the discovery that changed everything was Google's realisation that "*we are less valuable than others' bets on our future behavior*" (93; cf. 93–4, emphasis original).

20. Christl, "Everyday Life," 40–44, 47–48, 75–79; Daniela Gabor and Sally Brooks, "The Digital Revolution in Financial Inclusion: International Development in the Fintech Era," *New Political Economy* 22, no. 4 (2017): 423–36, Zuboff, *Surveillance Capitalism*, 8–12. Jain and Gabor, "The Rise of Digital Financialisation," 819: "The prize in digital financialisation is not revenue from lopping a small slice off cashless payments but *customer data* obtained through increased surveillance. Digital footprints are harvested and monetised by allowing companies to create more detailed profiles of customers for better targeting of products."

21. Jain and Gabor, "The Rise of Digital Financialisation," 819. Additionally, Michael Steinmann describes this reality in materialist terms as "alienation." Alienation means that both our

behavioural predictions to help its customers increase their profits by influencing and automating consumer behaviour.[22] Zuboff describes this as instrumentarian power—power that knows and shapes human behaviour towards others' ends—to manipulate and automate us.[23] The information or knowledge about us is used by others *for their own profit.* The superhuman knowledge of big data is for the benefit of those companies who control it so that consumer behavioural predictions can be sold and then used to influence and manipulate consumer behaviour more effectively.

The real-world effects of data surveillance should be noted. The "omniscience" of big data changes the world in which we live by seeking to shape and order "data sources"—that is us—to desired effects. Reichel has astutely noted that the questions about data surveillance bear a striking resemblance to the questions that have plagued the doctrine of divine omniscience over the centuries. For Reichel, the convergence between omniscience and digitisation is that both are world creating or world making.[24] Reichel uses the metaphor of a game to illustrate the reality-altering nature of big data technology. Not only do these technologies put new pieces on the board within the game, but they also manufacture the game board itself and fundamentally alter the rules according to which the game is played.[25] It is here that the heart of the issue of digital surveillance, its intrusion into our privacy, and its seeming omniscience become clear. What type of world is created by the omniscience of big data? A world in which people are dehumanised and impersonally reduced to sources of data to predict and manipulate future behaviour and who only matter for the benefit they can provide to those in power. When we theologically reflect on divine omniscience, it is in the context of *this* world that is powerfully created by surveillance capitalism's faux "omniscience," and we must exercise diligence and great caution to avoid allowing this world to influence and distort our theology of God.

"activities and their products are repurposed or controlled by others" (Steinmann, "Alienation in a World of Data," 10).

22. Christl, "Everyday Life," 73–5; Zuboff, *Surveillance Capitalism*; Jain and Gabor, "The Rise of Digital Financialisation," 818–20.

23. Zuboff, *Surveillance Capitalism*, 8.

24. Reichel, "Worldmaking Knowledge (I)," 3, 7–11.

25. Reichel, "Worldmaking Knowledge (I)," 11–12. Steinmann similarly argues that data is a new and additional reality that transforms reality (Steinmann, "Alienation in a World of Data," 5–10). Zuboff's animating concern is that surveillance capitalism dangerously disrupts and wreaks havoc on human nature in the same way that industrial capitalism destroyed nature (Zuboff, *Surveillance Capitalism*, 20).

The Privacy Meaningful Life Argument: No Opting Out of Divine Omniscience

This essay is briefly setting aside the issue of data surveillance to examine a recent axiological antitheism argument. Kirk Lougheed has developed a privacy version of the meaningful life argument against theism.[26] Although his argument cannot be explored in-depth, the following outline helps to transition from the issue of "omniscient" data surveillance to the doctrine of divine omniscience. Lougheed's argument states that no matter how one defines privacy, its contents, or the value of privacy, God violates human privacy. This argument is premised on several presuppositions: First, privacy is an *intrinsic* good to a meaningful human life and without privacy one is not able to live a meaningful life.[27] Second, if God exists, per the necessary definition of the divine attributes, God would violate our privacy.[28] Lougheed interacts with Linda Zagzebski's doctrine of omnisubjectivity as a particularly egregious example of the way God breaches human privacy.[29] Therefore, for those who value privacy, the superior world is the one in which God does not exist since God's existence would nullify the meaning of one's life by violating one's privacy.

At this point, it is important to pause and observe the similarities between Lougheed's argument and the reality of our digitally surveilled world. We do have our privacy violated through corporate surveillance. Although surveillance has been used for centuries, the extent and usage of surveillance has created a genuinely new reality as Reichel, Zuboff, and others have argued. Our experience with the "omniscience" of big data adds existential weight to Lougheed's argument. *We know in an unprecedented way what this supposed divine violation of privacy feels like through corporate surveillance.* Most people could probably articulate something similar to Lougheed's argument about God's omniscience based on their experience

---

26. Kirk Lougheed, *The Axiological Status of Theism and Other Worldviews*, Palgrave Frontiers in Philosophy of Religion (Cham: Palgrave MacMillan, 2020), 55–110. This chapter is a further development of an earlier argument by Lougheed, "Anti-Theism and the Objective Meaningful Life Argument," *Dialogue* 56, no. 2 (2017): 337–55. For a similar argument, see Guy Kahane, "Should We Want God to Exist?," *Philosophy and Phenomenological Research* 82 (2011): 674–96.

27. For the overall argument, see Lougheed, *The Axiological Status of Theism*, 75–89. For example, "Even if Sally continues to wish that her diary remain private, this is not within her control with respect to God. Sally necessarily lacks such control when it comes to God. Even if privacy is a derivative right, God violates some of the rights from which it is derived" (68); "Our sense of security may well be violated by God's surveillance even if our security is not in fact violated. This in itself constitutes a harm" (88); "The fact that God violates our privacy means that we are unable to choose which information about ourselves we disclose and hence hurts our ability to develop an intimate relationship with God (which according to many theists is one of greatest human goods)" (89).

28. Lougheed, *The Axiological Status of Theism*, 86.

29. Lougheed, *The Axiological Status of Theism*, 71–75.

with surveillance capitalism. The reality of the "omniscience" of surveillance capitalism serves as a powerful and transformative metaphor that shapes our thinking about divine omniscience: Is God some sort of cosmic voyeur or Peeping Tom collecting information about us? Whether we are responding to a philosopher of religion or the person attending church service, the reality of surveillance capitalism has created a world that requires carefully considering what it means to say God is omniscient.

Divine Omniscience: The Power and Presence of the Personal God for Us

"Where Can I Flee from Your Presence?": Sonderegger and Divine Privacy

The problem of divine voyeurism, or the terror of divine omniscience, is not a new worry for the theological tradition. Katherine Sonderegger and Karl Barth have both noted the dread associated with divine omniscience due to human sinfulness.[30] Sonderegger states:

> Our premodern teachers in the faith saw much further than we, for they tasted directly the guilt and terror of a holy God *inside* and not outside the devices and desires of sinners. This is the specter of the panopticon held in the hands not of a human guard or voyeur, but rather of a perfect, omnipotent, and holy Judge. The surveillance extends to the heart, . . . all these lie bare to the Lord's eye, and there is no hiding from its scorching heat.[31]

The point this essay emphasises, however, is that this worry is intensified since we daily live with surveillance capitalism's panopticon that imitates this exact fear of divine omniscience. *What if God's omniscience is in some way like or worse than surveillance capitalism's "omniscience"—knowing our darkest secrets and using that against us?* One possible response to the terror of divine omniscience would be to assert that God does grant us privacy. This section focuses on Sonderegger's provocative assertion that the personal,

30. Karl Barth, *Church Dogmatics*, ed. G. W. Bromiley and T. F. Torrance (Edinburgh: T&T Clark, 1957), II/1, 552–5; hereafter, *CD* II/1: "And so, since nothing that exists can be hidden from God, and since God knows everything, there is no self-concealment from God. There is, of course, a desire for self-concealment which is the direct consequence of sin and the unwilling, compulsory, impotent admission of it" (*CD* II/1, 553).

31. Katherine Sonderegger, *Systematic Theology*, vol. 1, *The Doctrine of God* (Minneapolis: Fortress, 2015), 356; hereafter, *ST1*.

omniscient God graciously and mercifully does just that, and briefly outlines Sonderegger's claim that God gives us privacy and the theological commitments that ground this assertion.

From the outset of her discussion of divine omniscience, Sonderegger makes clear that God's perfect knowledge is no "Divine Tyranny."[32] Rather, the attribute of knowledge is moral; therefore, it is good, holy, and humble.[33] This leads to her conclusion that

> the Lord can allow us a private life, a liberty and solitude, that does not abandon but elevates the creature. The Lord God can forgive in just this sense. No tyrant, He; no crushing Power. . . . God bends down to us and with us and in us such that our encounter with Him will be personal, living, free. He *respects* us and our inner life, our privacy—we might dare to say even this![34]

This is certainly a daring claim.

It is vital to recognise that this statement is staked on one of Sonderegger's central commitments in the doctrine of God—God as person *and* substance. How can a God with *perfect* knowledge grant us the privacy of an inner life? According to Sonderegger, it is God's *personal* nature that makes "relational space" between the Creator and creature.[35] There are two important features of Sonderegger's concept of divine personhood—divine liberty and agency—that are essential to establishing the Creator-creature distinction and God's *relatio* to the world, a *relatio* that includes granting privacy to the creature.

First, God's personhood indicates a type of liberty or freedom regarding God's relation to God's creatures. Since God is personal, God "is not imprisoned by His own objectivity" and is liberty precisely because God is able "to withhold, to withdraw, to resist and refrain, to exhibit the marks of the personal." Therefore, God can "veil His eyes in His omniscient Life

32. *ST1*, 337.

33. *ST1*, 335–79.

34. *ST1*, 361–62. It is also worth noting that when discussing the Trinitarian processions Sonderegger ascribes to God an immeasurable, inward depth and privacy that is the dignity of personal life. Katherine Sonderegger, *Systematic Theology*, vol. 2, *The Doctrine of the Holy Trinity: Processions and Persons* (Minneapolis: Fortress, 2020), 340–41; hereafter, *ST2*.

35. *ST1*, 361–62. Please note, *relational space* is my term and not Sonderegger's. Similarly, God's nature as Person *is* the basis of Sonderegger's willingness to affirm counterfactual possibilities in the divine life: "So we must affirm, in the end, that the Almighty Lord necessarily may impede His own Light, hindering and shielding It from springing into creaturely life. This too, we may dare to say, is what we mean by the Personal, the living mastery over one's own subjectivity" (*ST1*, 325; cf. 318–26).

within our lives."[36] In a phrase very much reminiscent of Barth,[37] God is not a prisoner of God's own nature—God is subject over God's objectivity. God's personal liberty means that God can refrain and compassionately self-veil so that the human is respected and not crushed. It appears that Sonderegger's understanding of the personal liberty of God allows God to "limit" Godself without impinging on God's perfect knowledge, and this *is* the humility, kindness, and goodness of God.[38]

Second, Sonderegger's theology of divine personhood seeks to establish a type of divine agency or relation to creation that pushes against certain causal accounts of God's relation to creation. On her account, the personal God is not compelled by some "mechanical or material impulse"[39] to create creatures as emanations, exempla, or imitations of archetypes in the divine knowledge.[40] God, as person, indicates the agency of God as the one who stands "outside" of the created world while being present "in" the world.[41] Sonderegger explicitly rejects the notion that God is the hidden cause underlying all creaturely occurrences[42] and is adamant that God is not caught up in some causal nexus with creation.[43] Rather, Sonderegger argues, "God *plants*, He speaks, He welcomes and commands; these agential forms of creation, spanning Genesis 1 and 2, ensure that the Creator stands 'outside' the world he brings into being." Divine omniscience teaches us that "God can make, bear in existence, and know what is not God, what is truly creature."[44] The personal God's

---

36. *ST1*, 361.

37. As one example, Barth makes very similar statements while discussing divine power and omniscience and critiques Schleiermacher for making God a prisoner of God's attributes, see *CD* II/1, 530, 566.

38. Of course, this *relatio* to creation does not exhaust the divine goodness, kindness, and humility. One of the central refrains of Sonderegger's systematics is "God is More" (cf. *ST1*, 112, 456–57; *ST2*, 68, 205).

39. *ST1*, 368.

40. *ST1*, 365–68.

41. *ST1*, 367; cf. 343, 350–53, 387–88.

42. It seems that one could interpret this as the rejection of the notions of primary and secondary causality since primary causality is that which underlies and makes possible *all* secondary causality; however, we must wait until her volume on creation for her conclusion on causality. After denying that God's relation to the world is causal in this sense, Sonderegger states: "Here we must underscore that the prime relation—God to the world—is utterly unique, beyond all category and causal sequence, because in the end the *Relatio* must be nothing else but God Himself. And just so we cannot say too much here. . . . But the Transcendental Relation allows us to give voice to what we must confess: that in each and all particulars, in their own mode and concrete life, God communicates His very Life and Light. He, this very One, is the utterly luminous Ground, the *Ratio*, the Hope and Healing of all that is" (*ST1*, 353).

43. For more on this, see Katherine Sonderegger, "Scripture and Metaphysics: A Response to Reviewers," *Pro Ecclesia* 27, no.1 (2018): 66–67.

44. *ST1*, 366.

liberty and agency are how Sonderegger explains God's gracious gift of "space" or privacy between the human and God.

Sonderegger's account of God respecting humans by graciously gifting us privacy is compelling, especially in light of the world of surveillance capitalism. For reasons outlined in the next section, this essay does not affirm the divine self-veiling of knowledge as the solution to the problem of the terror of divine omniscience.[45] However, Sonderegger's account helps us to think well about the doctrine of omniscience.

Although she does not use this term herself, Sonderegger's account of God's first-person knowledge of us advocates for what Zagzebski terms the divine attribute of omnisubjectivity. Sonderegger posits that God does not just know *about us*; rather,

> It is not my singularity or individuality that composes this Perfect Knowledge, but rather my *name*, my identity as this self, this person, this sinner. I am known by God not simply in a "third-personal" way, as if God were an exhaustive catalogue of all facts and dispositions and beliefs that are mine. No, the Lord God rather knows in a first-personal and inward way who I am, and the reach and texture of my inner world.[46]

God's knowledge is not the indifferent, propositional knowledge of surveillance capitalism. This intense, first-personal knowledge is based on Sonderegger's affirmation of the theological commitment that God *is* knowledge itself. Knowledge is not a faculty, nor is God a divine mind "to be filled with earthly, finite content."[47] Rather, "God is Light, perfect,

---

45. It is important to note that Sonderegger's claim that God grants privacy to us is not fully outlined in her current publications. She explicitly defers further conversation on this topic to her forthcoming doctrine of atonement (*ST1*, 361).

46. *ST1*, 359–60. Linda Zagzebski recently released her first monograph dedicated to defending and detailing the attribute of omnisubjectivity by exploring possible explanatory models: the empathy model (her preferred model), the perceptual model, and panentheism. Sonderegger's affirmation clearly does not fit either the empathy model or panentheism; however, while the perceptual model probably best describes her theology, it does not seem to fully encompass her claims either. There are certainly differences between Sonderegger and Zagzebski, but there is significant overlap in their understanding of God's "first-person" knowledge of us, including a willed empathy or passible impassibility, reliance on the metaphor of light to describe God's knowledge/consciousness and its relationship to the created universe, and an affirmation of the distinction between subjectivity and objectivity (i.e., personhood and substance/essence) in God. See Linda Trinkaus Zagzebski, *Omnisubjectivity: An Essay on God and Subjectivity* (Oxford: Oxford University Press, 2023).

47. *ST1*, 348; cf. 335–62. Since Sonderegger repeatedly emphasises that we humans "are not *items in Him*" (*ST1*, 349), and she rejects typical understandings of divine ideas to avoid any possibility of pantheism or threat to divine aseity (*ST1*, 386–67, 450), it is not clear what the exact relation is between God's knowledge of creatures and the divine act of creation. Sonderegger is keen

intellectual, and intelligible Light. . . . This dynamic Light that is God is altogether alive, personal, intelligible."[48] The theological claim that God is knowledge itself is vital for properly addressing the concerns raised for privacy and surveillance. Reichel highlights how this claim about divine knowledge explicitly rejects the definition of omniscience as God's complete knowledge of all true propositions. This is particularly important since big data is propositional, and this further illuminates the way surveillance capitalism only serves as a complete distortion of the God that *is* perfect, personal knowledge.[49]

Ultimately, God's omniscience is about God's intimate presence to God's creatures—God's humble, intimate, and indirect presence to all things in creation.[50] In Sonderegger's theology of God's personal, intimate knowledge of us, she completely rejects the notion of a competitive zero-sum relationship between God and the world. God's omniscient light descends humbly into the created world communicating being, knowledge, and power to each created thing.[51] This is vitally important for carefully considering the issue of privacy and omniscience. God is *not* observing and collecting information regarding God's creatures.[52] God's first-person knowledge of us means that God "sees through our eyes," while we can see *through* the divine light to know the material and intellectual world.[53]

Rejecting the Zero-Sum God-World Relation: A Christological Shaping of Divine Knowledge for Us and Our Personal Identities

It is here, on the basis of God's personal, intimate presence to the world as knowledge itself, that one can respond well to charges that God violates our privacy or that God in any way resembles the "omniscience"

---

to avoid saying too much on this exact issue. One possibility is that she will describe creation in terms of a radiating luminescence or a pouring forth, since she rejects the idea of a divine deliberative will (*ST1*, 197, 253–54, 266). Again, this is an area where God's personal nature is vital since Sonderegger uses the concept of the personal to explain how God *could* have stopped the divine life from generating all that is (*ST1*, 318–26).

48. *ST1*, 348.

49. Reichel, "Worldmaking Knowledge (I)," 4–7.

50. *ST1*, 350, 429–32, 460.

51. "It is the *living*, subjective intermixing and interceding that speaks most powerfully of what is generally true: that the One God is the life, the being, the knowledge, and the goodness of all that live. Yet not identical to them!" (*ST1*, 463; cf. 345). Given the importance of the metaphor of Light, it should not be surprising that Sonderegger affirms an Augustinian account of illumination that human acts of knowing are only possible because of God's humble and hidden light: "He is not the Object of our intellectual sight. Rather, He makes things known. He is the Light by which we see . . . He makes *others* to shine, to stand forth from the darkness, to appear. He, the Light, makes Himself *an instrument* in His own created world" (*ST1*, 425).

52. *ST1*, 349.

53. *ST1*, 359, 426.

of surveillance capitalism. The argument here agrees that God *is* God's knowing and that God's personal nature means that God's knowing of us is God's intimate presence and knowledge of us, but the argument departs from Sonderegger by reframing these claims in a christological manner.

First, instead of knowledge that is *about us* but *for* the profit of corporations, divine knowledge is always *for us* since it is the knowledge of the God who *is* love. Sonderegger repeatedly emphasises that divine omniscience cannot be pried apart from God's love.[54] But it is here that this essay goes further. Divine omniscience is christological. The theological tradition has often acknowledged the relation of the eternal Son to divine knowledge due to the biblical titles of "Word" and "Wisdom." Origen of Alexandria did not affirm an eternally existing creation; rather, he argued:

> In this Wisdom, therefore, who ever was with the Father, was creation always delineated and shaped, and there never was a moment when the prefiguration of those things, which were to be thereafter, was not in Wisdom.[55]
>
> And since within this very subsistence of Wisdom was every capacity and form of the creation that would come to be—both of those things which exist primarily and of those which occur in consequence, having been formed beforehand and arranged by the power of foreknowledge regarding these very created things, which has been as it were outlined and prefigured in Wisdom herself.[56]

Origen states that God the Father was always Almighty because all created things are prefigured and shaped in the eternal Son.[57] Origen points

54. *ST1*, 340–41, 361, 399, 405.

55. Origen of Alexandria, *On First Principles: A Reader's Edition*, trans. John Behr (Oxford: Oxford University Press, 2019), 1.4.4, 44. Sonderegger denies this notion of creation "in" God since she argues this threatens or challenges the aseity of God by making creatures necessary to God. If aseity is understood in its purely negative definition that denies God is from another, then even if some type of necessity is conceded concerning the creation (by no means is the conclusion of necessity a given in this situation), this does not negate the notion of God's *a se* life since God is eternally and unchangeably the same person *and* is the Creator of *all* that is (e.g., necessity in this case would not make God dependent on creation since God is the creative source of it). This in no way implies that God either relies on creation or that God's life is "exhausted" in the created temporal-spatial world.

56. Origen, *First Principles*, 1.2.2, 22.

57. Although the theology advocated here is not the same as that of Thomas Aquinas, his understanding of the eternal generation of the Son as an act of the intellect helps us to think through the Trinitarian theology related to this claim; see *ST* I, q.27, art.5. Aquinas explains the relation of the Son's personal title as Word to the divine intellect in this way: "Nothing belonging to the intellect can be applied to God personally, except word alone; for word alone signifies that which emanates from another. For what the intellect forms in its conception is the word. Now, the intellect itself, according as it is made actual by the intelligible species, is considered absolutely; likewise the act

to the importance of naming God as Father before Almighty—an ordering that is reflected in the later creeds.[58] As improper as it is to speak this way of an eternal God, the title Father is "older" than the title Almighty. This essay proposes that it is in the Son that God knows Godself and creation, including the personal, intimate divine knowledge of each one of us. In the generation of the Son, God knows Godself as divine love that ultimately is embodied and enacted in Jesus Christ's life, death, and resurrection.[59]

The divine omniscience has a christological shape—it is the centre point from which all things proceed. As eternal, God is never "without" the knowledge of all things in Christ. Unsurprisingly, Barth describes God's knowing similarly; however, Barth places his discussion of omniscience under the attribute of God's omnipotence: "It is the omnipotent knowing and willing that bears His name, the knowing and willing of the person designated by that name, *a knowing and willing which flows out from the place occupied by this person into all other places*."[60] Because we can be confident that we are known in and through Christ, the beloved Son who loves us, we do not need to fear that God uses knowledge against us or to manipulate or coerce us.

Second, instead of creating a world like big data that dehumanises us and reduces us to data sources for predictions of future behaviour, divine knowledge constitutes us as persons.[61] For Barth, God is *the* person, the

of understanding which is to the actual intellect what existence is to actual being; since the act of understanding does not signify an act going out from the intelligent agent, but an act remaining in the agent. *Therefore when we say that word is knowledge, the term knowledge does not mean the act of a knowing intellect, or any one of its habits, but stands for what the intellect conceives by knowing*. . . . The Word is conceived by the gaze of the divine thought" (*ST* I, q.34, art.1, ad.2; emphasis added). Essentially, while the divine intellect is the divine essence and not a property of any person in the Trinity, the Word is knowledge or what the divine intellect *conceives* by knowing–this is the unique relation of the Word to the divine intellect. Aquinas later affirms that the term *Word* implies a relation and the knowing of creatures, see *ST* I, q.34, art.3. Gilles Emery summarises this aspect of Aquinas's theology thus: "And the Word is the person whom the Father conceives when he knows himself. By his own mode of procession, that is, the property distinctive to him, the Word not only knows all the Father knows, but he *articulates* all that is contained in the Father's knowledge—a word is, by definition, *expression*. From one side, the Word is the perfect expression of the Father. From another, the Word is the expression of creatures contained in the Father's knowledge, and, because this is creative knowledge, the Word is also the creative cause of all that the Father does." Gilles Emery, OP, *The Trinitarian Theology of St. Thomas Aquinas*, trans. Francesca Aran Murphy (Oxford: Oxford University Press, 2007), 195–96.

58. Origen, *First Principles*, 1.2.10, 29–31.

59. It is important to note that Origen defines God's nature as Almighty based on the description in Philippians 2:5–11 of Christ's exaltation as the crucified and risen one. God's power and wisdom are not through force and necessity but Wisdom and Reason (Origen, *First Principles*, 1.2.10, 29–31). For Origen, the fullness of Christ's deity is demonstrated in his emptying (Origen, *First Principles*, 1.2.8, 27–28).

60. Barth, *CD* II/1, 605, emphasis added.

61. Note how Barth grounds all creaturely knowing and willing in God's knowing and willing

one who properly defines and grounds personhood, not humans. God, as the "personifying person,"[62] graciously gifts us our personhood through the love of the divine knowing, willing, and acting: "Man is not a person, but he becomes one on the basis that he is loved by God and can love God in return. Man finds what a person is when he finds it in the person of God and his own being as a person in the gift of fellowship afforded him by God in person."[63] By the Holy Spirit, the more one is aware and contemplates Jesus Christ and the divine love that knows one completely and thoroughly, in the words of Sonderegger, in a first-personal way, the more a person becomes who she truly is since who she is is found in Christ. God's eternal knowing of each person, including their *telos* to be in fellowship with God through Jesus Christ, is what makes each person who they are and holds them in existence.

Third, beyond God's knowledge constituting us as persons, divine omniscience is not completely opaque to us—God graciously reveals Godself to us and includes us in this knowledge.[64] This is in no way a claim that we have an exhaustive or comprehensive knowledge of God or divine omniscience; however, God does lovingly reveal Godself to us, and in revealing Godself we also learn who we are as well. This is part of what the apostle Paul means when he states that when the perfect comes, the partial will pass away. Paul frames this in terms of personal knowing: "For now we see in a mirror dimly, but then face to face. Now I know in part; then I shall know fully, *even as I have been fully known*."[65] This complete face-to-face knowing is the love that never ends—the completeness that does not pass away. We are already fully known and loved by God, but we have not yet reached our *telos* to love and know God perfectly. Privacy is the last thing needed from God, even in the darkest and most sinful crevasse of one's heart, because this would mean that one's identity and personhood would be separated from its loving source, and the gift of one's personhood withdrawn. It is here that we most need the divine light of God's loving omniscience that does not withdraw—while knowing the depth of our sinful thoughts and desires—but graciously sustains us.

(knowing, willing, and acting are essential to Barth's definition of personhood): "He is, in fact, the knowing and willing itself . . . the presupposition and creative ground of all knowing and willing, the personal Creator of all personal being, the spiritual Creator of all spirit" (*CD* II/1, 543).

62. *CD* II/1, 285: "He is not the personified but the personifying person—the person on the basis of whose prior existence alone we can speak (hypothetically) of other persons different from Him."

63. *CD* II/1, 284.

64. "Consciously or unconsciously it is thanks to the love of God in His revelation that we can describe man in this way [as a person]" (*CD* II/1, 285).

65. 1 Cor. 13:12 ESV.

In conclusion, privacy, just like the bedevilled questions about freedom, foreknowledge, and divine and human agency, often implies a zero-sum game between God and humans where God impinges and negates our "space." Although the worry that God could violate our privacy is completely understandable in light of our sinful hearts and the world of surveillance capitalism, this worry should be alleviated when we recognise that the relationship between God and human beings does not operate on the same plane as our human-to-human relationships.[66] Big data is ultimately a creature—an impersonal creation of propositional, disembodied data as the result of human programming. God's knowledge is the very source of our existence—it is personal, intimate, and loving. Barth summarises well why this worry melts away when we understand divine power, knowing, and willing from revelation and reconciliation in Jesus Christ:

> If we understand that God's omnipotence is the omnipotence of His knowing and willing, and if this is a genuine understanding because it has its source in the divine revelation and reconciliation, and therefore if the knowing and willing of His omnipotence is known as that of His love, the problem of competition, from which all the errors necessarily and constantly derive, withers away of itself.[67]

The lordship of God is not that God lords over us in a domineering way; instead, as defined by Christ, God's lordship is the power of God's love for us—us frail, sinful creatures—that God knows all the way down yet still chooses us, still loves us in Christ. In a world where "knowledge" is power—power in asymmetric relations that benefit those who have knowledge over us—the good news of the God for us is that divine power is perfectly demonstrated and fulfilled in Jesus Christ who knows us fully and chooses to give up our worldly notions of "power" and loves us.

---

66. Although I would not use this language, Zagzebski captures this idea in her response to the complaint that God violates our privacy: "The complaint is that God should not observe our sexual feelings or other states that we consider to be especially private. The problem is not that the feelings are creepy, but that God would be creepy if he observed them. God seems like a peeping Tom. If that is the image we have, I think it means that we are using the wrong image. God does not peer at us; God is within us. If consciousness flows out of God with God's own consciousness attached to it, God keeps our consciousness in existence" (Zagzebski, *Omnisubjectivity*, 112).

67. *CD* II/1, 598.

CHAPTER 6

THE IMPASSIBLE PERSONAL GOD

DANIELLE W. JANSEN

This chapter is concerned with one of the primary ways theologians understand the wrath of God: *as a divine emotion*. There is a long history of explicitly violent and emotive language employed when defenders of an angry God explain the nature of divine wrath. Common language from this theological discussion incorporates the idea that "God *must* be angry at sin" or "God *must* be wrathful in the face of injustice or God is not love." The highly emotive and appetitive rhetoric is meant to convey God's personal involvement in human affairs and commitment to God's holiness and justice. Sin necessitates wrath, and in some way, God *feels* this wrath.

Western conservative theologians who defend the emotive or appetitive account of divine wrath often collapse the discussion into the *justification* for the existence of God's wrath. However, those of this Western conservative ilk also adhere to some form of classical theism, particularly divine impassibility. The justification of divine wrath may be one concern, but the issue relating to *how* such a negative and seemingly volatile human emotion can be ascribed to an impassible God is rarely seriously engaged. Most crucially, I am concerned with the lack of attention to the definition of emotion and how these theological conversations center around widely held assumptions and folk psychology regarding the nature of human anger. The absence of a robust definition of emotion not only reveals the modern complacency regarding a so-called standard definition but also betrays an unease with attributing anger to an all-loving God.

The impassibility discussion almost certainly begins with the recognition that the biblical text provides a picture of the divine life that is in some meaningful way analogous to human life. What are often considered passages of anthropomorphisms and anthropopathisms attributed to God are understood along varying degrees of analogy or metaphor. Principles of equivocality and univocity delimit the discussion and are tools that guide one's interpretation of such biblical texts. Depending on where one lands in the debate, the difference or similarity of the corresponding depiction of God in human terms is emphasized. Ultimately, there is general agreement that all God-talk is, in some sense, a species of divine accommodation.

So, then, can God experience emotion? Is the Christian God an emotional being? More specifically, can God be angry? Is the wrath of God analogous to human anger? If so, in what respect? It seems to me that before we can approach the question of divine (im)passibility, we must understand what precisely an emotion is. Therefore, this chapter will examine a leading contemporary theory of emotion so we can begin to assess the intelligibility of the claim that God experiences anger. The remainder of the chapter will consider the implications of the current understanding of emotion and will engage issues concerning religious language and analogical predication. Ultimately, I will argue that (1) it is a category mistake to attribute emotions to the divine life, and (2) although God is without emotions, this does not mean that God is impersonal; in fact, God can and does relate to God's creatures through the use of psychological language that communicates divine values and judgments.

What Is an Emotion?

Contemporary theological discussions about the doctrine of divine impassibility have almost entirely avoided any formal definition of emotion, particularly one informed by modern-day psychology and/or philosophy.[1] This is with good reason, of course. The modern study of emotion is notoriously convoluted and highly contested, with no resolution in sight. Neuroscientists, psychologists, philosophers, and anthropologists are all producing groundbreaking work in the study of emotions. Yet it is difficult

1. Most troubling, Rob Lister, in his book *God Is Impassible and Impassioned: Toward a Theology of Divine Emotion* (Wheaton, IL: Crossway, 2013), gives a nod to the complexity of the impassibility debate and the convoluted use of language concerning emotion but refuses to engage. He writes, "I acknowledge at the outset that while I am interested, for instance, in what modern psychology and philosophy have to say about the definition of various terms in the vocabulary of emotion, I do not write on this topic as a specialist. . . . In the main, then, throughout this study, I intend to make use of the major terms of the vocabulary of emotion (e.g. emotion, passion, affection, feelings) with a degree of layman-like interchangeability" (35). Whether Lister's decision is due to ignorance or an effort to score points with his conservative evangelical readership, or both, it all but makes his aim *Toward a Theology of Divine Emotion* inconsequential.

to find any clear sense of agreement. Arthur Reber remarked that "no other term in psychology shares its non-definability with its frequency of use."[2] William Reddy, a leading scholar in the study of the cultural development of emotions, explains that there have been hundreds of studies on emotion in psychology alone since the 1970s, inciting a revolution of sorts in the theory of emotion. Yet, he observes, "despite the many positive findings this new research has generated, the revolution has done little to clear up the vexed question of what, exactly, emotions are. Disagreements persist, uncertainties abound."[3]

Nevertheless, in this sea of literature pertaining to what we call "emotion" today, a particularly helpful way of clarifying this complex field of research is to distinguish between two different approaches: *noncognitive theories* and *cognitive theories*.[4] Noncognitive theories are often viewed as the "traditional" or "classical" theories. These accounts assert that the somatic and neuroscientific states that accompany perceived emotions are explained independently of cognition or evaluations of judgment, beliefs, or values. Cognitive theories of emotion emerged in reaction to the noncognitivist insistence that emotions are in opposition to reason or the rational will.

Noncognitive accounts are varied and complex. Most importantly, however, these theories claim emotions are more or less preconscious, precognitive neurological arousals. But as philosophers and psychologists have cautioned, there is a lack of attention to how one's emotions seem to be determined, on some real level, by one's beliefs and evaluations.[5] In other words, a theory of emotion should attempt to explain, say, the relationship between anger and the evaluation of injustice or between sadness and the evaluation of loss. The cognitive approach to emotion seeks to address

---

2. Arthur Reber, *The Penguin Dictionary of Psychology* (London: Penguin, 1985), 234.

3. William M. Reddy, *The Navigation of Feeling: The Framework for the History of Emotions* (Cambridge: Cambridge University Press, 2001), ix.

4. While this demarcation may seem clumsy for theologians, this is a standard way in which emotion theorists have categorized the field.

5. Interestingly, the constructivist account and cognitive theories seem to have a significant overlap in how they conceptualize the impetus for the production of an emotional state. Both, at some level—either biologically or psychologically—acknowledge that the individual is influenced by particular situations that give rise to interpretations of outside stimuli that then produce emotion. For the constructivists, this is a neurological interpretation of changes in affective bodily states, whereas the cognitivist (appraisal theories) identifies the relationship between goal congruence and relevant concerns of the individual. See Brosch, "Comment," 369–73. As such, the categories of "noncognitive" and "cognitive" may not properly indicate the distinction between, say Ekman, Barrett, and Lazarus. Thus, perhaps the distinguishing factor that I am attempting to highlight is that in one set of theories the somatic and neurological functions are essential to what constitutes an emotion, and in the other set of theories they are not.

these particular concerns. Cognitive theories account for the "intentionality of emotion" and seek to incorporate belief structures and the evaluative process that accompanies emotion.[6] Although admittedly simplistic, here is a brief summary of these two classes of emotion theory:

Noncognitive theories. Although the noncognitive theories are varied and each approach is a distinct area of research, they all depend on the *physical* human body in that they are contingent on somatic or neurological markers by which emotions are identified and defined. Most importantly, these theories understand emotions more or less as preconscious, precognitive neurological arousals.

Cognitive theories. These accounts claim that beliefs, values, and appraisals (sometimes termed evaluations or judgments) are closely related to emotions or are emotions themselves. Often it is stated that emotions are value judgments. Additionally, particular appraisals correspond to particular emotions. Philosophers and psychologists in this vein seek to find a logical connection between one's emotions and one's beliefs.[7]

Given that one of the goals of this chapter is to find a fitting theory of emotion that may allow for analogy in some way to the divine nature, we can easily reject the noncognitive accounts of emotion due to the fact that the Christian God does not have bodily states. So let us now evaluate an example of a cognitive theory of emotion.

Richard S. Lazarus is an American psychologist known for his influential cognitive-motivational theory of emotion, CMRT. He explains that a revival of interest in the theory of emotion in the second half of the twentieth century was due to a number of contributing factors, including "the cognitive movement in social science and the more open epistemology that followed the loss of influence of radical behavioralism."[8] Terms used to indicate biological or evolutionary processes such as "instincts, drives, and needs" were replaced with motivational terms such as "values, goals,

6. Renee England, "The Cognitive/Noncognitive Debate in Emotion Theory: A Corrective from Spinoza," *Emotion Review* 11, no. 2 (2019): 103.

7. Cheshire Calhoun and Robert C. Solomon, introduction to *What Is an Emotion? Classic Readings in Philosophical Psychology*, ed. Cheshire Calhoun and Robert C. Solomon (New York: Oxford University Press, 1984), 16.

8. Richard S. Lazarus, "Progress on a Cognitive-Motivational-Relational Theory of Emotion," *American Psychologist* 46, no. 8 (1991): 819–34.

commitments, intentions, and plans."[9] Lazarus is only one of several psychologists who subscribe to some form of appraisal or attribution account of emotion. While there is strong disagreement within this body of work, what is most significant for this essay is that emotions are broadly understood to be cognitive appraisals of the world in which one lives and relates. In other words, emotions are the means by which humans interact with the world in a personal way.

According to Lazarus's CMRT, there are three fundamental elements that determine a particular emotion: (1) *relational*, in that emotions are always formed in "person-environment" relationships; (2) *motivational*, in that emotions are produced according to the individual's goal hierarchies (including a disposition toward particular responses) and environmental constraints or advantages of a particular situation; and (3) *cognitive*, in that there are both knowledge (beliefs) and *appraisal* (evaluation) of a particular situation that give rise to meaning and therefore produce a corresponding emotion.[10]

CMRT asserts that appraisals and emotions are inextricably connected: appraisals result in emotions. Appraisals consist of personal meaning, which is informed by the individual's evaluation of the significance of a particular person-environment relationship. For the emotion to occur, the evaluation of the environment must be appraised to have implications for personal well-being—whether positive or negative. Suppose the individual does not appraise the situation as holding personal meaning that affects or challenges their well-being (or the well-being of those for whom the individual cares). In that case, emotion will not be generated. Again, the appraisal is the mechanism by which an emotion is generated. Thus, appraisals serve as a "meditational role of linking emotional response to environmental circumstances on the one hand, and personal goals and beliefs on the other."[11]

The cognitive or appraisal element of Lazarus's theory first maintains reciprocity between cognition and emotion and emotion and cognition. While emotion is always in response to meaning, the subsequent meaning also informs the resulting emotion and meaning. Second, cognition is causal in that the appraisal of the situation results in an emotion; thus, once a particular situation has been resolved or removed, so too the

---

9. Lazarus, "Progress," 819–34.

10. Lazarus, "Progress," 819–34.

11. Craig A. Smith and Richard S. Lazarus, "Appraisal Components, Core Relational Themes, and the Emotions," *Cognition and Emotion* 7 (1993): 234.

emotion will dissipate. Third, an emotion will not be generated if there is not a goal or investment in personal well-being in the situation at hand.[12]

With this basic outline of CMRT, we can now consider the three elements of this cognitive theory of emotion with respect to the sort of classic theism and divine impassibility presumed by some Western conservative theologians who defend the notion of an emotionally wrathful God.

1. *Person-environment relationship:* Lazarus's person-environment relationship is strictly situated within the individual herself and the environment in which she finds herself. According to Lazarus, one cannot understand emotion solely from an analysis of the individual *or* environment; rather, these elements are inextricably linked. The person-environment relationship is crucial and gives meaning to the subject's relational concepts, such as threat, insult, or ego enhancement, which map onto their corresponding emotions, such as anxiety, anger, and pride.

   Accordingly, this is an *evaluative* process. Goals, desires, wants, and wishes all influence the emotion-producing process. Powerful environmental and personal influences shape emotional states, but it is in conjunction with the individual's perception of harm or benefit to their well-being. While humans will evaluate particular situations according to the positive or negative effects such situations may have on their well-being, it seems that, according to classical theism, God cannot possess such processes within the divine mind. God cannot change in any way, shape, or form, no matter the particular situation or environment—God is metaphysically incapable of being influenced to move or act. If God is pure act, then God is not assessing human affairs to determine how God may respond. Indeed, there cannot be an evaluative process for an "emotion" to be produced—there remains no potential in God to make such evaluation.
2. *Motivation:* In addition to the person-environment relationship, the concept of motivation is also central to CMRT. Motivation is understood in two distinct but interrelated senses: first, as a

12. While it may seem one could think of counter-examples to this statement, particularly concerning an instance of feeling an emotion without understanding why, it is important to note that Lazarus acknowledges that although the cognitive appraisal theory seems only to apply to conscious evaluations, he does address such counter-examples in his work. However, we will not examine his argument here.

latent disposition, and second, as a reaction to a specific environment, which is a responsive mobilization toward an intended goal. Unfortunately for the impassibilist, the concept of motivation is problematic when attributed to the divine. According to classic Christian doctrine, there is no deliberation process within the divine—God is a simple pure act. This means that there are no unrealized possibilities in God. Although one may conceptualize how God may or may not "act" within human history, God is not motivated by an evaluative process based on extenuating circumstances. Indeed, God most certainly does not need motivation to be God.[13]

3. *Appraisal:* This is understood to be the cognitive evaluation of the person-environment relationship, which gives rise to meaning and, therefore, the corresponding emotion. Due to the extreme difficulty in finding any worthy corresponding analog to the first two elements of Lazarus's theory of emotion addressed above, there inevitably results the impossibility of attributing the appraisal process to God. Both the person-environment relationship and the motivational element are necessary conditions in order to produce an appraisal. Without such appraisal, no emotion is generated. As such, appraisals link the individual's emotional response to a particular situation and that individual's personal goals and beliefs. The appraisal process is *meaning-making*, which results in a specific emotion. It is difficult to imagine that God would have any such process, let alone require such process in the divine life.

It should be clear that there is a significant amount of tension between leading theories of human emotion and the classical doctrine of God. Indeed, it seems that an attempt to apply emotion to the divine analogously would render "emotion" unrecognizable to contemporary neuroscience and psychology. As noted above, we can simply reject accounts that rely solely on neurological or somatic experiences to define human emotion, given that the Christian God is not embodied.

---

13. It has been increasingly popular in conservative Protestant circles to argue that God is a *qualified* (im)passibilist. Specifically, employing the idea that God "chooses" to feel an emotion. This line of thinking is in response to those on one end of the spectrum who argue that God must feel an emotion to be personal and on the other who claim God cannot be acted upon from without (implying that emotion is understood to be a passive experience—this in itself exposes the lack of attention to contemporary scholarship only briefly explored in this chapter). Yet, frustratingly, *how* God "chooses" to feel is often overlooked in theological discussion—it is simply defended by explaining *why* God chooses to do so. For example, Lister, *God is Impassible and Impassioned.*

However, cognitive appraisal accounts identify emotion as a meaning-making process. The individual experiences an emotion once an appraisal is made—based on values, judgments, and goals concerning particular situations. The process is inherently in flux, deliberative, and a learned experience. Cognitive accounts also seem to pose a considerable problem for the classical theists.

Nevertheless, there is still room for the use of analogical predication when it comes to divine anger. But first, let us look at an account of human anger before we see how analogical predication bears on the discussion.

Human Anger

Anger is a particularly troubling emotion. On the one hand, anger can be a valuable part of social and political life. Indeed, anger is, at times, an essential part of moral life. Defenders argue that without anger, a mockery is made of injustice, evil, and, in some cases, self-respect. Anger is an integral function of human life that helps guide and shift the structures that strangle human freedom and dignity. Yet, on the other hand, anger can be irrational and destructive. Thus, some argue that anger is problematic and counterproductive at best. In most cases, anger is nothing but a dangerous poison that produces irrational and violent behavior that lashes out in retribution or even vengeance. Anger serves no purpose other than inciting retaliation and harm against its object.

In the psychological discussion on the emotion of anger, the issue does not rest on identifying how anger is exhibited psychologically, physiologically, or neuroscientifically, but rather, the dominating issue when it comes to the emotion of anger is the *function* and resulting *behavior* of such emotion. Is anger a positive emotion that motivates a particular behavior or physiological response crucial to a just society, or is anger a destructive emotion that leads to more harm than good? Of course, these questions indicate that anger is often defined as a moral emotion. How does one determine whether or not an emotion is moral? Aaron Ben-Ze'Ev proposes two essential criteria for an emotion to be considered moral: first, whether the primary evaluative concern of the emotion is moral, and second, whether the resulting behavior or response of the emotion leads to beneficial moral consequences.[14] In the case of anger, it is a moral emotion

14. A. Ben-Ze'Ev, "Are Envy, Anger, and Resentment Moral Emotions?," *Philosophical Explorations* 5 (2002): 148, 152.

in that its core evaluative concern is moral (injustice), and the effects of the emotion lead to beneficial moral consequences (justice).[15]

So then, how does anger relate to moral character? Philosophical discussions tend to claim either that virtue requires some form of anger or that anger is incompatible with virtue. Common attitudes in North America lean toward the side of the argument in favor of virtuous or righteous anger in response to grave injustice. Thus, a virtuous person does indeed get angry, just at the right place and the right time. As such, this sentiment is consistent with the theological claims in favor of a wrathful God. We cannot explain away the considerable amount of the biblical text that depicts God as wrathful. Thus, we must seek to understand the value of wrath or anger in a human context, which aids in our understanding of the divine.

Those who argue that moral anger is a righteous or virtuous response to injustice often make an evaluative claim. If one responds in anger when someone or something of value has been unjustly harmed, this indicates the attribution of value to that someone or something. Conversely, if one does not respond in anger when someone or something of value is unjustly wronged, then this is an indication that one does not truly believe (a) that someone or something has value, (b) that someone or something has been harmed or (c) that a morally unjustified agent has perpetrated an act of injustice. Defenders of moral anger also insist that anger *communicates* important moral messages and *motivates* one to defend those things one cares about and bring about change. Additionally, an *epistemic* claim is made that anger signals that something is wrong with accepted social and political understandings of the way things are.[16]

Feminist moral philosophy has produced a significant amount of literature relating to the moral status of anger in the face of what Macalester Bell calls "non-ideal conditions," particularly oppression. So-called "negative" emotions, such as anger, serve a distinct and vital role in responding to oppression. In this sense, anger is an essential form of protest that helps women retain their "self-respect"; it provides women with unique access to emotions that the unoppressed cannot experience, exposes female oppression, and motivates social progress.[17] Anger is a valuable tool that should be developed and encouraged to achieve particular social and political goals in the face of sexist oppression.

---

15. Ben-Ze'Ev, "Moral Emotions?," 153.

16. Pettigrove, "Meekness and 'Moral' Anger," *Ethics* 122 (2012): 359.

17. Bell, "Anger, Virtue, and Oppression," in *Feminist Ethics and Social and Political Philosophy: Theorizing the Non-Ideal*, ed. L. Tessman (Dordrecht: Springer, 2009), 168.

Anger is argued to be a valuable tool for the oppressed due to the fact that anger has a particularly unique and effective way of capturing the attention of the one in receipt of the anger. Jennifer Lerner and Larissa Tiedens write,

> Once people perceive angry targets, a cascade of emotion-specific inferences automatically follows. Angry expressers are implicitly perceived as threatening, competent, powerful, and dominant. . . . In fact, differentiating the expression of anger from other negative emotions is so basic a skill that even 10 week old infants respond differently to angry faces than to sad faces.[18]

As such, anger's social function often forces a better outcome through the expression of threats, power, and authoritative communication.

Although most studies have concentrated on the maladaptive qualities of anger, specifically aggression, "various studies have also shown that the social functions of anger can be served when anger is expressed or regulated in a variety of less destructive and more strategic ways, for example, by just telling someone you are angry, by expressing criticism verbally, by temporarily ignoring someone, or by merely venting your anger against inanimate objects."[19] This point is particularly helpful: Anger can be expressed *without* physical aggression. The verbal expression of anger is just as strategic and effective in communicating disapproval and motivating change in others as, say, throwing a punch. In this sense, verbalizing the need for wrongs to be made right can have a constructive result on the hearers.

Of course, serious questions remain regarding the usefulness of anger in humans and its effects not only on the individual but also on the community in which the individual lives.[20] However, for our current purposes, we are most concerned with the positive function of anger as we seek to attribute such an emotion to the divine, given that, for classical theists, the wrath of God must be righteous.

According to Lazarus, the appraisal that results in anger is that the individual's "ego identity" is at stake, and the core relational theme is

---

18. Jennifer S. Lerner and Larissa Z. Tiedens, "Portrait of the Anger Decision Maker: How Appraisal Tendencies Shape Anger's Influence on Cognition," *Journal of Behavior Decision Making* 19 (2006): 116.

19. Agneta H. Fischer and Ira J. Roseman, "Beat Them or Ban Them: The Characteristics and Social Functions of Anger and Contempt," *Journal of Personality and Social Psychology* 93 (2007): 104.

20. Most prominently in Martha Nussbaum, *Anger and Forgiveness: Forgiveness, Generosity, and Justice* (Oxford: Oxford University Press, 2016).

"other-blame." He writes, "When this identity has been threatened or harmed, there is goal incongruence in what is deemed to be an unfair slight or insult. With anger, blame is also necessary, and it depends on the attributions that someone is accountable and has full control over the demeaning action."[21] Thus, if there is a lesser sense of culpability on the offender's part, the anger intensity is lessened, redirected, or dissipated. The individual experiencing anger is directing the emotion at the object they blame for being responsible for hindering or thwarting their intended goal.

Additionally, CMRT accounts for anger experienced when the offense is not directed toward the individual themselves. This is a situation when one evaluates a particular person-environment relationship that involves the well-being of someone else or a particular group. As such, this introduces issues concerning fairness and justice. In this case, the individual's well-being is connected to their values and beliefs, but the individual is not the subject of the unfairness or injustice, so anger is then vicariously felt by the individual.

Although there are instances when malicious intent of the offender may be missing, the perception of the offended individual is that they have been treated in a way that falls short of what they deserve. As Lazarus points out, this is why retaliation and vengeance are often connected to anger; there is a desire for reparations or just deserts to be exacted from the offender. As the individual forms meaning by observing the attack or injustice, the cognitive appraisal results in anger. The individual's ego is damaged (intentionally or unintentionally) on the basis of which the desire for retaliatory action is made known.

Let us review. Anger is the emotion produced when an individual perceives an unjust act committed against the individual herself or against a person or group of people with whom they profoundly identify and is accompanied by a desire for retaliation in order to right the wrong committed. Furthermore, anger is a moral emotion in that its core evaluative concern is moral (injustice), and the effects of the emotion lead to beneficial moral consequences (justice). Given the theological commitments of classical theism, the anger experienced or expressed by God is indeed virtuous and just.

Furthermore, there is a positive function of anger within society. Anger is uniquely effective in communicating instances of injustice

21. Lazarus, "Progress," 828.

perpetrated against an individual or group (particularly the oppressed), which signals important moral messages to others and their communities. Furthermore, anger motivates change in undesirable behavior by signaling hostility, aggression, power, and authority, which are all indicators to the object of anger that a change in circumstance should result. As such, anger can enact change in others relatively quickly and effectively. Thus, anger communicates and motivates others to change behavior in order to right perceived instances of injustice.

Analogical Predication of the Divine

The notion of analogy has been indispensable in exploring the doctrine of God. At the core of this issue lies concerns over how we can meaningfully speak about an ineffable God. An analogical view of theological language about God seeks to preserve the Creator-creature distinction, while simultaneously maintaining the claim that our language does indeed say something truthful about God.

The goal of the classical theistic appeal to analogical language is to avoid two poles: anthropomorphism and agnosticism. Anthropomorphism is the idea that God possesses properties that can only be possessed by a finite human being. That takes place, for example, in conceptualizing God as having spatial or material qualities or, in our particular case, human emotions and values. Thinking about God in human terms, however, is unavoidable. The inherent limitations of our language results in us using anthropomorphic language in order to communicate divine realities. We are confined to the finite and fallen state of our existence; thus, human terms will forever be "stretched" to speak about God this side of the eschaton.

As mentioned above, the primary way in which theologians conceptualize divine wrath is to draw on the existence of wrath that is present in humankind. However, speaking of God's wrath indicates a righteous wrath, or the purest form of wrath, because it is ascribed to God. So, in this sense, the anthropomorphic language found in the biblical text concerning the wrath and anger of God must be filtered through the idea that divine wrath is free of human limitations, such as human sin. However, this move seems to make God an ideal human who possesses the most excellent form of wrath humans can conceive.

On the other hand, there is a problem with agnosticism. This concern is not the validity of the existence of God but whether we can speak truthfully about God as God is. Does our language actually give meaning to what God is, or are we incapable of knowing and expressing God's nature? Is the transcendence of God insurmountable for postlapsarian humankind? For my present purposes, this concern highlights the difficulties in claiming that God's wrath is a holy extension of human wrath—what does this mean? How are we to understand "holy wrath"? What content can we give to the claim that God's wrath is like human wrath but without sin?

Many classical theists fall in line with a Thomist account of religious language and its relation to the names of God. In addition to the concerns with finding a balance between univocal and equivocal terms, the theological commitment to divine simplicity remains. So we may struggle to understand how language informs our understanding of the classical theist's God, but doctrines concerning divine perfections must be grounded in the claim that God is metaphysically simple or noncomposite. In other words, God *is* God's attributes. The doctrine of divine simplicity underpins Thomas's theory of analogy and is the foundation upon which he builds his notion of religious language.

In addition, Thomas's account of analogy distinguishes between analogy in terms of ontology and semantics. For Thomas, this can be mapped to his concepts of participation and predication, respectively. While there are serious debates surrounding his theory of analogy and whether or not it was linguistically focused or metaphysical in intention, it is the case that he sought to find a middle ground between univocity and equivocity and argued that analogy provided the means by which we speak about God.[22]

Thomas Aquinas on Analogy

For Thomas, distinguishing between the multitude of perfections within the divine life is a merely conceptual matter. It is a means by which humankind can, in a meaningful but imperfect way, come to know God's transcendent and hidden nature, but it does not imply any real distinctions in God's being since God is noncomposite.[23] God's essence and being are one and the same; thus, all that God freely chooses to reveal of Godself is accommodated so far as to bring the finite a glimpse into the infinite.

22. R. M. McInery, *The Logic of Analogy: An Interpretation of St. Thomas* (New York: Springer, 1971), 76–77.

23. Thomas Aquinas, *Commentary on the Sentences of Peter Lombard*, I.2.1, a. 2., at https://aquinas.cc/la/en/~Sent.I.

Human apprehension of divine perfections depends in important respects on our epistemic vantage.[24] Thomas writes,

> Plurality of notions arises from the fact that the reality that is God surpasses our intellect. For our intellect cannot receive diverse modes of perfection by means of one conception. . . . Whence, since God is perfect in all ways according to one and the same reality, one cannot apprehend his perfection in an integral way by a single conception, and consequently neither can one so name him. . . . Those names are not synonyms, inasmuch as they signify diverse notions.[25]

Thomas's theory of analogical predication makes certain ontological claims relating to God's essential properties. In doing so, God's perfections or names provide a means by which humankind can speak intelligibly about the ineffable God and yet, paradoxically, fall infinitely short of the true nature of the divine.

He uses a number of arguments to defend his position, but particularly central to his thesis is the idea of divine causality and participation. We know God by God's effects. Goodness, justice, wisdom, and so on are known by the work of God in creation. So when creaturely instances of goodness, justice, and wisdom are made known in created things, they are understood to reflect (in some sense) the essential and maximal good, just, and wise nature of God. The claim is not that God creates or merely causes goodness, justice, or wisdom. Instead, the idea is that God's supreme nature is reflected in creation so that these creaturely attributes resemble their source in the one true God.[26] Thus, these perfections, in a sense, flow from God to creatures—preexisting in God in a more excellent and perfect way—so that God causes goodness in things because God is good, not that God is good because he causes goodness.[27] The creaturely correspondence to these conceptions signifies something is truly and properly divine.[28] This is a central plank of Thomas's account: Analogy gives ontological priority to the attributes of God over and against those found in humankind.

24. Aquinas, *Sentences*, I.2.1, a. 3.

25. Aquinas, *Sentences*, I.2.1, a. 3.

26. Thomas Aquinas, *The Summa Theologica* (hereafter *ST*), trans. Thomas Laurence Shapcote and Daniel Joseph Sullivan, ed. Daniel J. Sullivan (Chicago: Encyclopedia Britannica, 1952), I.13, a. 2.

27. Aquinas, *ST*, I.13, 6.

28. Aquinas, *Sentences*, I.2.1, a. 3.

Furthermore, Thomas attempts to make sense of the fact that we must use human language to speak of God. Therefore, as there is an ontological priority of the analogy of terms attributed to the divine, Thomas also argues for a linguistic priority. Thus, although meaning and knowledge of human terms are derived from the created realm—for we can only attain knowledge through created things—we can and do apply what is learned empirically in order to name God.

Thomas contends that the perfections of God exceed our intellect, because of God's mode of being and because of our postlapsarian epistemological condition. Yet there is still a level of correspondence or analogy that gives content to the language we use in relation to God—even as this infinitely falls short of perfection. For Thomas, analogy allows the referent to be a transcendent perfection (ontological priority), and yet the human term can, in some important way, signify a derivative notion (linguistic priority).

Nevertheless, we cannot forget that the divine attributes are predicated primarily of God, not humankind. Thomas writes:

> Sacred Scripture sometimes recalls the likeness between [God] and his creatures. . . . However, according to this likeness, it is more fitting to say that the feature is like God than vice versa. For one thing is like another when it possesses a quality or form of it. Since, then, what is in God perfectly is found in other things by way of an imperfect participation, that in which likeness is observed is God's simply, but not the creature's. And thus the creature has what is God's, and therefore is rightly said to be like God. But it cannot be said in this way that God has what belongs to his creature; therefore, it is not fitting to say that God is like his creature, as neither do we say that a man is like his portrait, although we declare that his portrait is like him.[29]

Accordingly, then, when we speak of wisdom, we can only come to distorted, defective, and ambiguous concepts of wisdom. Wisdom is only measured according to God and not according to the creature. This is due to the fact that, first, we cannot know what true wisdom actually is because we simply cannot know what God is. Second, there are no created means by which humankind can learn, experience, or name what

---

29. Thomas Aquinas, *The Summa Contra Gentiles*, first book (hereafter *SCG* I), trans. Laurence Shapcote (New York: Benziger, 1928–29), c. 89.

true wisdom is because we cannot access the divine nature. While this move guards against theological language collapsing into mere anthropomorphism, these two claims seem to leave us with no positive content to name God.

As such, as has been noted by many, while anthropomorphism is rejected, agnosticism seems to be waiting around the corner. Of course, Thomas aims to find a middle ground between those two dangerous poles. Appealing to analogy allows him to stress the vast epistemological gap between the divine and human while retaining some intelligible correspondence between God and the created world which humankind inhabits.[30]

However, Thomas does not argue that analogy is the only way by which we talk about God. So, while some perfections such as goodness, wisdom, justice, and the like signify the divine substance, although in an imperfect manner,[31] other perfections are metaphorically signified. There are some names which signify perfections flowing from God to creatures in such a way that the imperfect way creatures receive the divine perfection is part of the very signification of the name itself, as *stone* signifies a material being, and names of this kind can be applied to God only in a metaphorical sense.[32]

The distinction he makes is due to an ontological claim that undergirds Thomas's theory of analogy. Janet Soskice writes,

> Because of the particular theory of meaning with which [Aquinas] worked, these linguistic relations were also ontological ones. Analogical relations all refer to the same thing, they all have the same *res significata*, but they refer to it in different ways. . . . [However,] Aquinas does not claim that everything we say about God is said analogically. . . . Because of the ontological relation involved in "naming" things analogically, only a select group of the perfection terms can be so applied to God. We say analogically of God that he is one, wise, good, and so on.[33]

This is important and, for our current purposes, is a critical point in Thomas's understanding of religious language and one that has retained particular prominence in subsequent Western Christian theology.

---

30. Roger White, *Talking About God* (Aldershost: Ashgate, 2010), 100.
31. Aquinas, *ST*, I.13, a. 2.
32. Aquinas, *ST*, I.13, a. 3.
33. Janet Martin Soskice, *Metaphor and Religious Language* (Oxford: Clarendon, 1987), 65.

The relationship between divine perfections and the creature's ability to know God has been the foundation for classical theistic accounts of speaking intelligibly about God while, at the same time, insisting on the unknowability of the divine essence. As Thomas insists, the ontological priority of the term rests in God, yet the linguistic priority still acknowledges the failure of such language. These two principles are integral in maintaining, among other things, the Creator/creature distinction.

Thomas aligns with a long history of Christian theologians who applied the method of the *viae*. As such, the means by which terms are deemed worthy of ascription to the divine is according to the *summum bonum*, which relies on the understanding that God is utter perfection. Thus, names attributed to God are those that attribute to God "every discernible good to the highest possible degree, and den[y] of him completely every discernible limitation."[34] This includes the idea that God is omnipotent, infinite, just, wise, and good. While the names of God are the preeminent perfection of such terms, this is not to be understood as a mere extension of our creaturely conceptions of power, infinity, justice, wisdom, and goodness—one that could be understood as merely void of sin or confusion. It is only by analogy that these terms can signify anything close to the thing signified.

However, Thomas's use of metaphor is also helpful in identifying and clarifying theological language. He writes: "These names which are applied to God literally [analogously] imply corporeal conditions not in the thing signified, but as regards their mode of signification; whereas those which are applied to God metaphorically imply and mean a corporeal condition in the thing signified."[35]

One way metaphorical language is utilized is when psychological terms are attributed to the divine. However, for Thomas, there are no passions of the appetite in God.[36] First, these passions are only known through the senses. Since God has no knowledge through the senses, God cannot experience passion. Second, every passion is accompanied by somatic change. Increased and decreased heart rate, for example, cannot possibly occur in God.[37] Furthermore, a passion is said to move the subject from

---

34. Stephen R. Holmes, "The Attributes of God," *The Oxford Handbook of Systematic Theology*, ed. Kathryn Tanner (Oxford: Oxford University Press, 2009), 56.

35. Aquinas, *ST*, I.13, a. 3.

36. As mentioned previously, passions do not indicate the contemporary concept of emotion. Although there remains overlap in Thomas's account of "passion" and how emotion theorists understand "emotion," they must remain distinct. In this instance, we can see that Thomas is concerned with the somatic and neurological nature of perceived passions.

37. Aquinas, *SCG* I, c. 89.

its original disposition. Thus, since there is no potency nor mutability in the divine, passion can be attributed to God. Accordingly, Thomas argues because of its genus, there are no passions in God.

Thomas also argues that some passions are absent from God according to species. In this move, passions that are unfitting according to the essence of God cannot be properly ascribed to the divine. This is with respect to their specific mode of relation to their proper objects, for example, sorrow and pain, whose object is some present evil. There are various ways sorrow is manifested: repentance, whose object is a change in the will; envy, whose object is grief over the good of another; and anger, an effect of sorrow, whose object is revenge for the harm inflicted.

By way of contrast, passions of the intellect, or will, are fitting to God. Thomas states,

> Now, the operations of the appetite take their species from their objects. Accordingly, we find in the intellective appetite (which is the will) operations specifically similar to those of the sensitive appetite, though differing in this: in the sensitive appetite they are passions on account of its connection with a bodily organ, but in the intellective appetite they are pure operations.[38]

Here, we see Thomas make a linguistic move. On the one hand, he argues that particular psychological or emotive language, passions of the *senses*, can only be improperly attributed to God. According to Thomas, God is metaphysically simple, immutable, and incorporeal. Thus, for example, repentance cannot be adequately spoken of God because it indicates a change in will. Classical theists reject the idea that God experiences emotions that would necessitate somatic or neurological changes within God (however conceived) since God is simple, immutable, and incorporeal.[39] Thus, biblical language, which seems to indicate particular human experiences that are dependent upon corporeal realities and the senses, is not a form of ontological analogy but is metaphorically applied. The metaphor does, however, point to some higher perfection, but this is shrouded in mystery and obscurity.[40]

---

38. Aquinas, *SCG* I, c. 90.

39. Aquinas also argues that such passions of the senses are also unfitting due to divine blessedness. *ST*, I.26.

40. Herwi Rikhof, *The Concept of Church: A Methodological Inquiry into the Use of Metaphors in Ecclesiology* (London, Sheed & Ward, 1981), 186–187.

Analogical Predication and Psychological Language

At this point, it is time to turn to the discussion concerning how divine wrath, emotion, and a Thomist perspective on religious language can converge. In the case of analogical predication, if we say divine wrath is predicated of God in an analogical manner, traditionally speaking, we are saying that God is literally (analogically) wrathful. However, one would be inclined, as Thomas was, to avoid claims that biblical instances of God's wrath indicate wrath as a divine perfection, which, for him, entails the creaturely experience of bodily changes and changes of the will. This is why Thomas opts to place God's wrath in the metaphorical category.

However, as I have shown, emotions are not simply a somatic or neurological experience—nor are emotions behavior. Emotions are the means by which humans communicate values and judgments. And in the case of anger, values and judgments are not only communicated but enable individuals to motivate others either to acknowledge injustice or to motivate individuals to bring about justice. In this sense, I am arguing that the *communication* of value judgments is the fundamental element to an emotion, and particularly anger.

If we use psychological language to construct an analogical concept of divine wrath, we are not claiming wrath is a divine perfection, which is analogous to the divine essence in the same way that the *emotive process* of human individuals is analogous to that of the divine. No, what is analogous to the divine life is that the values and judgments of the human individual are communicated to others just as psychological (or emotive) language in relation to God is analogous to the communication of God's values and judgments. The metaphysical claim is not that God is emotional in the colloquial sense (i.e., the somatic and neurological effects of being sad, repentant, or angry, or even the idea of "feelings" obtain within the divine life). Rather, the claim is that God has values and judgments (i.e., the divine expression of being sad, repentant, or angry communicates the reciprocal values or judgments in relation to human activity).

This way of analogical predication allows such use of psychological, emotive language to be appropriately ascribed to God without implying the corporeal realities of what we know to be essential to the cognitive emotion process—namely, the need for a body and brain. Furthermore, analogy in this respect allows us to retain emotive terms concerning the divine without constructing a concept of emotion that is purely and entirely based on folk understandings of emotion or manufacturing a unique and privatized definition of emotion that has no neurological or psychological footing. As such, divine wrath, which is often said to be God's judgment on human sin, is not God's action but God's *value judgment*—perhaps it could be understood as an extension of divine perfection. For the impassibilist, there is neither an emotional process nor feeling or behavior or change therein, given the simplicity, immutability, and aseity of the divine nature. The biblical use of wrath in relation to the divine does not signal a change or reaction in God but God's moral judgment, which is consistently held in the divine life. God is eternally against sin yet not eternally emotionally angry.

As such, we can say that God's anger communicates to multiple audiences: those who are the perpetrators of injustice, those who are victims of injustice, and those who are witnesses to the injustice.[41] While one may argue this is not novel, this is, I believe, *the* revelatory purpose of divine wrath. God, in God's perfection, reveals God's moral evaluative judgment of sin through analogical language, which communicates to victims and their communities that their suffering is the result of those who have sinned against God.

So then, our knowledge of God is grounded in the revelation of God, but due to our finite epistemological status as fallen creatures, God has accommodated such revelation to provide analogical language that gives human creatures a mediated access to the infinite being of the divine. While the ontological priority remains the essence of God, the analogy of terms finds its linguistic priority in the created realm. The use of analogy is the *function* of the emotion, not the process therein. The analogy of terms allows the referent to be a transcendent perfection (goodness, justice, wisdom), understood in psychological terms as wrath or anger. Although we may not fully grasp or even come close to comprehending the divine predicate, what we can say is that God *communicates* and motivates the need for justice.

---

41. Although he has a different take on divine wrath, Cristian Mihut has a similar understanding of the communicative value of divine anger. See *Gracious Forgiveness: A Theological Retrieval* (Oxford: Oxford University Press, 2023), 89.

CHAPTER 7

THE GOD WHO IS KENOTIC LOVE

BRUCE L. MCCORMACK

I want to begin with a few passages from the writings of Karl Barth which serve to bookend his career as a dogmatic theologian and which, in doing so, give us reliable insight into his deepest-lying intentions. This is not, to be clear, an essay on Barth, though anyone who knows me knows that he is one of my primary sources of inspiration. So it was almost an inevitability that he would appear somewhere—and he will do so again later in the chapter.

The first two passages come from Barth's *Göttingen Dogmatics.* Both are found in the prolegomena volume written in 1924, when Barth first set sail on the vast ocean of dogmatic thinking. Here they are: "The relation of God to human beings is not accidental; it is necessarily contained and grounded in God's *essence.* . . . God would not be God if his relation to human beings were not originally inherent in him."[1] And again:

> The content of God's Word is God alone, God as a whole, God himself. . . . The new thing which is added to the concept "God" by the concept "Word" is that he is God in relation. But [and now notice!] the second concept is only an analysis, a making more precise, an unfolding of the first. The content of the concept "Word" is precisely this, that God is never and nowhere *without* relation, without his turning towards human beings; that the *foedus*, the covenant as the decree of his will is eternal in God himself. And God never ceases to be God, wholly and completely God, in the relation.[2]

1. Karl Barth, *"Unterricht in der christlichen Religion", Erster Band: Prolegomena, 1924* (Zürich: TVZ, 1985), 156–57; ET: *The Göttingen Dogmatics: Instruction in the Christian Religion*, trans. Geoffrey W. Bromiley (Grand Rapids: Eerdmans, 1990), 128.

2. Karl Barth, *"Unterricht in der christlichen Religion", Zweiter Band: Die Lehre von Gott / Die Lehre vom Menschen, 1924/1925* (Zürich: TVZ, 1990), 12; ET: *The Göttingen Dogmatics*, 326.

The original relation that God is, according to Barth, the relation that God is essentially, is not described here in strictly intra-Trinitarian terms (as modes of origin, perhaps, or as the perichoresis of persons as defined by the Neo-Chalcedonians); the Word of God *is* his turning towards the human race in the covenant of grace.

A second passage, this time from *Church Dogmatics* IV/2 (completed in 1955):

> It is only the pride of man, making a god in its own image, that will not hear of a determination of the divine essence in Jesus Christ. The presupposition of all earlier Christology has suffered from this pride: already the Church Fathers suffered from it as did the later Reformed and Lutherans. The presupposition was a philosophical concept of God, according to which God was far too exalted for His turning towards human beings, His incarnation, and therefore the reconciliation of the world with Himself, to mean anything at all for Himself, or in any way to affect His Godhead. In other words, He was the prisoner of His own Godhead. As if transfixed by this conception, the older theologians thought that they should close their eyes entirely to this aspect. They were only to speak of what happened to human essence in this turning. . . . Godhead was supposed to remain untouched by its union with humanity.[3]

To speak of a "determination" of the divine essence at all in theologies of Hegelian provenance is to speak of a relation which makes essence to be more than an abstract Idea, which makes it to be concretely realized through identification with either the world as a whole or with a part or portion thereof. In Barth's case, the "determination" of the divine essence consists in identification with Jesus Christ; even more precisely, it is a relation to a human being in the midst of history which renders divine essence concretely real in our world.[4] So real, in fact, that "Godhead" has itself been rendered *affective*—an ontological affectivity by any other name. Barth does not speak of an original relation in this context, as he did in Göttingen, but the linking of a "determination" of divine essence

3. Karl Barth, *Church Dogmatics*, 4 volumes in 13 parts, ed. G. W. Bromiley and T. F. Torrance (Edinburgh: T&T Clark, 1956–75), IV/2, 84–85.

4. So Barth can also say, "What makes God to be God, the selfhood and essentially, the *essentia* or 'essence' of God—we will either encounter there where God acts as Lord and Savior or we will not encounter it at all." Karl Barth, *Die Kirchliche Dogmatik*, 4 volumes in 13 parts (Munich: Chr. Kaiser, 1932; Zürich: EVZ, 1938–65), II/1, 293; ET: *Church Dogmatics*, II/1, 261.

to ontological affectivity achieves the same end. Indeed, I would go so far as to say that it is only that relation which can be conceived as rendering God affective.

Two sets of passages, then—one from the beginning of Barth's dogmatic career, one from very nearly its end—both testify to the same foundational intentionality and place Barth's thinking in an altogether different sphere than that in which, as he puts it, *all earlier Christology* from the Fathers to both Reformed and Lutheran orthodoxy took place. My contention is this: We will not be able to understand Barth's deepest-lying intentions throughout the whole of his career if we ignore the *Grundentscheidung* ("basic decision") announced in these two sets of passages. Barth deliberately changed his nomenclature on occasion (in part, to prevent his formulations from becoming uncritically employed slogans in the hands of fan boys), but that does not mean that he changed his mind in doing so in every instance. Clearly, he has not changed his mind here.

In what follows, I am going to set forth a brief sketch of a doctrine of the Trinity I am in the process of constructing. I will begin with a description of the received doctrine of God still celebrated by strict adherents to the dogma of the Trinity as definitively formulated at Constantinople in 381 CE. I will then introduce my alternative conception.

I. The Role Played by Divine Simplicity in the Construction of Trinitarian Dogma

The orthodox dogma of the Trinity as formulated by the Council of Constantinople in 381 is unthinkable apart from the controlling influence of the idea of divine "simplicity" in its metaphysical definition as "non-composite." The conception of eternal generation as purely intellectual, immediate, and productive of a relation that is both one and undivided (so that all that the Father is, he gives to the Son) led to a host of conclusions where the Trinity is concerned: first, "consubstantiality" as the focal point of the unity of the Three; second, the inability to distinguish the "persons" *materially* and, therefore, to define what it meant to be a Trinitarian "person"; third, the "principle of inseparable operations" (i.e., the idea that if one "person" does something in relation to that which is "outwith" God, they all do it), a principle which led quite directly to the inescapable conclusion that any of the Three might have become incarnate had the

Three so decided (it did not have to be the Son[5]); and, eventually, fourth, the idea of a "perichoresis" of the "persons"—all of these items of belief were carefully formulated under the strict control of the idea of simplicity. To these building blocks of the orthodox doctrine of the Trinity should be added items necessarily derived from the prior understanding of the "one God" as utterly simple: "unity" as the necessary consequence of a divine "essence" rendered ultimately undefinable by simplicity and transferred directly into Trinitarian discourse to play the role of "oneness"; "eternity" as timelessness and immensity as "spacelessness," the omni-attributes which render divine power, knowledge, and presence to be unlimited; and "incomprehensibility" defined without reference to God's self-revelation in Christ so that it becomes another principle, this one governing whether, how, *and to what extent* revelation can take place (thereby placing significant constraints on how the orthodox christological dogma would be formulated in the fifth century).

Now I should point out that it has not been critics of the Nicene-Constantinopolitan Creed who have, nearly for the last two decades, been demonstrating the regulative character of the concept of simplicity. It has been, instead, defenders of simplicity belonging to the guild of patristic historians who have been making this case: Lewis Ayres, Andrew Radde-Gallwitz, and (most recently) Pui Him Ip. Ayres drew upon the earlier work of David Burrell, CSC, to establish that

> we do not include "simpleness" in that list of terms we wish to attribute to God—classically, "living," "wise," "willing." It is rather that simpleness defines the manner in which such properties might be attributed to God. . . . "Formal features" [like simplicity] are not so much said of a subject, as they are reflected in a subject's very mode of existing, and govern the way in which anything whatsoever might be said of that subject.[6]

5. Saint Augustine, *The Trinity*, 2nd ed., trans. Edmund Hill, OP (Hyde Park: New City, 2015), 232: "The only reason, it seems, why we do not call the three persons together one person, as we call them one being and one God, but say three persons while we never say three Gods or three beings, is that we want to keep at least one word for signifying what we mean by trinity, so that we are not simply reduced to silence when we are asked three what, after we have confessed that there are three." Cf. Augustine, *The Trinity*, 197.

6. Lewis Ayres, *Nicaea and its Legacy: An Approach to Fourth-Century Trinitarian Theology* (Oxford: Oxford University Press, 2006), 288, here citing David Burrell, CSC, *Knowing the Unknowable God: Ibn-Sina, Maimonides, Aquinas* (Notre Dame, IN: University of Notre Dame Press, 1986), 46–47.

While noting that Burrell makes this assessment of the theology of Thomas Aquinas, Ayres says that it is in the "pro-Nicene theology" that gave rise to the Constantinopolitan Creed that "we first see simplicity functioning in the manner Burrell describes so well."[7] Pui Him Ip demurs in one important respect with this judgment. Ip holds that simplicity was already functioning as a regulative principle, as "second-order" discourse, in the writings of Irenaeus in the late second century.[8] Of course, this means that simplicity was already playing this role in Christian theologizing about God more than a century before Nicaea—so that the results of this regulated thinking about God could be taken for granted when attention turned to the Trinity in the wake of the Arian crisis. Even more significant, perhaps, is the fact that simplicity, precisely as a metaphysical principle (and not as an ethical principle as in Plato himself), was already functioning as a "pattern for biblical interpretation" by Philo of Alexandria (20–15 BCE to 45–50 CE).[9] And so it comes as no real surprise to find Radde-Gallwitz saying of simplicity that although it is a principle which cannot be found in Scripture, it does help one to "make sense of what is in scripture."[10]

It seems clear on the basis of the scholarly research just cited that simplicity had, at a minimum, two functions by the time of Origen: (1) to govern the construction of the Christian God first on the side of the "one God" and then (much later) on the side of the "triune God," and (2) to provide a criterion for interpreting biblical texts which bear witness to the nature and activities of God. But of course, this sets up a rather vicious circle since simplicity is often used as the primary criterion for interpreting texts that might seem at odds with it (e.g., those which speak of God as "repenting" or "changing his mind").

My questions about all of this—and I speak now as a committed "Protestant" theologian who thinks the Reformation will remain a powerful "protest" so long as its challenges have not been adequately addressed—are two in number. The first is this: Should a concept which everyone agrees was borrowed from that eclectic movement in philosophy known as "Middle Platonism" have ever been allowed to attain to the status it did? Please do not think for even a minute that I am protesting

7. Ayres, *Nicaea and its Legacy*, 46–47.

8. Pui Him Ip, *Origen and the Emergence of Divine Simplicity before Nicaea* (Notre Dame, IN: University of Notre Dame Press, 2022), 53–68.

9. Ip, *Origen*, 38–47.

10. Andrew Radde-Gallwitz, *Basil of Caesarea, Gregory of Nyssa, and the Transformation of Divine Simplicity* (Oxford: Oxford University Press, 2009), 20.

against the use of philosophies in theology. Karl Barth never did that either, though that has long been a story told of him, a fictional tale which will undoubtedly continue to find eager ears among the pragmatically inclined who care little for probity and truth.[11] Borrowings from philosophies which provide something like an academic "lingua franca" in any age are necessary not only for communicating accurately with one's contemporaries but also for working out solutions to theological problems. But I am not asking whether the early church did well to draw upon Hellenistic philosophies; that much was an inevitability. I am asking whether a borrowed concept should ever have been allowed to become so all-controlling, so all-determinative. And should a concept have been allowed to function as *the* key that controls how the Scriptural witness to the reality of God is to be read and understood? Can simplicity find any support in Scripture that a zealous defender has not first read into biblical concepts like divine "unity," "constancy," "steadfast faithfulness," and so on?

"Unity" is a most interesting problem in this context since David Burrell holds that it too is a "formal feature" that describes the ontological constitution of God, but he understands it as *derivative* of the primary "formal feature" of simplicity[12]—which means that simplicity is controlling the meaning of "unity" or "oneness." If so, it must remain highly questionable whether any putative biblical exegesis which hopes to find a biblical root for the concept of simplicity in passages which speak of the "oneness" of Jesus and his Father in the New Testament (John 10:30)—or even of the singularity and universality of the God of Israel in the Old Testament—can be at all persuasive if it must first be read *into* those very passages in order to be read out of them.

"Simplicity" is, in my judgment, the very pinnacle of speculative theology—as well as the source from which additional entailments are derived. Unity, impassibility, incorporeality, incomprehensibility—these are all terms whose definitions *had to be* controlled by simplicity once simplicity had been affirmed. But simplicity also set the limits for understanding incarnation when the time came to address conflicts in that realm of reflection. Simplicity as "noncomposition" demanded that hypostatic "union" be conceived in such a way as to preserve and uphold

11. Against this myth, consider the following: Robert W. Jenson, response to "The Significance of Karl Barth's Thought for the Relation of Philosophy and Theology," by Jonathan E. Smith, *Union Seminary Quarterly Review* 28 (1972), 31–34; D. Paul LaMontagne, *Barth and Rationality: Critical Realism in Theology* (Eugene, OR: Cascade, 2012); Kenneth Oakes, *Karl Barth on Theology and Philosophy* (Oxford: Oxford University Press, 2012).

12. Burrell, *Knowing the Unknowable God*, 49.

the ontological non-affectivity of God. That meant, in turn, that "separation" of the so-called "natures" was a requirement that no distinction of "person" from "nature" (or *hypostasis* from *ousia*[13]) could finally overcome.

In the modern period, reflection on Christology was only able to retain a connection to the Chalcedonian dogma by making it a conclusion, not a starting-point. One attended closely to life-of-Jesus research, not giving it complete credence without further thought but through critical engagement. But taking history seriously at all had wider ramifications. For it was bound up with another development, this time in theological epistemologies. German idealism and Romanticism, however dramatic their differences, both held that the Absolute (in the case of the Idealists) or the Infinite (in the case of the Romantics) could become thinkable and speakable only where a relation existed that rendered the one or the other concrete either in a particular or in the whole of the "real." Both were thought to be "living" by those who made appeal to them and, therefore, as *naturally* generative, creative, and self-disclosive. For theologians impacted by one or the other of these movements, "God" came to be thought of as essentially living, as person-forming or indeed as "Personality."

To give just one example, a "mediating" theologian like H. L. Martensen could oppose the idea that God is incomprehensible "not merely for us, but absolutely incomprehensible in God's self" on the grounds that revelation would be impossible were that the case. For Pseudo-Dionysius, Martensen noted, God is an "absolute mystery which is above all names because every name would pull God into the circle of relations" known to us if (as Pseudo-Dionysius insisted) God "is the simple One (τὸ ἁπλας ἓν), the pure light which is no different than pure darkness."[14] To conceive God rightly means, Martensen argued, to understand God in his relations: "If it did not belong to the essence of God to give himself in relations, thereby making himself comprehensible, then he has not revealed himself. Only in the inner relations of the self-consciousness does God possess God's deity and only in that he sets himself in a variety of relations to his world does he reveal his essence to the world."[15]

13. Basil of Caesarea, "Letter 38," in *The Letters* (New York: Putnam, 1926), 197–201. The question of whether it was, in fact, Basil who wrote this letter or his younger brother Gregory is a matter of concern to patristic scholars but need not detain us here. My interest—not here in this essay but in the long run—lies rather in the significance of the distinction, its presuppositions and consequences for thought, and its role in helping Constantinople I to find the widespread (though not universal) acceptance it did.

14. H. Martensen, *Die christliche Dogmatik* (Berlin: Verlag von Gustav Schlawiz, 1870), 81.

15. Martensen, *Die christliche Dogmatik*, 81.

The truth is that "God *is* personality. i.e. he is the Absolute *centered* in itself, the eternally founded essence which knows itself as the centerpoint, as the *I* in his infinite majesty, and as the *Lord* over this, his majesty."[16] If, for Martensen, we wish to

> speak rightly of knowledge of the divine essence, then we must hold together the tensive statements of Scripture. We know the truth [1 Jn 2:20] and yet our knowledge is partial (1 Cor. 13:12); we know him and yet we will only see him as he is there [eschatologically] (1 Jn 3:2). We investigate the depths of deity (1 Cor. 2:10), and yet no one has seen God (1 Jn 4:12) for God dwells in a light that is inaccessible (1 Tim. 6:16).[17]

And so "we have a true but not an adequate knowledge of the essence of God."[18]

Karl Barth would later reduce the number of relations through which God discloses God's "essence" to one: the christological. That did not mean that he could not provide a fulsome account of creation and providence (to which Martensen was pointing)—and indeed he did so, albeit christologically grounded ones. The great advantage of his reduction, though, was that it made possible a much more fundamental critique of the metaphysics which had informed the formation of the Trinitarian dogma at every point than was carried out by even the very best of nineteenth-century theologians. This is not to say, however, that Barth's critique was as thorough or complete as it was fundamental; it was not—as we shall now see.

II. The Doctrine of the Trinity After Barth

The standard work on Barth's doctrine of the Trinity remains Eberhard Jüngel's *God's Being Is in Becoming*, a work completed before his thirtieth birthday.[19] Already in the first foreword to the book, the tensive character

16. Martensen, *Die christliche Dogmatik*, 74.
17. Martensen, *Die christliche Dogmatik*, 83.
18. Martensen, *Die christliche Dogmatik*, 83.
19. Eberhard Jüngel, *Gottes Sein ist im Werden: Verantwortliche Rede vom Sein Gottes bei Karl Barth, Eine Paraphrase*, 2nd ed. (Tübingen: Mohr, 1967); ET: *God's Being Is in Becoming: The Trinitarian Being of God in the Theology of Karl Barth*, trans. John B. Webster (Grand Rapids: Eerdmans, 2001). This is a work which really needs first to be read in German. For a thorough contextualization of the book and its argument, see Bruce L. McCormack, "God *Is* His Decision: The Jüngel-Gottwitzer 'Debate' Revisited," in *Theology as Conversation: The Significance of Dialogue in Historical and Contemporary Theology, A Festschrift for Daniel L. Migliore*, ed. Bruce L. McCormack and Kimlyn Bender (Grand Rapids: Eerdmans, 2009), 48–66.

of Jüngel's interpretation emerges clearly into the light of day, reflecting (quite accurately, I would argue) the tensive character of Barth's own thinking about the relation of Trinity and election, above all. Jüngel writes:

> The title of this treatment may alienate some readers. Nonetheless, I ask that it be read carefully. I am *not* speaking here of a "becoming God." God's being is not identified with God's becoming; much rather is it the case that God's being is ontologically localized. . . . The becoming in which God's being is, can . . . mean neither an elevation nor a lessening of the being of God. Elevation and lessening are, as evaluative categories, to be kept far away from the concept of being, if one does not wish to be forced yet again to think God as *summum bonum* and, in this way, as the highest value. For the God whose being is in becoming can *die* as a human! "Becoming," therefore, indicates the way *in* which God's being is, and can, for that reason, be understood as the ontological place of God's being.[20]

The conspicuous tension in Barth's thinking—as interpreted by Jüngel—is that between a "being" of God which does not "become" and the emphasis on an ontological "localization" of God's being "in" becoming. To be faithful to the first side of this tension, God's "being" would surely have to be somehow preserved in an ontic space "above" becoming and, therefore, would not be "in" becoming at all in any sense other than that of self-disclosure—which would be saying nothing at all new, thereby removing the need to talk about offense. On the other side, however, if being "in" becoming is meant seriously, there could be no absolutized opposition to talk of a "becoming" God. One would need only to specify the conditions under which "becoming" occurs as well as its limits. But this only makes it seem as though Jüngel (and Barth before him) are speaking out of both sides of their mouths at the same time. How did it come to this? How can two of the more obviously brilliant theologians of the twentieth century find themselves in such a dilemma?

The answer, I think, has everything to do with Barth's basic move of making the act of election to be the ontological ground of God's "being" as God—without sufficient integration into his doctrine of the Trinity,

---

20. Jüngel, *Gottes Sein ist im Werden*, iii.

a move which left him room to say (as occasion seemed to him to require) that the triunity of God is complete in and for itself alone (with or without a world, with or without human beings). We catch sight of the always-to-be-contested side of this ontologically more fundamental tension in the following statement by means of which Jüngel explicates the first statement in his foreword:

> The ontological place of God's becoming is the place of his decision. In that God is understood as the electing God, God's being has already been thought of as a being in becoming. This hermeneutical circle is grounded in an ontological circle which has been gestured towards with the localization "God's being is in becoming." The ontological localization of the being of God in becoming tries to *think* theologically to what extent God *is the Living One*. Without the courage to *think* the living-ness of God, theology will end in becoming a mausoleum of the living God.[21]

John Webster, too, found in such statements a basis for the tension I am describing. Webster wrote:

> What Jüngel attempts in Part I of *God's Being Is in Becoming* is an anatomy of Barth's account of the triune God as self-communicative, the one who is incontestably Lord in the self-differentiated action of revelation, and therefore *equiprimordially for himself and for us*. . . . For Barth, God is God's act: God's being is not, as it were, reconstructed by going back behind the economic action of God, for God's being is the self-moved, free act of God's self-communicative presence in history. More specifically, the act in which God is, is the act of God setting himself in relation to us, an act which "reiterates" God's innertrinitarian being. Jüngel demonstrates that for Barth this is closely related to the way in which the doctrine of election is drawn back into the being of God. Placing election there . . . means that election is God's self-election, God's decision to be God in this way, in and as the man Jesus.[22]

This is, in my judgment, a completely sound interpretation of Jüngel's reading of Barth—and, I would argue, of Barth himself. This is indeed the way election is brought by Barth into his doctrine of God.

---

21. Jüngel, *Gottes Sein ist im Werden*, iii.
22. Jüngel, *God's Being is in Becoming*, "Translator's Introduction," xv, xvii.

But—I should add—Jüngel himself was not content in the long run with this state of affairs in his own theology. In his magisterial work *God as the Mystery of the World*, he would identify the "ontological place of God's becoming" not with the act of eternal election but with the event of the cross—with his famous analysis of "the unity of God with perishable man" as a "union of death and life for the sake of life."[23]

This is not the place to enter into the so-called "debates" over the relation of Trinity and election. I will set forth my final word on both the interpretive and the theological questions surrounding that problem in my forthcoming book on the Trinity. Here, I wish only to say that the tensions I have just identified in Barth's thinking might well have been understood as an invitation to each side to make appeal to those passages and those alone which served the interests of their constructive work; so long as they acknowledged the existence of the tension, there would have been no need for much, if any, "debate." But the self-styled "traditionalists" have always insisted that there is no tension, that Barth was always self-consistent.[24] Or, even worse, that it is "uncharitable" to suggest that anyone as intelligent and gifted as he could ever be inconsistent—even as the same critics reserved to themselves the right to claim that Barth's treatment of the Christian rites of baptism and the Lord's Supper was inconsistent with the basic commitments of his theology as a whole.

Before leaving Jüngel, one final comment on his claim that talk of an enhancement or a lessening of divine being is appropriate only on the grounds of treatments of God as "supreme being" (the Absolute, we might say, or the Unconditioned), and that it is *not* appropriate in the context of Barth's localization of theological ontology in divine election. That, I would say, is almost true—and it really ought to have been true. Had Barth specified the relation of eternal generation of the Son to the eternal act of election more exactly than he did—and in a way that allowed for a christologically grounded and carefully delimited becoming in God—that claim would have been unquestionably true. As things stood, however, the overcoming of Barth's tension had to remain aspirational.

---

23. Eberhard Jüngel, *God as the Mystery of the World: On the Foundation of the Theology of the Crucified One in the Dispute Between Theism and Atheism* (Grand Rapids: Eerdmans, 1983), 299.

24. George Hunsinger, *Reading Barth with Charity: A Hermeneutical Proposal* (Grand Rapids: Baker Academic, 2015), xii–xiv.

III. On the Significance of My Version of "Reformed Kenoticism" for the Doctrine of the Immanent Trinity

In what follows, I want to *think* the livingness of the triune God, as Jüngel put it.[25] To do so, I must first identify for those who have not read it, the primary moves made in my Christology (published in 2021), since it is that Christology and not some other which will ground my efforts to reconstruct the doctrine of the Trinity.

A. Christology

In my Christology, I made three foundational moves. First, whereas Barth drew the divine election back into the being of God (as Webster put it), I drew the relation of the Son to Jesus up into the eternal generation of the Son-Jesus, an eternal act of self-differentiation on the part of the triune Person, *the* act of divine self-constitution. Eternal generation is thus seen as teleologically ordered, as purposive. And it establishes an ontologically basic *relation* of the Son to Jesus, such that the Son is never the Son without this relation. Second, I tried to think through what it would mean to understand the *kenosis* of the Son in terms of what I call "ontological receptivity."[26] The element of "receptivity" means that the mode of the Son's relating to Jesus is not that of a sovereign or omnipotent activity upon and through the latter but is instead a receiving, a taking up of all that comes to him from the side of Jesus into himself, all of Jesus's human activities and experiences. It is an ongoing act of self-constitution "inside," so to speak, the inner life of Jesus—feeling what he feels, knowing what he knows as he knows it, willing what he wills, and so on—on the basis of an eternal relation which joins the two. Third, the "unity" of the Son and Jesus as a single "composite person" which arises though the living of their eternal relation can be described as a kind of "hypostatic uniting"—an interpretive phrase which owes much to Schleiermacher, Dorner, and Barth and which is intended to replace the traditional concept of a "hypostatic union" that is fully complete in that conception by the Holy Spirit by which the flesh of Jesus was made concretely. All that is required for this claim to be intelligible is the understanding that the *relation* of the Son to Jesus has always been real in the Son and *immediately*

25. See above, n19.

26. Bruce Lindley McCormack, *The Humility of the Eternal Son: Reformed Kenoticism and the Repair of Chalcedon* (Cambridge: Cambridge University Press, 2021), 246–95.

so because it is proper to him—which also means that, having never been without a self-realizing relation to Jesus, the second person of the Trinity is the "Son-Jesus" and never the Son alone.[27]

I turn now more directly to the Trinity. Please keep in mind that what follows is the briefest of sketches intended to serve as a sort of road map by means of which I will flesh out the doctrine of the Trinity in my forthcoming book. For my readers, this is but a first look at what I am thinking.

B. Trinity

The self-differentiation of God is, I want to say, a *psychological* event with ontologically constitutive significance. That is to say, self-differentiation is a fully conscious activity, taking place in the lived existence of God and not behind it in a realm of (humanly postulated) "being" which has been abstracted from the lived existence of God. The reason for this claim is simple: God's "being" should be seen as a being-in-act is the consequence of the kind of love that God is. God is self-giving, self-donating, self-emptying love. Or, more simply still, God is *essentially* kenotic love.

Notice that I used the word *essentially* here only in its adverbial form. I think the time has come for us to abandon all talk of the divine "essence" in its substantive form since it has invariably been construed in a highly formal, impersonal way that devalues the personal in God and postpones treatment of the life of God to a clearly derivative treatise on Trinity. This would also mean abandonment of all talk of God as "being itself" or "pure being" since God's being is always *lived* "being," "being" as the Trinitarian event of God's self-constitution/self-revelation.

And so, God is *one* self-differentiated *Person.* In the strict sense, there are not three "persons"; there is but one Person or "Subject" whose personhood is "expressed" fully and completely in three "ways of being."[28] Barth was right, therefore, to insist that it is the *one* Person of God that is self-differentiating precisely in his living-ness; that is, he is the one God Jesus of Nazareth called "Father." But if the one Person is self-differentiating in his self-conscious life as "Father," then self-differentiation cannot be captured by means of metaphysical abstractions (i.e., the strictly formal

27. See on the last point, Alexandra Pârvan, "Kenoticism in the Erotic God: On the Psychological Ontology of the Christic Person," *International Journal of Systematic Theology* 24 (2022): 15–46; Bruce Lindley McCormack, "Response to Alexandra Pârvan," *International Journal of Systematic Theology* 24 (2022): 47–56. The denominator "Son-Jesus" is Pârvan's.

28. See n5 above. If the only reason Augustine had not to speak of "one Person" is that to do so would have meant having no different term for the three, that is a problem that can be remedied.

"modes of origin"). For that reason, Barth desperately needed to move forward to a *material* differentiation of the "ways of being."

Eberhard Jüngel makes the same basic claim as the one I am making here: "God *differentiates* himself in that He loves himself. . . . In John's language, He is God the Father *and God the Son*."[29] But the love of God the Father for the Son cannot remain a self-love in which God is both lover and beloved. For in loving, God does not remain an "I" which is only "I"; the love of God radiates beyond the Father-Son relation to include us. "God is the radiant event . . . of love itself."[30] Or as I put it twenty years ago on the occasion of Jüngel's seventieth birthday, "The love of the Father for the Son spills over to the world of human beings."[31] That is what distinguishes divine love, precisely as self-love, from all self-loves found in the human sphere. It is an expansive, capacious love which renders God selfless. Thus, the event of God's "being" as God is, Jüngel says, the event of a love which completes itself "*in the midst of an ever so great self-relatedness as still greater selflessness* and in this way is *love*."[32]

But now the concrete realization of the love of God in this world is met by human lovelessness, by the human refusal to love God in return, by a resistance that leads to the separation of Father and Son and the inevitability of death at the hands of those who refuse God's love. And so the spilling over of God's love means the sending of the Son into this world to certain death. The role of the Spirit, then, is to maintain the unity of Father and Son in their separation and, indeed, in death itself. Jüngel writes, "We are . . . speaking of God *as Spirit* when we have to interpret the separation of lover and beloved leading to death in such a way that God does not cease to be the *one* and *living* God in the midst of this most painful separation, but rather is supremely God in this situation."[33] The aforementioned formula "the union of life and death for the sake of life" is meant to convey the understanding that death did not have the final word but was followed by resurrection, that the Spirit of the Father raised Jesus from the dead.

My own reflections move on a track parallel to Jüngel's and embody

---

29. Jüngel, *Gott als Geheimnis der Welt*, 448; ET: *God as the Mystery of the World*, 327.

30. Jüngel, *Gott als Geheimnis der Welt*, 449; ET: *God as the Mystery of the World*, 327. It should be noted that the language of "being itself" is nicely supplanted in this formulation by "love itself."

31. Bruce McCormack, "Participation in God, Yes, Deification, No; Two Modern Protestant Answers to an Ancient Question," in *Denkwürdiges Geheimnis: Beiträge zur Gotteslehre, Festschrift für Eberhard Jüngel zum 70. Geburtstag*, ed. Ingolf U. Dalferth, Johannes Fischer, and Hans-Peter Großhans (Tübingen: Mohr Siebeck, 2004), 366.

32. Jüngel, *Gott als Geheimnis der Welt*, 408; ET: *God as the Mystery of the World*, 298.

33. Jüngel, *Gott als Geheminis der Welt*, 449; ET: *God as the Mystery of the World*, 328.

many of the same theological values. We both make the "missions" of Son and Spirit to be the interpretive key for understanding the "processions." We both make the love that God is the wholly necessary link between "missions" and "processions." But the Christologies upon which we base our respective reflections on Trinity differ. Jüngel's Christology found its focus in the Crucified; my own places greater emphasis on the ongoing *life* of receptivity—and, as I have learned now to say from recent work by Alexandra Pârvan, Jesus's "engagement" of that receptivity.[34] Both sides of that lived relation need to come into view in order for "hypostatic uniting" to be more fully conceptualized—though I cannot do that here.

If "Jesus Christ" (the second "person" of the Trinity) is the name of a "composite person," then it is already clear that "composition" is not alien to the innermost being of the one personal God. The one Person is "composite" in his second "way of being." His life "presses" towards unity with human life in Christ as Karl Barth once put it. "*His* life, which is his life in himself, the original and one and only life, presses towards [*drängt nach*] . . . union with our life. The goodness of his being as God is so great that it overflows as good gifts to us who are not God."[35] Barth here speaks more expansively than I am at the moment. He is looking forward to what Jüngel thinks of as the overflow of divine love to the "others." But I would like to reflect for just a moment on the "sending" of the Son into this world.

Up to now, I have spoken of the Son's "sending" as the "necessary" overflow of the kind of love that God is. But in God "necessity" is not opposed in any way to willing. In fact, "sending" is also rightly understood as willed activity. The Father wills the "sending" in self-love, in a self-love which consists in willing the kind of love that God is—namely, kenotic love. So "sending" is a metaphor which reminds us that the self-giving love is personal activity, not impersonal. Love is intentional, it is willed. Self-willing as the willing of self-giving love also introduces an element

34. Alexandra Pârvan, "Romanticism in the Kenotic God: Receptivity, Engaging, Affective Unity, and the Psychological Ontology of the Christic Person," *International Journal of Systematic Theology* 26, no. 4 (2024): 12–16.

35. Barth, *Kirchliche Dogmatik*, II/1, 308; ET: *Church Dogmatics*, II/1, 274. The German phrase which I have translated "presses towards" is *drängt nach*. The root verb is *dringen* which connotes compulsion, drive, urgency. What Barth has in view here is an inner compulsion, a desire that accompanies love. This is hardly the stuff of a "free decision" if conceived as contingent. But it is fully compatible with the understanding that the eternal will of God is at once "necessary"—as a "necessity" of the kind of love God is—and freeing insofar as the fulfillment of the love that God is makes God maximally free to be himself. The attentive reader will have noticed that this passage from II/1 reflects the basic decision I discussed in my introduction above on the passages brought forward there.

of desire and even longing for the "other" who is the "necessary" object of that love. You might think of what I am trying to do now as joining an impulse from the Romantics (which I take from the work of Pârvan) with an impulse from a kind of Christianized existentialism (which I find in Barth).

I will begin with the Romantic impulse. Pârvan, with whom I have engaged in dialogue on Christology for a number of years now, has appealed to the Romantic understanding of poetic "expression" to elaborate a vision for how the one Life of God has three "expressions":

> I want to propose a new term and speak of the triune God in his three *life-expressions* rather than three persons, or three "modes of being." . . . The way I see it, expression is God's self-constitution as triune: it makes be; it is not a partial bringing out . . . of something already there. Father, Son-Jesus, and Spirit do not formulate or express partially or imperfectly an ontological content that lies deeper and remains "silent," that pre-exists or is more basic than their expression. . . . As triune, God is relation, and therefore self-communication between the related terms, and therefore expression; he "presses himself out"—which is the Latin meaning of the word "expression" ("to take out by pressing," *exprimo*). God is in himself a pressing out, a "life extended towards" his own self but also the other, the human Jesus, who, in this movement, is made Godself. A person can rest in himself, expression cannot.[36]

What I like in this passage are three things. First, God is essentially self-communicative—which secures the fact that the divine Word is divine *reality*, not merely a "speaking" (as Barth had it[37]), which must always be partial and incomplete. Second, there is nothing behind or beneath the three "life-expressions," which is why the focus is placed on *life*. There is no metaphysically abstract "essence" that would somehow "ground" triunity. Third, Pârvan speaks of God as a life extended not only towards himself but towards an "other"—that is, the human Jesus. She puts forth this thesis to extend and enrich my concept of kenotic love. What Pârvan has added is the basic definition of *expression* as "pressing out." What I

---

36. Alexandra Pârvan, "The Princeton Creed: Expanding the Underlying Romanticism in Bruce McCormack and Karl Barth—on Dogmatics, Trinity, and Kenosis," in *Karl Barth and Reformed Theology: Tradition, Dialogue, and Construction*, ed. Paul T. Nimmo (Eugene, OR: Cascade, 2025), p. 11 of forthcoming essay.

37. Barth, *Kirchliche Dogmatik*, I/1, 136–48; ET: *Church Dogmatics*, I/1, 132–43.

value most highly in that addition is that she has made the divine Word to be more than speech, more than cognitive—a divine mind speaking to a human mind, divine reason communicating with human reason. What she has added are the full depths of divine Personhood which come to expression in the Word as the Son-Jesus, including above all *feeling*, desire, the inner compulsion of which I spoke earlier. This is the Romantic element I have taken up from Pârvan and which I want to make basic to the second "way of being" in the one Person of God or "second life-expression," as Pârvan has it.

But Pârvan herself does not rest content with having made feeling basic to that divine love by which God is self-constituting and self-communicating. The divine "love" (precisely as self-communicating) is, she says, "intentional." She writes that God's "self-constitution as expression is unique, not replicable; it has no equivalent; it reveals in perpetuity; there is no end to its meanings which emerge anew in relation to the receivers; it is intentional, not indifferent, committed to the purpose of revealing both what is expressed and the one expressing it (which in God are one and the same); it seeks to make its content accessible, 'visible.'"[38] By this, she means, the Word is "made flesh." I see this claim as the bridge from her own Romantic inclinations to Barth's more nearly existential orientation.

A final word on what I am calling the "existential" element in Barth's thinking. For Barth, there is *nothing* in God that is not being expressed. And so it is also right to say that God is what God does—and to mean that in an existentialist way. I call Karl Barth a Christian existentialist because he can say, "That God's being is event, the event of God's act [*Tat*], must mean (if, when we speak of him, we look nowhere else than to His revelation), that it is his own conscious, willed and executed *decision*."[39] And he can also say: "The Godhead of God consists . . . also in this, that it is an event—not any event, not events in general, but precisely the event of His action, by which we are engaged in revelation."[40] Barth made the identification of self-communication in eternity with self-revelation in time (as one event viewed from two perspectives) to rest on "decision." I have backed away from use of this word a bit in recent years, but only because so many misguided Barth readers want to understand the "decision" in

38. Pârvan, "The Princeton Creed" (manuscript, 12).

39. Barth, *Kirchliche Dogmatik* II/1, 304; ET: *Church Dogmatics* II/1, 271.

40. Barth, *Kirchliche Dogmatik* II/1, 294; ET: *Church Dogmatics* II/1, 263. Barth immediately follows this statement with this: "The definition from which we must begin is that God's being is *Life*" (294; ET: 263). The deep connection of Barth's Christian existentialism with Pârvan's romanticism is clear in this passage.

question as contingent, as accidentally related to what God is and not as a necessary act of self-constituting as Barth did. In any event, I see Pârvan's romanticism and Barth's Christian existentialism as two sides of the same coin. The one allows me to speak of the "necessity" contained in kenotic love; the other allows me to think of that love in terms of its driving purpose, a willed "end" which is continuously being realized.

There is much that has been left out of account here. I have said nothing of pneumatology, for example, which will play a prominent role in my book on Trinity. But this much allows me to reckon critically with the dogma of the Trinity with which I began.

C. *Some Much-Needed Critical Adjustments*

A doctrine of the Trinity which is grounded in Christology and, therefore, in the lived existence of the triune God does not require that we speak of three "persons" or even of three "modes of being." *Seinsweisen* was always poorly translated as "modes" of being. What Barth had in view were "ways of being": "ways" which connote a path entered, a history in which one lives. For me, "ways of being" and "life-expressions" are both viable formulations for getting at my meaning.

If I am right in the criticisms I brought against the degree of control exercised by simplicity in forming the dogma of the Trinity, and if there is promise in the alternative I have sketched here, then there is much in the sphere of ideas surrounding the dogma that we may now surrender. If it is the case that the one Person of God is "composite" in his second "way of being," then "composition" is not alien to the innermost being of God. Simplicity has been rejected without remainder. And that has consequences.

We may surrender the distinction between "common properties" and "personal properties." *Properties* in any case is a word describing "traits" belonging to a "nature" conceived substantially. There being no metaphysical "essence" behind the self-constituting, self-communicating life of God, there are no "common *properties*." There are no "personal *properties*" either since the "persons" too would have to be considered substantively in order to have properties. What we can do is to describe the One Person in terms of his three life-expressions as they continue to emerge.

We may also surrender our use of the Trinitarian principle of inseparable operations in its classical form. "Appropriations" ceases to be a "hermeneutical rule"[41] which prevents us from falling silent with

41. Jüngel, *Gottes Sein ist im Werden*, 49; ET: *God's Being Is in Becoming*, 49.

respect to individuation but becomes a description of ontologically constitutive life-expressions that can be distinguished materially in time. And, finally, we can also do without "perichoresis." "Perichoresis," defined as the "interpenetration" of each individual "person" of the Trinity by the other two, requires at a minimum that the "persons" be substantively conceived. And so I say again, "ways of being" are not substantive entities in and for themselves but are "pressed out" of the one divine Person by the one divine Person as his "expression" (as Pârvan has it).

If we were to agree that God is essentially kenotic love, then the "processions" would have to be understood as both simultaneous (and ongoing!) and carefully coordinated to each other. Which has the priority? That is finally an impossible question to answer. Seen from the angle of originary activity, the "Father" who breathes forth the Spirit is called "Father" because he is not without the Son in doing so. That might lead one to expect that both Father and Son breathe forth the Spirit. Seen from the angle of ongoing effects, the principle reason the Father breathes forth the Spirit is to equip the Son-Jesus for his mediatorial work. That might lead one to expect that the breathing forth of the Spirit precedes (logically) the generation of the Son. But the simultaneity and ongoing nature of both processions forbids talk of "principles" on both sides. Neither the "Father" alone nor the "Father and the Son" are principles; "principles" are incapable of willed activities. I will draw the appropriate conclusion for arguments about the *filioque* on another occasion.

CONCLUSION

All of this is a work in progress: a programmatic statement of hopes and dreams laid out in what I hope was a systematically clear form. I could still change my mind about this or that in the writing of my book on Trinity. For now, you would do well to consider this a thought experiment—and not get too excited (positively or negatively).

CHAPTER 8

SPEAKING OF INCARNATION

Modern Predicaments and Ancient Paradigms

JOHN BEHR

That "God is *for us*" is surely at the heart of the proclamation of the Gospel. And equally indisputably the doctrine of the incarnation embodies this fact in a particularly clear, if not paradigmatic, manner, for now we are not only talking about "God for us" but "God with us" (Matt 1:23; Isa 7:14). But what, in fact, are we talking about when we speak of "the incarnation"? The answer might seem obvious; it is that which Matthew describes by citing the verse of Isaiah: "Behold, a virgin shall conceive and bear a son, and his name shall be called Emmanuel, which means God with us." The "classical shape" for describing this, arrived at "under the influence of the controversies of the 4th–5th centuries," in the words of the *Oxford Dictionary of the Christian Church*, is that "the eternal Son of God took flesh from his human mother and that the historical Christ is at once both fully God and fully man."[1] What is said here, however, leaves a lot unsaid, just as the term *incarnation* tends to evoke a lot more than is here said. This essay will consider Ingolf Dalferth's observations regarding the extra freight that the term *incarnation* carries; his analysis of the different problems perceived in the classical doctrine of the incarnation, many of which still beset the task of theology; and then his own positive and constructive contribution to the discussion as a way of passing beyond the impasses of the classical doctrine. We will then turn to the classic exposition of incarnation, that is, the work by Athanasius, noting a striking resemblance to Dalferth's insight as well as a way of framing the subject matter that might take us one step further.

1. *The Oxford Dictionary of the Christian Church*, 4th ed., ed. Andrew Louth (Oxford: Oxford University Press, 2022), s.v. incarnation.

Restructuring the Grammar

Dalferth begins his book *Crucified and Resurrected: Restructuring the Grammar of Christology* with an examination of the controversy surrounding the publication *The Myth of God Incarnate*, edited by John Hick.[2] The reason why this book caused such a furore, according to Dalferth, was the new place and expansive definition that the term *incarnation* had come to assume since the nineteenth century:

> Since the Oxford movement for restoration . . . had focused Anglican spirituality and theology so rigorously on the mystery of the incarnation, the concept of incarnation had become something of a neo-Anglican "shibboleth, exempt from reasoned scrutiny and treated with unquestioned literalness." Across the entire theological spectrum, there was an environmental shift to a "religion of incarnation," with the concept of incarnation as the all-encompassing paradigm of theological thinking.[3]

There are, in Dalferth's analysis, four main structural elements in this paradigm. I give the first in full:

> The doctrine of the incarnation, as the most concentrated expression of the gospel, holds the dominant theological position among the articles of Christology. In that God's Son, the Second Person of the Trinity, entered our human existence, God took on himself the human condition in such a way that we humans are now in touch with God through the human nature of Jesus Christ. It is therefore not the cross and resurrection but the fact that Christ became human that is the decisive soteriological message of the Christian faith.[4]

The second element is its connection to ecclesiology; that is, as Oakley put it in 1843, Christ "is (what an awful thought!) *continually* incarnated in his church."[5] The third element is the way in which, in the context of a debate with Darwinism, this emphasis on incarnation expanded into "a theology

---

2. John Hick, ed., *The Myth of God Incarnate* (London: SCM, 1977).
3. Ingolf U. Dalferth, *Crucified and Risen: Restructuring the Grammar of Christology* (Grand Rapids: Baker Academic, 2015 [German 1994]), 3; citing John Hick, preface to *The Myth of God Incarnate*, xi.
4. Dalferth, *Crucified and Risen*, 3–4.
5. Dalferth, *Crucified and Risen*, 4, quoting F. Oakley, "Sacramental Confession," *The British Critic and Quarterly Theological Review* 33 (1843): 314. (The English translation of Dalferth's work, in which Oakley's statement is quoted from another German work, renders this statement slightly differently.)

of creation immanentism. . . . God is to be sought in the world, not above the world."[6] And fourth, especially in the context of the First World War, there was a distinctive emphasis on the suffering of God: "If Christ is God made man, then his earthly life provides insight into God's being. The suffering of the Son on the cross, which the church commemorates in the eucharistic offering, is to be understood as the temporal realization of that which is done by God the Father in eternity: he is a suffering God."[7] Developed in these dimensions, Christianity was held to be essentially "the religion of the incarnation," as it is put in the subtitle of the collection of essays, edited by Charles Gore, entitled *Lux Mundi*.[8]

Against this background, in which the term *incarnation* had become so expansive that it could stand for Christianity itself, it is not surprising that the publication of *The Myth of God Incarnate* caused outrage. There were, in Dalferth's assessment, four different kinds of argument advanced by the authors contributing to *Myth*.[9] First, the "fundamental-theological argument" that belief in Jesus Christ is not the same as assenting to certain doctrinal and creedal formulae. Second, the historical argument, that while *incarnation* as a theological concept became increasingly dominant from the second century onwards, it was never the only way to express faith in Jesus Christ: "Christology has *not always* been incarnational Christology. . . . It is therefore historically inadequate to equate Christology with incarnational Christology." Third, the "exegetical-hermeneutical argument" that "Christology is *never purely* incarnational Christology" anyway, for any account of the person and work of Christ must take into account other features beyond descent or incarnation, aspects such as ascension and exaltation which in fact may well claim to be earlier. And, fourth and finally, the theological argument proper, which, as Dalferth puts it, holds that "the incarnational Christology that has become the standard paradigm since Nicaea and Chalcedon and was given its classic presentation by Athanasius has never been satisfactorily explicated theologically," and, moreover, "the idea of a being who, because God has taken human form, is fully human and fully God, is deemed self-contradictory." Dalferth further summarizes the theological argument this way:

---

6. Dalferth, *Crucified and Risen*, 4.

7. Dalferth, *Crucified and Risen*, 5.

8. Charles Gore, *Lux Mundi: A Series of Studies in the Religion of the Incarnation* (London: John Murray, 1889).

9. For what follows, see Dalferth, *Crucified and Risen*, 7–8.

> Every attempt to demonstrate its consistency, such as the Cappadocians' doctrine of an- and enhypostasia and its assimilation into modern (Protestant) theology; assumptus, habitus, and subsistence theories of Scholastic theologies; or the kenosis theories of Lutheran and Anglican origin, has called into question either the humanity or the divinity or the unity of the person of Jesus Christ.[10]

The Cappadocians, of course, did not have a "doctrine of an- and enhypostasia," and even with regard to later figures such as Leontius of Byzantium, it is debated whether their teaching has been assimilated into later modern Protestant theology or whether the presuppositions of the latter have been read back into the former.[11]

There are weaknesses and conceptual confusion in all of these arguments. For instance, as Dalferth notes, "The fact that the concept of the incarnation did not dominate christological discourse from the outset does not mean that the subject matter that this concept sought to comprehend was not already present."[12] But it is in turning to an analysis of the grammar of the most basic confession, that "Jesus is the Son of God," that Dalferth makes his own constructive and positive contribution. Of the four ways in which Hick suggested that the word *is* can be taken—that is, as predication, as indicating class membership, as giving a definition, and as identification—after identifying problems with the latter three, Dalferth focuses on predication.[13] In the confession that "Jesus is the Son of God," the question as to which is the subject and which the predicate is not simple. If Jesus is the subject of predication, then it is he who is being said to be the Son of God, and this then demands a historical assessment of whether Jesus of Nazareth actually demonstrated and possessed all the divine attributes (resulting, as Dalferth points out, in the intense research into the life of Jesus carried out since the nineteenth century and the revival of kenotic Christologies in Lutheran and Anglican theology). If, on the other hand, we take the confession the other way round,

---

10. Dalferth, *Crucified and Risen*, 8.

11. Cf. F. LeRon Shults, "A Dubious Christological Formula: From Leontius of Byzantium to Karl Barth," *Theological Studies*, 57 (1996): 431–46; Matthias Gockel, "A Dubious Christological Formula? Leontius of Byzantium and the *Anhypostasis–Enhypostasis* Theory," *Journal of Theological Studies* 51, no. 2 (2000): 515–32. For a full survey of the patristic period, see Benjamin Gleede, *The Development of the Term* ἐνυπόστατος *from Origen to John of Damascus*, Supplements to *Vigiliae Christianae* 113 (Leiden: Brill, 2012).

12. Dalferth, *Crucified and Risen*, 9.

13. Dalferth, *Crucified and Risen*, 13–19; drawing upon John Hick, "Christ and Incarnation," in John Hick, *God and the Universe of Faiths: Essays in the Philosophy of Religion* (London: Macmillan, 1973), 148–64, at 154.

then, as Dalferth puts it, "it is not Jesus but the Son of God (i.e., 'Son of God' according to the understanding of the term in classical incarnational Christology), the Logos, the Second Person of the Trinity, who is the subject and of whom it is said that he is Jesus of Nazareth."[14] In this case, "this analysis imposes, as it were, another subject on the life story of Jesus of Nazareth, with the result that this life story becomes the predicate of a divine person."[15] And here resides the disquiet that many have had with what is described as the "classic doctrine of the incarnation":

> Even the orthodox solution, as presented to us in the doctrine of an- and en-hypostasia, leaves open the question of whether the full individual humanity of Jesus remains assured. For if what constitutes the person of Jesus is the Logos, the Second Person of the Trinity, so that Jesus is not a self-individuating human subject, then it is not surprising that "Christologies designed around the theme of incarnation have never ever led to the historical and concrete humanity of Jesus of Nazareth."[16]

In other words, when analysing the confession that "Jesus is the Son of God" in terms of predication, depending on which part of the confession we take to be the subject and which the predicate, we end up with either a Christology from below or from above, and both are unsatisfactory.

Finally, turning to Hick's use of the language of myth, Dalferth argues that Hick's characterization of the confession that "Jesus is the Son of God" as a metaphor, using "a mythical concept for the historical Jesus of Nazareth in order to express his meaning for us," results in "a double misidentification."[17] That is, the confession, according to Dalferth, is not concerned merely with the tangible, historical Jesus of Nazareth, nor is it based on "any significance he has for us," but rather it is concerned with his *soteriological* significance. It is here that Dalferth begins his restructuring of the grammar of Christology:

> The only reason these confessions have soteriological significance is that they do not speak merely of Jesus of Nazareth; they speak of the *Jesus Christ who was raised from the dead by God*. "Jesus is the Son of

14. Dalferth, *Crucified and Risen*, 18–19.
15. Dalferth, *Crucified and Risen*, 19.
16. Dalferth, *Crucified and Risen*, 19; quoting W. Pannenberg, "Christologie und Theologie," in *Grundfragen systematischer Theologie*, Gesammelte Aufsätze II (198): 129–45, at 134.
17. Dalferth, *Crucified and Risen*, 21, referring primarily to Hick's "Jesus and World Religions," in *The Myth of God Incarnate*, 167–85.

> God" is not a metaphor because a mythological predicate is here being applied to a Jew who belongs to a distant past; rather it is a metaphor because it attempts to speak of the one who has been crucified and raised in such a way that he is presented as the living one who is constantly present. Jesus Christ has soteriological relevance for us solely because he mediates our relationship with God *in the present*. So the principal flaw in Hick's analysis is that he equates the Christ to whom the Christological confessions refer with the historical figure of the man Jesus of Nazareth.[18]

Salvation, Dalferth further argues, "does not stem primarily from *what* the Christological confessions declare concerning Jesus; it stems from the fact that they declare it *concerning him*. Christians confess Jesus as Son of God, Lord, Savior, Word of God, and so on, for this reason: they know him to be *the one who was crucified and whom God raised from the dead*."[19] And so, in turn, if we want to understand the logical structure of christological confessions coherently, "their content must always be reconstrued as a statement *concerning the one who has been crucified and raised*. In other words, it is not the tangible historical Jesus in isolation who is the point of reference, and thus the topic, of Christological confessions, but Jesus Christ raised from the dead by God."[20] This is an inescapable fact for Dalferth, and it holds for all confessions and statements, as well as all narrative and discursive texts in the New Testament, including the Gospels, which are, in his words, "no more and no less than interpretations of the resurrection message as proclaimed in the events of Jesus's life."[21]

Recognizing the cross and resurrection as the starting point for all theological confession shapes, in turn, the way we then speak about God and about ourselves:

> Right from the outset, therefore, the Christian faith has never doubted that the one who has been raised is *the crucified Jesus of Nazareth* (resurrection of *Jesus*) and that to speak of his having been raised by God is to acknowledge the occurrence of *an eschatological event that affects not only him but God himself and each one of us* (resurrection of Jesus *Christ*).[22]

18. Dalferth, *Crucified and Risen*, 21–22, italics original.
19. Dalferth, *Crucified and Risen*, 24, italics original.
20. Dalferth, *Crucified and Risen*, 24, italics original.
21. Dalferth, *Crucified and Risen*, 24.
22. Dalferth, *Crucified and Risen*, 24–5, italics original.

It is as crucified and risen that Jesus of Nazareth is Jesus Christ. So "the real subject matter of Christology," Dalferth concludes, is not "the historical, tangible Jesus of Nazareth and his exemplary and religious significance for us" but rather "God's *firstborn raised from the dead*."[23]

A final point that Dalferth makes in the opening chapter to his book that is of interest for this essay is that "whereas statements concerning the *raising* of *Jesus by God* belong to the primary historical and epistemological definition of the topic of christological confessions, to state that *God has taken human form* is a continuation of this primary definition."[24] As such "incarnational Christology is a secondary interpretation of the resurrection confession which seeks to explore the implications of specific interpretations of the resurrection for Jesus' life story and to explain how it is integrated into fellowship with God's community of life."[25] It is, as such, as Dalferth continues, a "supplementary interpretation of the christological topic, but it is not the christological topic."[26] The subject matter for Christology is primarily and essentially God's firstborn raised from the dead, a subject matter which remains to be expounded in different dimensions—in relation to God, to the Spirit, to us—in the same way that the evangelists narrate the life of Jesus as a proclamation of the resurrection.

ATHANASIUS, *ON THE INCARNATION*

Turning now to what is universally acknowledged—certainly by Dalferth—to be the classic statement on the theme from the fourth century, Athanasius's treatise usually referred to simply as *On the Incarnation*, we will find that not only does it *not* present the subject matter in the manner that is usually assumed to be the "classical shape of the doctrine of the incarnation," but in fact it resonates profoundly with the argument of Dalferth and in fact even enables us to explicate the subject matter in a more pointed and expansive manner.

The full title of the work is in fact *On the Inhumanization of the Word and His Manifestation to Us Through the Body*.[27] But before we turn to the two parts

23. Dalferth, *Crucified and Risen*, 31, italics original.
24. Dalferth, *Crucified and Risen*, 30–31, italics original.
25. Dalferth, *Crucified and Risen*, 31.
26. Dalferth, *Crucified and Risen*, 31.
27. Περὶ τῆς ἐνανθρωπήσεως τοῦ Λόγου καὶ τῆς διὰ σώματος πρὸς ἡμᾶς ἐπιφανείας αὐτοῦ. Although the word used here is more properly rendered "inhumanization," I will treat it here as equivalent to "incarnation" (which would more properly render ἐνσάρκωσις), for the term *incarnation* is the standard term in modern theological discussion, leaving to another time a full exploration of

of this title, it should first be noted that, opening with the words "In what preceded we have sufficiently treated a few points from many regarding the error of their Gentiles and their superstition . . . ," it is clearly the second part of a two-part work.[28] The first part, *Against the Gentiles*, as is indicated here, is devoted to the error of idolatry, and specifically the prevalence of idolatry before the coming of the Christ, so that it forms a barometer of the human state and the background for the work of Christ. More specifically, Athanasius states that although "the sacred and divinely inspired Scriptures are sufficient for the exposition of the truth," and there are also "many treatises of our blessed teachers" which show how to interpret the Scriptures, yet as these works are not to hand, Athanasius claims, the task now is to expound what he has learnt from them:

> I mean the faith in Christ the Saviour, that no one may regard the teaching of our doctrine [λόγου] as worthless or suppose faith in Christ to be irrational [ἄλογον]. Such things the pagans misrepresent and scorn, greatly mocking us, though they have nothing other than the cross of Christ to cite in objection. It is particularly in this respect that one must pity their insensitivity, because in slandering the cross they do not see that its power has filled the whole world, and that through it the effects of the knowledge of God have been revealed to all. For if they had really applied their minds to his divinity they would not have mocked at so great a thing, but would rather have recognized that he was the Saviour of the universe and that the cross was not the ruin but the healing of creation. For if, after the cross, all idolatry has been overthrown, and all demonic activity is put to flight by this sign, and Christ alone is worshipped, and through him the Father is known, and opponents are put to shame while he every day invisibly converts their souls—how then, one might reasonably ask them, is this matter still to be considered in human terms, and should one not rather confess that he who ascended the cross is the Word of God and the Saviour of the universe? [ὁμολογεῖν Θεοῦ Λόγου καὶ Σωτῆρα εἶναι τοῦ παντὸς τὸν ἐπὶ τοῦ σταυρôυ ἀναβάντα] (*Gent.* 1)

the different shades of meaning of the words ἐνανθρώπησις (inhumanization), ἐνσάρκωσις (incarnation), and ἐνσωμάτωσις (embodiment).

28. John Behr, ed. and trans., *Athanasius: On the Incarnation*, Popular Patristics Series 44a (Crestwood, NY: St. Vladimir's Seminary Press, 2011), 1. For Athanasius's *Contra Gentes*, see Robert W. Thomson, ed. and trans. *Athanasius: Contra Gentes and De Incarnatione*, Oxford Early Christian Texts (Oxford: Clarendon, 1971).

Athanasius opens the second part of the treatise, as we will see, with a similar statement. It is clear that these works of Athanasius "are first and foremost an *apologia crucis*."[29] The order of identification is important, and consistently rendered thus by Athanasius: It is the one who ascended the cross that is the Word of God and Saviour, a point that we have seen made by Dalferth, though in Dalferth's case it is expanded to include the resurrection ("the one who was crucified and whom God raised from the dead" is the subject of Christology, something to which we will return).

Opening the second part of the two-part work by recapitulating what he had done in the first part, Athanasius then specifies his present task:

> Let us, with the faith of our religion, relate also the things concerning the inhumanization of the Word and expound his divine manifestation to us, which the Jews slander and the Greeks mock, but we ourselves venerate, so that, all the more from his apparent degradation, you may have an even greater and fuller piety towards him, for the more he is mocked by unbelievers by so much he provides a greater witness of his divinity, because what human beings cannot understand as impossible, these he shows to be possible (cf. Matt 19.26), and what human beings mock as unseemly, these he renders fitting by his own goodness, and what human beings through sophistry laugh at as merely human, these by his power he shows to be divine, overturning the illusion of idols by his own apparent degradation through the cross, invisibly persuading those who mock and disbelieve to recognize his divinity and his power. (*Inc.* 1)

It is likely that these two tasks—to expound the inhumanization of the Word and his divine manifestation—generated the title of this work, if he did not give it a title himself. The specification that these things are slandered by the Jews and mocked by the Greeks, a clear allusion to 1 Corinthians 1:23, makes it clear that the "apparent degradation" is not that of a divine person kenotically assuming a human condition, but rather, as he makes clear, the "apparent degradation through the cross"—"apparent" because, although foolishness and weak by worldly standards, this is in fact the power and wisdom of God, by which he "invisibly persuades" those who mock and disbelieve to recognize his divinity, here,

29. Cf. Khaled Anatolios, *Athanasius: The Coherence of His Thought* (London: Routledge, 1998), 28.

on the cross. As is already clear, the stated aim of the classic text on the incarnation has little to do with what is assumed to be the classic shape of the doctrine of the incarnation but in fact is already focused on that towards which Dalferth aims to reorient christological reflection.

This becomes indisputably clear when we turn to the content of the treatise itself. The work is clearly divided, by Athanasius's own words, into five main sections, together with introductory and concluding paragraphs:

Introduction (*Inc.* 1)
I: The Divine Dilemma Regarding Life and Death (*Inc.* 2–10)
II: The Divine Dilemma Regarding Knowledge and Ignorance (*Inc.* 11–19)
III: The Death of Christ and the Resurrection of the Body (*Inc.* 20–32)
IV: Refutation of the Jews (*Inc.* 33–40)
V: Refutation of the Gentiles (*Inc.* 41–55)
Conclusion (*Inc.* 56)

After the introduction, which we have already considered, Athanasius develops his *apologia crucis*, defending the rationality of the Christian faith by demonstrating that the one on the cross is the Logos, by offering two "divine dilemmas": First, while God had created human beings for life, they had succumbed to death, so what was God to do other than take a body capable of death so as to conquer death and give life to the body. Second, as God also created human beings for knowledge of himself through the Word, yet they turned their attention to things of perception, what, again, was God to do other than take a physical body so as to catch their attention and then, through the works done in the body, demonstrate that he is in fact the very Word of God. It is possible that these two "divine dilemmas" are matched by the two "refutations," giving the work as a whole a chiastic structure, with the third part, on the death of Christ and the raising of the body, being the central element.

The wording of the first analysis is particularly rich and subtle. Athanasius speaks of how the Word, having mercy upon the human race, having pity on our weakness, condescending to our corruption, not enduring the dominion of death, lest what had been created should perish and the work of the Father be in vain, "takes [λαμβάνει] for himself a body and that not foreign to our own" (*Inc.* 8). He then continues:

> He takes [λαμβάνει] that which is ours, and that not simply, but from a spotless and stainless virgin, ignorant of man, [a body] pure and unmixed from intercourse with men. Although being himself powerful and the creator of the universe, he prepares [κατασκευάζει] for himself in the Virgin the body as a temple, and made it his own, as an instrument, making himself known and dwelling in it. And thus, taking from ours that which is like, since all were liable to the corruption of death, delivering it over to death on behalf of all, he offered it to the Father, doing this in his love for human beings, so that, on the one hand, with all dying in him [πάντων ἀποθανόντων ἐν αὐτῷ] the law concerning corruption in human beings might be undone (its power being fully expended in the lordly body [ἐν τῷ κυριακῷ σώματι] and no longer having any ground against similar human beings), and, on the other hand, that as human beings had turned towards corruption he might turn them again to incorruptibility and give them life from death, by making the body his own and by the grace of the resurrection banishing death from them as straw from the fire.
>
> For the Word, realizing that in no other way would the corruption of human beings be undone except, simply, by dying, yet being immortal and the Son of the Father the Word was not able to die, for this reason he takes [λαμβάνει] to himself a body capable of death, in order that it, participating in the Word who is above all, might be sufficient for death on behalf of all, and through the indwelling Word would remain incorruptible, and so corruption might henceforth cease from all by the grace of the resurrection. Whence, by offering to death the body he had taken to himself, as an offering holy and free of all spot, he immediately abolished death from all like him, by the offering of a like. For being above all, the Word of God consequently, by offering his own temple and his bodily instrument as a substitute for all, fulfilled in death that which was required; and, being with all through the like [body], the incorruptible Son of God consequently clothed all with incorruptibility in the promise concerning the resurrection. And now the very corruption of death no longer holds ground against human beings because of the Word indwelling in them through the one body [διὰ τὸν ἐνοικήσαντα Λόγον ἐν τούτοις διὰ τοῦ ἑνὸς σώματος]. (*Inc.* 8–9)

So when Athanasius speaks of the body which the Word takes (in the present tense) from the Virgin, or the body as the temple which he prepares for himself in the Virgin, in which he might dwell and make himself known, the body which he offers to death, so that with all dying in him, the law of death and corruption might be loosed, and the body as that which he makes his own by giving others life from death through the grace of the resurrection, and, above all, all this happening "because of the Word indwelling in them through the one body"—it is clear that Athanasius is not describing here how Jesus was born from his mother; indeed, he never mentions the name Mary in this work. Rather, his analysis of the rationality of the cross speaks of the life-giving death on the cross and the corporate mystery in which this is effected, involving the whole human race.

Athanasius concludes this section by saying: "This, therefore, is the first cause/reason [αἰτία μὲν δὴ πρώτη] of the incarnation of the Savior. One might also recognize that his gracious advent consistently occurred from the following" (*Inc.* 10). As already mentioned, Athanasius turns in the second account of the rationality of the cross to examine it through the dilemma of knowledge and ignorance: Having been created to know God through his Word, human beings turned rather to things of sense-perception, and so "the Word himself submitted to appear through a body, so that as a human he might bring humans to himself and return their sense perception to himself, and then, seeing him as a human being, he might, through the works he effects, persuade them that he is not human only but God and the Word and Wisdom of the true God" (*Inc.* 16: λοιπὸν ἐκείνους ὡς ἄνθρωπον αὐτὸν ὁρῶντας, δι᾽ ὧν ἐργάζεται ἔργων, πείσῃ μὴ εἶναι ἑαυτὸν ἄνθρωπον μόνον, ἀλλὰ καὶ Θεὸν . . .). Athanasius says that this persuasion culminates in the cross, for while the disciples continually misunderstood, what is most wonderful is that:

> Even at his death, or rather at the very trophy over death, I mean the cross, all creation confessed that he who was made known and suffered in the body was not simply a human being but Son of God and Savior of all. For the sun turned back and the earth shook and the mountains were rent, and all were awed. These things showed the Christ on the cross to be God [Ταῦτα δὲ τὸν μὲν ἐν τῷ σταυρῷ Χριστὸν Θεὸν ἐδείκνυον] and the whole of creation to be his servant, witnessing in fear the advent [παρουσίαν] of the Master. In this way, then, the God Word showed himself to human beings by his works. (*Inc.* 19)

Athanasius again maintains his consistency in the order of identification: It is the Christ on the cross who is shown to be God, and it is this way that the God Word reveals himself to human beings by his works.

In what we have seen so far, it is clear that there is indeed a great deal of alignment between Athanasius's treatise and Dalferth's constructive proposal for "restructuring the grammar of Christology" by taking seriously that the one confessed to be the Son of God, Word, Lord and Saviour is always already the one who was crucified and raised from the dead by God. It might also be that the sequence of the two analyses provided by Athanasius (the dilemma of life/death followed by knowledge/ignorance) traces the logical and epistemological point made by Dalferth, that the taking of human form by the Word is in fact a continuation of the primary definition regarding the raising of Jesus by God. It is only after dealing with the dilemma of life and death that Athanasius turns to how the Word is made known through the body, by the works that he does, principally, again, the cross.

There is, nevertheless, a difference. While Dalferth emphasizes that it is the crucified and risen Jesus who is the subject of christological statements, Athanasius instead simply identifies the subject as the one on the cross: "He who ascended the cross is the Word and Saviour of the universe" (*Gent.* 1), and the whole of creation witnesses that "the Christ on the cross is God," shaking with fear at his *parousia* there (*Inc.* 19). In the following chapters Athanasius focuses his attention on the form of Christ's death, "because this is the chief point of our faith and absolutely all human beings discuss it, so that you may know that also from this, the more rather than the less, Christ is known to be God and the Son of God" (*Inc.* 19). After playing with his readers, speculating about whether Christ might have died, for instance, from old age or why he had not died a more glorious death, in human terms, only to dismiss such speculations as being "for outsiders" (*Inc.* 25), Athanasius gives various scriptural reasons for the cross (such as "becoming a curse"; Gal 3:13; Deut 21:23) and then turns his attention to the resurrection of the body. Strikingly, he does not here turn to the gospel reports of seeing the risen Christ, nor Paul's words about this, but instead focuses all his attention on Christians in the present, for by taking up the faith of the cross they are the ones who witness to the reality of the resurrection:

> That death has been dissolved, and the cross has become victory over it, and it is no longer strong but is itself truly dead, no mean proof but an evident surety is that it is despised by all Christ's disciples, and everyone tramples on it, and no longer fears it, but with the sign of the cross and faith in Christ tread it under foot as something dead. Of old, before the

> divine sojourn [ἐπιδημίαν] of the Saviour, all used to weep for those dying as if they were perishing. But since the Saviour's raising the body, no longer is death fearsome, but all believers in Christ tread on it as nothing, and would rather choose to die than deny their faith in Christ. (*Inc.* 27)

Athanasius concludes this central section of his treatise by emphasizing that, with the witness of Christians now taking up the cross and with even the demons bearing witness to Christ, it should be clear that

> the Saviour raised up his own body, and that he is the true Son of God, being from him as the Father's own Word and Wisdom and Power, who in the last time took a body for the salvation of all, and taught the world about the Father, destroyed death, granted incorruptibility to all through the promise of the resurrection, raising his own body as the first-fruits and showing it as a trophy over death and its corruption by the sign of the cross. (*Inc.* 32)

Athanasius's treatment of the resurrection takes us back to his analysis of the first dilemma and "the one body" spoken of there: The resurrection is not only that of the body of Jesus of Nazareth, but "the lordly body" (τοῦ κυριακοῦ σώματος, *Inc.* 31; cf. 8), the body of Christ, the whole Christ.[30]

Refracting the Light of Pascha

Athanasius's treatment of his subject matter in the treatise whose title we shorten to *On the Incarnation* is clearly as different to what passes as "the classical doctrine of the incarnation" (despite it being continuously referred to as the classical exposition of this doctrine), as is Dalferth's restructured grammar for confessing the crucified and risen one, in ways which are both similar and slightly different. Yet while Dalferth wants to make sure that incarnational language is grounded in a prior confession about the crucified and risen one, for Athanasius these—the incarnation and the cross—have not yet been separated into two different "events," nor for that matter has the cross and resurrection. Perhaps the most striking aspect of

30. Origen, *Commentary on John* 10:229: "The Resurrection of Christ, who followed on from his Passion on the Cross, also contains the mystery of the Resurrection of the whole body of Christ." Erwin Preuschen, ed., *Origenes Werke* 4, GCS 10 (Leipzig: Hinrichs, 1903); trans. R. E. Heine (Washington: Catholic University of America, 1989), 80.

Athanasius's treatise is that it makes no mention of or allusion to the birth narratives in Matthew and Luke, which is typically thought of as being the incarnation. But then one should also note that when Athanasius wrote *On the Incarnation*, the church in Alexandria did not as yet celebrate a feast for the nativity of Christ.[31] Indeed, it took a long time for the full liturgical calendar to develop. This process began in the late second century with the expansion of the original single-night Quartodeciman celebration of Pascha on 14 Nisan expanded into a triduum, and this, in turn, as Thomas Talley puts it, "contained the seeds that would eventually yield the refraction of the single mystery of redemption into a series of commemorations of discrete historical moments in that mystery."[32] By the early third century, the coincidence of 14th Nisan with March 25 had already been noted in Rome, and the dating of the birth of Christ to December 25 appears a century later, in what might seem to be an unusual place: the earliest authentic document to give this as the date of the birth of Christ is the *Depositio martyrum* (354 CE). This list of martyrs honoured in Rome is arranged by the date of their death and begins with the simple statement: "Christ is born on the eighth of the Calends of January, in Bethlehem of Judea."[33] This notice is placed at the head of the list, marking it out as the starting point for the list of martyrs that follows.

That the death of the martyr is their "birth" (not new/spiritual birth) is ubiquitous in the early centuries of Christianity.[34] For instance,

---

31. Cf. T. Talley, *The Origins of the Liturgical Year*, 2nd ed. (Collegeville, MN: Liturgical, 1991), 140–41; according to John Cassian, the Egyptians celebrate the feast of Epiphany on January 6, and this feast commemorated both the baptism of the Lord and his birth in the flesh (*Conference* 10.2.1, written between 418 and 427), though in the fourth century the feast of Epiphany was exclusively focused on Christ's baptism, so that the sixteenth of the *Canons of Athanasius* (of disputed attribution, but dating from the second half of the fourth century) does not even mention the Nativity. W. Riedel and W. E. Crum, *The Canons of Athanasius of Alexandria* (London, 1904; repr., Amsterdam: Philo, 1973), 26–27.

32. Talley, *Origins of the Liturgical Year*, 39.

33. Cf. Susan K. Roll, *Toward the Origins of Christmas*, Liturgia condenda 5 (Leuven: Peeters, 1995), 79–84. The connection between 14 Nisan and 25 March is made on the Paschal Tables at the foot of a statue, a Roman copy of a Greek woman philosopher, dating to 222–235 CE; on this see also Talley, *Origins*, 9–10 (and 71 for notes). Plates of the statue and tables are included in Allen Brent, *Hippolytus and the Roman Church in the Third Century: Communities in Tension before the Emergence of a Monarch-Bishop*, Supplements to VC 31 (Leiden: Brill, 1995), plates 1–4. The *Depositio martyrum* is the second document in what is known as the "Chronograph of 354": *Das Kalenderhandbuch von 354: Der Chronograph des Filocalus*, ed. Johannes Divjak and Wolfgang Wischmeyer, 2 vols. (Vienna: Holzhausen, 2014). The *Deposition martyrum* begins on 2:497.

34. See Stéphanie Machabée, "Life and Death, Confession and Denial: Birthing Language in the Letter of the Churches of Vienne and Lyons," in *Coming Back to Life: The Permeability of Past and Present, Mortality and Immortality, Death and Life in the Ancient Mediterranean*, ed. Frederick. S. Tappenden and Carly Daniel-Hughes, with Bradley N. Rice (Montreal, QC: McGill University Library, 2017), http://comingbacktolife.library.mcgill.ca; and John Behr, "Our Mother Church: Mary and Ecclesiology," *International Journal for the Study of the Christian Church* 22, no. 4 (2022): 333–44, DOI: 10.1080/1474225X.2023.2168868.

describing the events in Lyons in 177 CE, Irenaeus reported that those Christians who had previously denied their faith were restored by seeing the witness of Blandina and Attalus, and then, strengthened in their faith, went to their own martyrdom. And so, as Irenaeus continued: "There was great joy for Virgin Mother in receiving alive those who she had miscarried as dead [ὡς νεκροὺς ἐξέτρωσε], for through them many who had denied retraced their steps and were again conceived and brought to life [ἀνεμετροῦντο καὶ ἀνεκυΐσκοντο καὶ ἀνεζωπυροῦντο] and learnt to witness."[35] The trials of their martyrdom are their conception and birth-pangs, resulting in their birth into life. Similar language is used in Peter's speech in Acts regarding Christ, in which God did not simply raise Christ from the dead, but rather "God raised him from the dead having loosened the birth-pangs of death, because it was not possible for him to be held by it" (Acts 2.24: ὃν ὁ θεὸς ἀνέστησεν λύσας τὰς ὠδῖνας τοῦ θανάτου). Ignatius, who also saw his own coming martyrdom as "birth-pangs," brings together the birth of the head together with the rest of the body: "Through it [the cross], in his passion, he invites you to be parts of his body, as a head cannot be born without body-parts, because God promises unity, which he himself is."[36] It is as "the beginning [ἀρχή], the first born of the dead" that Jesus is the "head of the body, the church" (Col 1:18); he is the "Amen, the faithful and true witness/martyr, the beginning [ἀρχή] of God's creation" (Rev 3:14) and indeed as "the firstborn of many brethren" (Rom 8:29). The death-defeating, life-giving death of Jesus upon the cross is followed by the birth of the body of Christ, those who follow him in taking up the cross, the beginning of God's creation. As the martyrology of Jerome (in the version of Tallaght) puts it: On March 25, "Our Lord Jesus Christ was crucified, and conceived, and the world created."[37]

This connection between the passion and conception, followed by the birth of the body, would seem to be based on Isaiah 53–54:1, a connection already made by Paul in Galatians 4:21–31, an "allegory" which is preceded by Paul's statement regarding the "sending" of the Son of God,

---

35. Eusebius of Caesarea, *Historial ecclesiastica*, ed. and trans. K. Lake, 2 vols, LCL (Cambridge, MA: Harvard University Press, 1989), 5.1.45–6, modified.

36. Ignatius of Antioch, *Letter to the Romans* 6: Ὁ δὲ τοκετός μοι ἐπίκειται. And *Trallians*, 11.2: δι' οὗ ἐν τῷ πάθει αὐτοῦ προσκαλεῖται ὑμᾶς ὄντας μέλη αὐτοῦ· οὐ δύναται οὖν κεφαλὴ χωρὶς γεννηθῆναι ἄνευ μελῶν, τοῦ θεοῦ ἕνωσιν ἐπαγγελλομένου, ὅ ἐστιν αὐτός. Both texts are found in A. Stewart, ed. and trans., *Ignatius of Antioch: The Letters*, Popular Patristics Series 49 (Yonkers, NY: St. Vladimir's Seminary Press, 2013).

37. Richard Irvine Best and Hugh Jackson Lawlor, ed., *The Martyrology of Tallaght: From the Book of Leinster and Ms 5100–4 in the Royal Library Brussels* (London: Harrison and Sons, 1931), 27. Cf. H. Quentin, ed., *Martyrologium Hieronymianum*, in *Acta Sanctorum*, Tomus II pars posterior, ed. H. Delehaye, P. Peeters, M. Coens (Brussels: Bollandists, 1931), 159.

in which perhaps now we can see an important nuance: "In the fulness of time God sent forth his Son, who had come to be [γενόμενον] of a woman, who had come to be under the Law, so as to redeem those under the law, so that we might receive adoption" (Gal 4:4). God did not send his Son to be born of a woman, but rather the Son, who had come to be from a woman, is sent to redeem and effect adoption, implying a contrast between coming-to-be (γένεσις) and birth (γέννησις). And as such, it is now Paul, who was received by those to whom he preached the gospel as "an angel of God, as Christ Jesus" (Gal 4:14), who is now in "again in travail [ὠδίνω] until Christ be formed in you" (Gal 4:19).

The connection between the passion and the birth is also clearly presented in the iconography for the birth of Christ which subsequently developed: Christ, already with a cross in his halo, wrapped in swaddling clothes like a corpse, placed in a manger, shaped as a tomb or altar, placed in a cave where the Virgin and cave form one artistic shape, just as the crucified Christ had been placed in a new-hewn tomb in which no one had been laid, that is a virgin tomb, owned by (the other) Joseph. "To the tomb, in which no body had been laid before or after," as Augustine observes following the order of identification, "corresponds the womb in which he was conceived, where no mortal body was sown before or after."[38] Indeed, as Raymond Brown points out, the themes of the passion are already given in the infancy narratives themselves: "The story of Jesus' conception is no longer just an item of popular biography; it is the vehicle of the good news of salvation; in short, it is gospel. . . . The process [of arriving at these birth narratives] was literally an interpretative one of reading back later insights into the birth stories, and those later insights involved an adult Christ who had died and risen."[39]

A similar point might be made with regard to the contrast between Athanasius's focus on "the one on the cross" and Dalferth's emphasis on "the crucified and risen Jesus." Although the unitary Paschal celebration had refracted into a Triduum by the end of the second century, the iconography for the death and resurrection of Christ developed more slowly. The earliest depictions show the living Christ on the cross (as seen in the fifth-century ivory crucifixion in the British Museum and on the doors

---

38. Augustine, *On The Trinity*, 4.2.9; trans. E. Hill (Brooklyn, NY: New City, 1991).

39. Raymond E. Brown, *An Adult Christ at Christmas: Essays on the Three Biblical Christmas Stories; Matthew 2 and Luke 2* (Collegeville, MN: Liturgical, 1978), 8; and more fully, Raymond E. Brown, *The Birth of the Messiah: A Commentary on the Infancy Narratives in the Gospels of Matthew and Luke*, Anchor Bible Reference Library (New York: Doubleday, 1993).

of St. Sabina in Rome, and from the sixth century, the Rabbula Gospels and the Lateran reliquary box), and this is then refracted into an image of the dead Christ and the image of the resurrection, where the latter still depicts the cruciform Christ drawing all to himself: "When I am lifted up from the earth, I will draw all to myself" (John 12:32).[40] The images of the "anastasis" thus do not depict the crucified Jesus coming out of the tomb but rather his raising of Adam and Eve, representing the whole human race. The apparent anomaly of this is such that these images are often described as "the harrowing of hell." But they are clearly not![41] Indeed, in some of the earliest depictions it is labelled simply as "The Resurrection of Adam."[42] It is exactly in this way, as we have seen, that Athanasius treats the resurrection: not referring to the resurrectional appearances of Christ as described in the Gospels (just as he does not refer to the birth narratives), but rather as the raising of those who now have taken up the faith of the cross to be the body of Christ: It is indeed "the one on the cross" who is the Lord and Savior, the Word of God. Similarly Paul, at the beginning of Romans (1:3–4), writes that Christ, descended from David according to the flesh, is "designated Son of God in power according to the Spirit of holiness by resurrection of the dead ones" (ἐξ ἀναστάσεως νεκρῶν; not "from the dead," as is it regularly mistranslated). As Crossan notes, referring to this passage and its connection to 1 Corinthians 15:13, "Christ's Resurrection and the universal resurrection stand or fall together: 'if there is no resurrection of the dead [ἀνάστασις νεκρῶν], then Christ has not been raised.'"[43]

Conclusion

There is indeed a great deal of similarity between what Dalferth proposes as a "restructuring" of the grammar of Christology and what we find in the classic christological text *On the Incarnation* by Athanasius. However, there are also differences, differences which in large part derive from

40. Plates of these images appear in Anna D. Kartsonis, *Anastasis: The Making of an Image* (Princeton, NJ: Princeton University Press, 1986).

41. Cf. Kartsonis, *Anastasis*, 4, 6: "But any designation of the subject matter of this iconography as the Descent or Harrowing of Hell misrepresents and distorts the message of the chosen label Anastasis. The title and subject matter of this image refer, not to the Descent of Christ into Hades, Limbo, or Inferno, but to the rising of Christ and his raising of the dead. . . . Thus in the image of the Anastasis, Adam stands for Everyman."

42. For example, the Chudov Psalter, 63v. The image is reproduced, with many others, in John Dominic Crossan and Sarah Sexton Crossan, *Resurrecting Easter: How the West Lost and the East Kept the Original Easter Vision* (New York: HarperOne, 2018), 109, figure 7.7.

43. Crossan and Crossan, *Resurrecting Easter*, 174.

different starting points: the Paschal mystery, unveiling Scripture by the Cross to reveal the eternal mystery, and then tracing how the different aspects or moments it contains are brought into distinct focus and feasts within a liturgical calendar, yet always bearing the imprint of the Paschal mystery itself, or starting from our present theological frameworks, with its distinct elements now thought of as different historical events (incarnation, crucifixion, resurrection), reading Scripture now in a linear manner (with an Old Testament followed by a New Testament beginning with the birth of Jesus), with the predicaments into which we are then led (how to give full weight to Christ's humanity and divinity and yet the unity of person), with theories of en- and anhypostasis which, as Dalferth points out, echoing many others, ultimately fail.

Dalferth's reconstructive proposal that we should always begin by recognizing that confessional statements always already speak of the "Jesus Christ who was raised from the dead" is salutary, but I would suggest that if instead of trying to put the elements (as we think we already know them) back together again, we rather reflect on how the various elements of Christian theology were originally (and for centuries) all held together in the Paschal mystery and refract from that pure white light into the spectrum of theological loci and liturgical feasts, we might find a greater and more dynamic coherence and that the problems we are attempting to resolve look very different: the Paschal death overcoming death such that it is birth into life (γέννησις), contrasted with mere coming-into-being (γένεσις), and incarnation as the birth of the whole body of Christ.

CHAPTER 9

THE LABORED GOD

Freedom, Incarnation, and Discipleship

AMY PEELER

To proclaim "the God who is for us" sounds like very good news—certainly better than to deal with "the God who is against us." Moreover, it is a title that arises out of Christian sacred Scriptures, explicitly Romans 8:31, but also Paul's letter to the Galatians, the focus of this chapter. Paul says there that "God sent forth his Son" (Gal 4:4), that the Son of God is the one who "loved me and gave himself for me" (Gal 2:20), and that "God sent forth the Spirit of his Son into our hearts" (Gal 4:6).[1] Such statements form the core of this letter, a power-packed proclamation of good news. Dense in its brevity and expansive in its impact, Galatians has filled the vision of exegetes as its embers ignite numerous theological insights.

For those who are blessed with a penchant for inquisitiveness, however, uncomfortable questions persist amidst its glory. This essay will ask two: Why and who? If God is for us, why? And if God is for *us*, who is included in the "us" and under what conditions? These questions are intricately connected. If God acted in this way for salvation, freely as a revelation of God's character, then God is deeply committed to human embodiment and all the gritty particularities of it. Galatians provides a powerful affirmation of the value God places on human bodies, and consequently, it presses the potential dangers associated with this affirmation. Wrestling with those dangers results in the blessing of seeing how the salvific imagery in Galatians compels Christian communities to include the embodied testimony of all members so that the free exercise of mutual dependence can result in maximum fruitfulness. This ecclesial ethic should not be surprising because these communities are following the example of God, the God

1. Translations of the biblical text are my own.

who is for all, freely, by choosing to exercise divine dependence to bring about salvific abundance. I attend to the Galatian revelation of this God who is for us in three movements: freedom, incarnation, and discipleship.

The Why Question: Divine Freedom

Why did God send forth his Son? Did God have to? Does God's sending forth of the Son arise out of a divine need, a lack in God? Alternatively, is God responding out of duty to some law? Since God is perfect and good, *must* God have saved creation to act in alignment with that goodness? Consequently, is God not free? If God loves us, can we as creation cause God to suffer or change? If the answers to these questions are negative, and God did not *have* to create and redeem and care, then another disturbing question arises: Is the salvific revelation of the Son and Spirit arbitrary, selected at whim with no connection to the true nature of God?

Theologians recognize these questions as those that occur within discussions of divine freedom, divine impassibility, and divine simplicity. Although those discussions are much more complex than I can summarize here, a broad view is that one trajectory says that unless God is free, God is needy. A needy being would not be sovereign and, therefore, would not be God. Another position says that unless it is God's nature to be in relationship with creation, then God acts arbitrarily and cannot be trusted.[2] Those choices are unpalatable, forcing a selection between an insufficient or an arbitrary God. Clearly, then, the correct answer lies somewhere in the middle. It might sound like I am setting up a stalemated theological argument so that I, as a biblical scholar, can show how simply reading the Bible would provide the answer.

This is not the case for two reasons. First, I believe the theological problem is a real one. These questions arise organically out of serious reading of the Scriptures.[3] Second, I have found that once the questions are posed, deeper attention to the Scriptures press the problem more acutely. The God who is for us elected to suffer death for us, even death on a cross (Phil 2:8), and in order to die on that cross, God first chose to take

2. This is my summary of the treatment of the issue catalogued in *Divine Impassibility: Four Views of God's Emotions and Suffering*, ed. Robert J. Matz and A. Chadwick Thornhill, Spectrum Multiview Book Series (Grand Rapids: IVP Academic, 2019).

3. My own exegetical investigations of the incarnation, articulated in the book *Women and the Gender of God* (Grand Rapids: Eerdmans, 2022) caused me to make assertions that opened the door to the curtailment of God's freedom. Insightful critiques propelled me to investigate it more carefully. In short, it was attention to Scripture that propelled me to ask questions about divine freedom.

on human flesh in the person of the Son and chose to do so by being conceived, labored, and born. Few if any moments press the question of divine dependence upon humanity than when the Son of God is a fetus and an infant. Certainly, it is the incarnate Son who, in his humanity, is dependent, but since his humanity reveals God, might that process indicate, in some way, God's dependence upon humanity? Moreover, in Galatians Paul not only affirms the way the incarnation came to be with more clarity than anywhere else in his writings, saying explicitly that the Son was born of a woman (Gal 4:4), but he also asserts that this process is replicated in the community. The God who is for us has chosen to be the God who continues to be labored, the God who is birthed by Christian communities in the process of evangelism and discipleship. Due to this relationship with humanity, a relationship that includes divine dependence upon human acceptance and action, the question of divine freedom, impassibility, and simplicity is not only *not* solved by Scripture but is instead made more difficult by it.

Scriptural exegesis, disciplined by theological thinking, also shows the way through the questions. It is true that Paul does not enter into divine freedom debates explicitly. He does not contemplate why God redeemed humanity or if God could have done differently, but simply states that God did redeem. In so doing, Paul provides a window into the concept of freedom. I see his logic working in this way. Paul uses much of the ink in this letter to assert the reality of the Galatians' freedom in Christ. They are no longer bound but free, having been rescued and adopted into the family of God (Gal 4:4–6). Their birth story has been rewritten; Paul can now proclaim that they are children of the free woman (Gal 4:21–31). Those who seek to enslave them are acting contrary to the work of God (2:4) because "for freedom Christ has set us free" (Gal 5:1). It is a salient expression of Christian paradox, then, when Paul concludes his statements on Christian freedom with the teaching that their freedom should be expressed in loving slavery to one another (Gal 5:13). They are now free to serve, free to live in the way God intends for humanity to live, bearing one another's weights (Gal 6:2).[4]

This is exactly what the incarnate Son of God did: He served. He entered into the human condition in which he shouldered the law (4:4). In his appeal to family dynamics in chapter 4, Paul portrays him as the

4. This is an echo of the creational mandate that humans are not to work alone, but together (Gen 1:28), and even more specifically, an echo of the divine pronouncement that it was not good that the man was alone, and so God created a woman to shoulder the task with him (Gen 2:18).

young son who is indistinguishable from the slave, by being in a position of boundedness before reaching the fullness of time, the time of maturity (Gal 4:1–2). When he was mature and completed the work of bearing the law's curse (Gal 3:10–13), he did so as a servant. As slaves do, he gave himself on behalf of others (2:20; See also Phil 2:7).

If the Galatians' God-given freedom should manifest in service to others (Gal 5:13), and the Son of God served others, then it follows that his service, as the law they should follow (6:2), also arises from a place of freedom. In other words, it is logical to conclude that divine service unto salvation was an expression of divine freedom. That means that there was no lack in God, nor compulsion; God did not save because God had to do so. Paul affirms that God is not motivated by social pressure (2:6). This is why Paul can describe God's work as a gift, as grace (1:15; 2:9, 21; 6:18).[5] Those who are in relationship with God through Christ by the Spirit are not the fulfillment of God's need nor the completion of God's duty. The Son of God's redemptive service to creation is the fitting expression of God's inherent and most perfect gracious freedom. This protects interpreters from seeing God as subservient to something external to God. This New Testament letter offers exegetical support for the theological conclusion in favor of divine freedom.

Galatians also aids theologians' ability to perceive that God's salvific act is not arbitrary but is instead an outflow of God's nature. Paul speaks of God's pleasure (1:15) and many times of God's love (2:20; 5:13–14, 22–23) as that which motivated God's actions. These emotive terms need not impinge upon God's freedom or sovereignty or simplicity, for God is the fullness of desire.[6] The terms do indicate that God's salvific work was not disconnected from God's being and, therefore, random, or subject to change, but was instead a consistent expression of the fullness of God's nature.[7] The redeemed are the recipients of God's holy, consistent, and trustworthy desire. There is no lack in God, and at the same time there is divine pleasure in creation's union with God.

---

5. John Barclay notes that for Paul "Christ and gift are rhetorically and logical merged," *Paul and the Gift* (Grand Rapids: Eerdmans, 2015), 332.

6. James Dolezal summarizes, "As impassible, God could not possibly be more loving, caring, or opposed to sin than he is from all eternity." Dolezal, "Strong Impassibility," in *Divine Impassibility*, ed. Matz and Thornhill, 36. This is not an endorsement of Dolezal's entire position, but only to demonstrate that even an author most committed to divine impassibility agrees that actions humans associate with emotions are most fulsome, not lacking, in God.

7. John Peckham states succinctly, "God's relational love for creation is rooted in God's essential nature of love." Peckham, "A Qualified Passibility Response," in *Divine Impassibility*, ed. Matz and Thornhill, 159.

The epistle's revelation of the divine nature mitigates against the arbitrariness of God's salvific choice, as do Paul's statements concerning God's will. At the beginning of the letter, Paul notes that Jesus's rescue operation happened according to God's *will* (1:4). The divine will freely opts for a salvific plan out of God's desiring nature. Moreover, finite humans must acknowledge that there could have been other wills in line with God's nature. So God is the most free because God chooses in line with the perfect divine nature, and God is also free in the sense of having options to will. What God chose God freely desired and willed to choose.

When theologians allow the honesty of the why question—as in "why did God save?"—God rewards frankness with a deeper revelation of divine goodness. The nature of a person's character appears with more clarity through freely desired choices than through actions arising out of necessity or constraint. As an expression of free divine desire, God sent forth his Son to serve.

This is not, however, all Galatians says about God's free salvific choice. The entire sentence reads: "When the fullness of time came, God sent forth his Son born of a woman, born under the law in order that he might rescue those under the law, in order that we might receive adoption" (Gal 4:4–5). In addition to the fact of the sending, Paul also proclaims the timing, the mode, and the result. Space constraints prevent me from explicating all these aspects, and so I will focus on one, the way in which the Son was sent, by being born of a woman. If this modality was not demanded of God but was God's free choice, then interpreters learn much about God's desire to honor human embodiment.

Divine Honor for Women

The grammar of Galatians 4:4 allows a debate concerning the way God is involved in this pregnancy. In the influential book, *Christology in the Making*, James Dunn demonstrated the confluence of "sending" language with a prophetic motif. He argued that God's "sending" "underlines the heavenly origin of *commissioning* but not of the one commissioned." In other words, Galatians 4:4 is primarily concerned with function not ontology. The emphasis, according to Dunn, is Jesus's humanity and his participation in a bound condition so that he might redeem other humans out of that condition. Given that there is "little real precedent for such an idea as incarnation," Galatians 4 cannot "rule out this possibility," but it does not provide "firm evidence in favour" as readers trained by the Christian tradition might assume. Instead, this verse asserts that he was divinely commissioned to do the work of redemption, but not necessarily divine. Put differently, he is God's "Son" only as a way of pointing to a special relationship this human messenger has with God.[8] In this reading, God commissions a human who is born of woman, as are all other humans.

Conversely, for other exegetes, Paul's phrasing does gesture toward the doctrine of the incarnation. These interpreters are clear that the phrase cannot bear the weight of proving that Paul was aware of the claims made by Matthew and Luke that Jesus was born of a virgin. (Neither does this verse stand at odds with such claims.) Instead, they see this verse as an affirmation of God the Son *becoming* human, as opposed to God establishing intimate relationship with a previously existing human such that he is *like* God's Son. Richard Hays comes to the gentle conclusion, "It seems likely that Paul did think of the son as preexistent, sent forth from Heaven on a rescue mission."[9] Kavin Rowe is bolder: "There can be no question that the 'fullness of time' read in conjunction with 'born of a woman . . .' assumes a relationship of prior existence between the Father, Son, and Spirit and a doctrine of incarnation, however nascent."[10] As is Tom Wright: "For Paul to say in our present passage that God 'sent' his Son, that this resulted in his being 'born,' . . . leav[es] no room for adoptionist speculations."[11]

Both readings have Paul portraying Jesus in intimate relationship with God, either an intimacy which always existed or an intimacy which Jesus, like Isaiah (Isa 49:1, 5), Jeremiah (Jer 1:5), and Paul (Gal 1:15), traced all the way back to the time of his gestation. Both acknowledge the presence of God, the Son, and the necessity of birth in the verse, but only in one does God choose to work through the mother as well as through the Son.

To be clear, if Jesus were only human as opposed to fully human and fully divine, then God's sending of the Son takes place after his conception. If God commissioned him from the womb, the woman who carried

---

8. *Christology in the Making: A New Testament Inquiry into the Origins of the Doctrine of the Incarnation*, 2nd ed. (Grand Rapids: Eerdmans, 1989), 38–44. Dunn remains frequently cited in the literature of this discussion. See also Michael Peppard's agreement with Dunn concerning preexistence in this passage: "It is possible that Paul meant that, but it is not very likely." Peppard, "Adopted and Begotten Sons of God in John and Paul," *CBQ* 73 (2011): 98.

9. Richard B. Hays, "Galatians," in *New Interpreters Bible* 11 (Nashville: Abingdon, 1994), 283.

10. C. Kavin Rowe, *Method, Context, and Meaning in New Testament Studies* (Grand Rapids: Eerdmans, 2024), 305.

11. N. T. Wright, *Galatians*, Commentaries for Christian Formation (Grand Rapids: Eerdmans, 2021), 268.

him is necessary but inconsequential. God is calling the one who will be his intimate "Son"; the woman is simply the way he is human. In other words, she is the way he can exist and perform God's commission.

Alternatively, if the Son exists in relation with the Father eternally, and the Father freely chooses out of love to send the Son *through pregnancy*, then God is choosing a woman to be the one from whom and through whom God the Son takes on flesh and enters creation. The mother is necessary and consequential. A lower Christology needs a mother because every prophet had to have had a mother to be human, but it is the prophet whom God selects, not the mother. Conversely, a high Christology needs a mother because God elected a mother as the beginning of the salvation her incarnate Son would achieve. In this reading, God did not select a human son, who obviously but without special emphasis was born of a woman. Instead, in a high Christology it is a mother who God selects to provide the humanity for the eternal Son.

I acknowledge the christological ambiguity of this particular verse. It allows but does not demand preexistence. What is not ambiguous is the result. A lower Christology is worse for women. To repeat, if God sent his Son who *had been* born of a woman, that woman is necessary, but only a presupposition for the divine plan. If God sent his son *to be* born of a woman, partnering with that woman is the first step of the divine plan.

If Galatians 4:4 affirms incarnation and indicates that the sovereign God chose *this* method, then this verse provides a powerful insight into an aspect of divine freedom. If God *had* to choose this method, theologians could attend to the results of it, but would learn little about God's character. That God chose this method—freely—speaks powerfully of God's preference to interact with and save humanity *in this way*. Within the framework of the relational preexistence between God the Father and God the Son, interpreters can say that God the Father sent forth his willing Son through the process of being born from a woman. God freely chose—God wanted—to make a woman's body the location from which salvation would begin.

Pregnancy

As Paul describes it in Galatians, salvation via the womb is not a one-time occurrence. The theme of motherhood is a prominent one in the letter,[12]

12. Gal 1:15, 16; 4:4, 19, 21–31.

but for the argument at hand, I will focus on when Paul and the Galatians are mothers, when they do the laboring.

This imagery begins with Paul's autobiography in chapter 1. He recounts that God extended a call to him as an act of grace.[13] That grace was manifest in God's pleasure to reveal his Son. One might expect that Paul would say God revealed his Son *to* Paul, but that would not be the best translation. With no variants here, the manuscript tradition indicates that Paul wrote God revealed his Son ἐν ἐμοί (*en emoi*). The preposition ἐν (*en*) can serve as "the marker denoting the object to which something happens,"[14] hence the translation "to" adopted by the ESV, NRSV, and NLT is a possibility. God's revelation happened to Paul, and he recognized that revelation.

It is also the case that the preposition ἐν can indicate, and does most often, an object "by which something is recognized, or in which something shows itself."[15] Paul is the one in whom God's revelation of the Son appeared. The NKJV, NIV, Holman Christian Standard, and NASB, for example, adopt this translation. Not only is the locative sense of "in" the most dominant meaning of the preposition, but to translate it in this most natural way also allows the reader to hear with clarity the continuation of the familial theme, even more precisely, to hear the continuation of the *pregnancy* theme.[16] God set Paul apart when he was within the womb of his mother, and then God revealed the Son *within Paul*, so that Paul might, as it were, "birth" Christ by proclaiming the gospel to the gentiles (1:16).

This interpretation is not a flight of fancy but is instead justified by Paul's own adoption of this imagery for his work with the Galatians. He later says to them that he has worked hard for them (4:11). He uses a general term for labor (*kopiaō*), but he then specifies his commitment to them in 4:19. Addressing the Galatians as his children,[17] he says that he is again laboring. This time he uses the term for the birthing process, not the

---

13. This phrase "calling through his grace" is missing in some early witnesses, namely P[46], B, F, and G, but included in others such as X, A, and D. The idea of God calling by grace aligns with Pauline language for God's call (Gal 1:6; see also 2 Tim 1:9), so it is plausibly original. If it is not, then the phrase about being set apart from the womb stands right next to the phrase that describes God's revelation of the Son in him, heightening the proximity of the pregnancy references.

14. "ἐν," *A Greek-English Lexicon of the New Testament and Other Early Christian Literature*, hereafter *BDAG*, third edition, ed. F. W. Danker (Chicago: University of Chicago Press, 2000), 329.

15. "ἐν," *BDAG*, 329.

16. Susan G. Eastman, noting her agreement with commentaries by Lightfoot, Betz, Gaventa, and Hays, states that "all of these commentators emphasize the notion that Jesus Christ is revealed 'in' and 'through' the apostle's transformed life." Eastman, *Recovering Paul's Mother Tongue: Language and Theology in Galatians* (Grand Rapids: Eerdmans, 2007), 32n31.

17. A textual variant emphasizes the pregnancy and birth motif even more when it has Paul address them as little children, as τεκνια.

general term which could apply to any kind of labor, but the word for labor pains, *ōdinō*.[18] Even more, this time he says not that he is laboring *for* them, but he is laboring them.[19] They are the direct object of his birth pains. He can describe his work for and love of the Galatians as giving birth to them. Paul is setting himself as a mother to this community.[20]

There is more. The metaphor in Galatians 4:19 is not a simple one.[21] If it were, Paul might have said, I am laboring you *until you are born*. That could have allowed him to cast the Galatians as being formed in *his* image, an option he rejects.[22] Instead, the goal of his labor of the Galatians is that *Christ* is formed. Notably, Paul explicitly chooses *not* to cast himself as a father in this situation.[23] He has cast himself as mother, a mother who brings forth Christ.

He is not alone. Paul's life story is that God revealed Christ *in him* so that he might birth Christ to the gentiles (1:16), and this has happened among the Galatians. Paul is laboring them, so that Christ might be formed among them. The location of Christ demands attention. The goal of Paul's labor of the Galatians is that *Christ* is formed *in them*. Certainly, this indicates that the community should take the shape of the life of Christ.[24] In several other instances, Paul invites other congregations, as well, to see Christ in themselves (Rom 8:10; 2 Cor 13:5; Col 1:27). In none of these instances, however, does Paul use the verb μορφόω

18. In the New Testament the term is associated with cataclysmic and cosmos-altering events (Matt 24:8; Mark 13:8; Acts 2:24; Gal 4:19, 27; 1 Thess 5:3; Rev 12:2). See Gaventa's treatment of the apocalyptic nature of this term in Gaventa, *Our Mother Saint Paul* (Louisville: Westminster John Knox, 2007), 32–34.

19. Eastman states, "ὠδίνω . . . [has] a corporate people as its concrete direct object." Eastman, *Recovering Paul's Mother Tongue*, 92.

20. The presence of the term *again* (4:19) suggests that Paul saw his role with the Galatians in a maternal way from the beginning, even when he stated earlier that he was laboring (κοπιάω) for them using the general term (Eastman, *Recovering Paul's Mother Tongue*, 90). Several interpreters in the early Church reflect upon Paul as mother, including Origen, Methodius, Nyssa, Guerric of Igny, and Anselm. See discussion in Gaventa, *Our Mother St. Paul*, 14–15.

21. It is, instead, as Beverly Gaventa has noted, a "metaphor squared." *Our Mother St. Paul*, 4.

22. Philip Ryken calls attention to this possibility and its pastoral implications, noting that "It is important that Christ is being formed in them, not Paul." Ryken, *Galatians: The Gospel of Free Grace* (Phillipsburg: P&R, 2005), 178. So too does Yung Suk Kim, "The goal of his labor pains is not to produce little Pauls but to form Christ in them." Kim, *Rereading Galatians from the Perspective of Paul's Gospel: A Literary and Theological Commentary* (Eugene, OR: Cascade, 2019), 79.

23. As he does in other places, such as 1 Corinthians 4:15. Bridget Kahl writes, "What at first sight seems to be the voice of a patriarchal Pauline rule demanding obedience, in an ironic twist becomes the birth-cry of a woman in labor pains. In the same way, just a few verses before, Paul's apparently 'authoritarian' demand to become like him turns out to mean the imitation of 'unmanly weakness.'" Kahl, "No Longer Male: Masculinity Struggles Behind Gal 3:28," *JSNT* 79 (2001): 45–46.

24. Nijay Gupta, *Galatians*, Story of God Bible Commentary 9 (Grand Rapids: Zondervan, 2023), 186.

in the description, a term associated with the formation of an embryo.[25] Interpreters notice as well the lack of a subject in this second clause. Paul is actively laboring them (4:19a), as a mother would, but he is not doing the forming. Instead, the formation of Christ in them appears as a passive construction (μορφωθῇ). This aligns with the way Paul typically uses this term, as a vehicle to point to the work of God (2 Cor 3:18; Phil 3:10).[26] Paul is laboring the Galatians to birth Christ among them, but it is ultimately *God* who is forming Christ in them.[27]

In light of this term and the pregnancy imagery throughout the letter, I, along with many other interpreters, conclude that Paul applies the maternal metaphor not only to himself but also to the Galatians.[28] The metaphor, I would posit, is not of maternity generally but to a very specific birth. Because a new age has dawned with the birth of God's Son from the mother God selected (Gal 4:4), Paul is able to replicate that birth in this community. In describing his ministry in this way, Paul is setting himself as similar to the mother from whom Christ came. As she brought forth Christ into the world, Paul is bringing forth Christ among the Galatians. His hope is that they too might follow him as he follows her and allow the formation of Christ in them to reach its perfection. As was true with Mary's pregnancy, God serves as the source of Christ's life in them and forms the Son in these mothers. The Galatians' gestation of Christ is

---

25. See "μορφόω," *BDAG*, 659.

26. This language also appears in Jeremiah (1:5) and Isaiah (44:2, 24; 49:5) from whom Paul has been drawing. See discussion in Eastman, *Recovering Paul's Mother Tongue*, 87–88.

27. Sam Williams concludes, "Who is responsible for Christ 'taking shape' in the Galatian congregations? Not the Galatians themselves. Not even mother Paul. It is rather *God* who is doing the 'forming,' the One who sent his son in the first place (4:6)." Williams, *Galatians*, ANTC (Nashville: Abingdon, 1997), 122–23.

28. Unsurprisingly, this includes interpreters especially attentive to maternal themes such as Gaventa, *Our Mother Saint Paul*, 37; Eastman, *Recovering Paul's Mother Tongue*, 57, 154; Cynthia Long Westfall, who writes, "Paul depicted himself in labor, yet it was the Galatians themselves who were pregnant: Christ was 'being formed' in them like a fetus," in *Paul and Gender: Reclaiming the Apostle's Vision for Men and Women in Christ* (Grand Rapids: Baker Academic, 2016), 53; and Nancy Elizabeth Bedford, who states, "If they become like Paul, then they in turn will become maternally generative and Christomorphic." Bedford, *Galatians*, Belief: A Theological Commentary on the Bible (Louisville: Westminster John Knox, 2016), 141.

This is not lost on other interpreters as well. For instance, Timothy George comments, "Paul now suddenly shifted his metaphor again, doubtless producing a note of jarring dissonance in the minds of his readers. Paul has just described himself as a pregnant mother determined to carry the Galatians to full term. The anguish of his labor over them had to continue, he said, 'until Christ is formed in you.' The Galatians who a moment ago were described as being formed in the womb were now spoken of as expectant mothers who themselves must wait for an embryonic Christ to be fully developed . . . within them." George, *Galatians: An Exegetical and Theological Exposition of Scripture*, NAC 30 (Nashville: B&H, 1994), 65. Matthew Harmon notices, "the imagery portrays the Galatians as the ones who are pregnant, with Christ being formed inside of them." Harmon, *Galatians*, EBTC (Bellingham, WA: Lexham, 2021), 253.

divinely wrought by God the Father through the power of the Holy Spirit via the labor of Paul. It is God who is making them mothers, mothers who will bring forth Christ.

Appealing to labor as the place where God shows strength for their salvation aligns with the way God chose to begin salvation with the human conception, pregnancy, and birth of the Son. God has freely elected to save humanity by serving them, and this service begins with dependence upon them, as they birth the Son into the world.

Laboring Sons

That God freely chose to save in this way by honoring the process by which human life began is incredibly good news, but that penchant for inquisitiveness rears its head once again. There are questions that press for an answer in God's decision to save in this way, and the answers point the way forward toward flourishing Christian discipleship.

The second person pronoun in this statement—until Christ is formed in "*you*"—is a plural (ὑμῖν *umin*), and yet the pregnancy imagery is applicable to individuals within the community, for it is distinct persons who make up the body.[29] Individuals are caught up into this reality—for it is not just an image, but a reality—Christ, by the power of the Spirit is within each of them (see also Rom 8:9–10). It is a phenomenal gift that they get to be the mothers of Christ.

This reality also raises a concern. For these members, their rebirth as mothers is radically transformative to the degree that interpreters have wondered about the obliteration of each member's distinct humanity. All in the community might be tempted to lose themselves in attention to their child, as mothers often have been. With this particular pregnancy, moreover, the concern for erasure is compounded in an intense way. For within this pregnancy there is an unusual transformation of the mother. In the reversal of what would be true in a simply human biological process of conception and pregnancy, the Galatians will not pass on their image to Christ, the one in them, but he will make the Galatians into his. When they are reborn in the faith as mothers of Christ, they take on the identities of God's Son. Paul declares that as converts, they are seed of Abraham (3:29), heirs of the promise (3:29), and "sons of God" (3:26).

29. Eastman states what seems best to me: "4:19b also should be translated to refer to both individuals and the corporate community so that Christ is formed 'in and among' the Galatians." Eastman, *Recovering Paul's Mother Tongue*, 154n2.

It seems correct to say, then, that in some significant way Paul also views them all as free Jewish males.[30] Even more, to become like this Son is to follow the pattern of his life, to take up the cross, to die to oneself.[31] In addition, then, to the common concern that mothers can become overly attentive to their child to their own detriment, in this pregnancy, because of the particular Son in them, the mother takes on the image of her son and is then crucified.

The adoption of filial and maternal imagery raises the concern that the letter asks listeners to deny their embodied individuality and even to eliminate their very personhood. Readers are not wrong to wonder if the distinct identity of the person is at risk of being obliterated in the process of bearing and becoming like Christ.

Persons Not Obliterated

Instead of confirming that concern about personal annihilation, Paul's argument defuses it. The metaphors of bearing and being clothed with Christ, I posit, work against the idea of personal obliteration. To bear Christ, there must be the retention of the person who is his mother. Similarly, the picture Paul uses for becoming like Christ is that they are clothed with Christ (Gal 3:27). *Being clothed* assumes that the person remains to put on the clothes. In both of the Christ-imageries then, clothing and bearing, the person does not become Christ but retains bodily distinction from the Messiah, the one in whom they are clothed and the one whom they bear. In sum, persons are not obliterated by Christ; they are enveloped by Christ, inside and out.[32]

Set out of bounds by Galatians then is any kind of religious system that denies the body. The waters of baptism are not metaphorical, but tangible. Literal water is applied to actual bodies. Christian salvation is

---

30. As observed by Ed Miller as well: "Thus, there is a sense in which those who are in Christ—a Jew, a freeperson, and a male—are all Jews, all free, and all males." Miller, "Is Gal 3:28 the great Egalitarian Text?," *ET* 114 (2002): 11.

31. Gaventa, *Our Mother Saint Paul*, 37; Wright, *Galatians*, 288.

32. In disagreement with Daniel Boyarin's assessment that Paul urges a "coercive sameness," John Barclay counters: "But if unity is derived from common allegiance to an unconditioned event (the Christ-gift), there is no devaluation of particularity in principle, only an insistence that every difference is shorn of prior connotations of worth"; and "In common solidarity with Christ baptized believers are enabled and required to view each other without regard to these influential classifications of worth" (Barclay, *Paul and the Gift*, 397–98n23). Eastman summarizes Kasemann's interpretation of Paul's body language by suggesting that the members of Christ's body remain "individuals [who] become 'partisans' in God's liberating army, each living out a unique calling under God's lordship." Eastman, *Paul and the Person: Reframing Paul's Anthropology* (Grand Rapids: Eerdmans, 2017), 105.

spiritual, *and* it is physical. Hence, any concept of salvation is anemic and even non-Christian if one's body is dismissed.[33]

The persistence of the body in Christianity is supported by the fact that Galatians eliminates any pretense that bodily differences do not continue to exist postbaptism. Those baptized as mothers who are clothed with Christ remain Jew, gentile, male, and female. In this letter and others, Paul does not forget that reality. He will name the specificities of those Christians in these particular embodied states.[34] He and Peter are Jewish (Gal 2:15). After conversion, Titus remains Greek and is not compelled to be circumcised (2:3). Peter is eating with believers recognized as gentiles (2:12). Although Paul would say of these converts that they are now sons of Abraham (3:7), he is also clear about their ethnic heritage and indicates that it remains known to the congregations.[35] This continuation is also true with sex. Paul's intense instructions against circumcision demonstrate that he recognizes the persistence of the male body (5:2–6). Gentile men should not take on circumcision, which also implies that gentile women should not desire to take up this practice for their sons. In sum, none in the community must expunge their embodied and cultured identity nor pretend that their natural status has ceased to exist. It is still present even as they have embraced the identity of Christ. Laid over their old identity is the fact that they have *put on* Christ and empowering their particular identity is the fact that they have become Christ's mother. This transformation has occurred for them through the somatic ritual of baptism. While the worry about personal or bodily obliteration is understandable, it does not actually materialize in Paul's teaching.

The Cost of Sex

That being true, it seems important to say more regarding the specifics of sexed embodiment. The rite of baptism is open to all and equally practiced on all. By going through this transformation, males and females are not asked to obliterate themselves, but they are asked to reconceptualize

33. Mayra Rivera summarizes the position made clear in Tertullian: "No one can be saved except in the flesh. It is the flesh that is washed, anointed, signed, 'overshadowed by the imposition of hands,' fed with the body of Christ, and so on—the very means by which the soul becomes closer to God." Rivera, *Poetics of the Flesh* (Durham: Duke University Press, 2015), 53.

34. Susan Eastman summarizes the continuity of the body in Paul's cocrucifixion life in this way, "As the subsequent imperatives make clear, it is not bodily existence that is done away with but the body qualified in some way by sin as a distinct entity, or perhaps sin as it takes hold of embodied existence." Eastman, *Paul and the Person*, 89.

35. See the discussion by John Barclay, *Paul and the Gift*, 397.

their embodied identities. New members of God's family will join as the Galatians have, through faith and baptism, and they will join by being born, gestated, labored, delivered as God's Son was. They all get to think of themselves as being clothed with the honor of the Son. This is not limited to the men. They also all get to play the role of mothers, and these spiritual wombs are not limited to the women. At the very least, the schema Paul utilizes could present confusion, as baptizands are admonished to see themselves in Christ with nomenclature and actions of both male and female embodiment.

More pernicious threats than confusion are present as well. Because the imagery is distinctively sexed, because Paul says they are clothed with the identity of a male savior and are pregnant with him, the confessional identity impacts males and females in distinct ways. The particular threat to women is twofold. First, it might be more natural for women to fall into the trope of detrimental self-denial as they follow a common script for motherhood. Second, females are asked to find their identity in a male Messiah, raising the concern that women will be subsumed or lost, in him.[36] Men in the community, on the other hand, are being asked to follow a feminized leader, the mother Paul, and see themselves participating in a female action of pregnancy and labor, different than what their own created body could do. In addition, men may be more tempted to sacrifice themselves for their community following the model of men dying on behalf of women and children.

In addition to being different, the embrace of these disjunctive identities is also less socially valued. Men, when invited to conceive of themselves as mothers, are being asked to demote themselves, taking on the often less-esteemed female identity. Women too are being asked to take on the socially lower identity of a crucified Jewish male.[37]

In light of these threats, each member of the community is precariously poised to fall back into the temptation of self-denial in the sense that

36. This is the path followed by several non-canonical writings including the *Gospel According to Philip*, where the end of death arrives when Eve is joined again with Adam, or *The Gospel of Thomas*, where in saying 114 every woman who makes herself male will enter the Kingdom of Heaven. Peter Brown describes the Valentinian literature, in which "the female would be swallowed up in the male. It would not simply be disciplined by the male; it would become male," *The Body and Society: Men, Women, and Sexual Renunciation in Early Christianity*, second edition (New York: Columbia University Press, 2008), 109–116. Daniel Boyarin sees an eschatological androgyne also as "a reinstatement of masculinism: The androgyne in question always turns out somehow to be a male androgyne," "Gender," in *Critical Terms for Religious Studies*, ed. Mark C. Taylor (Chicago: University of Chicago Press, 1998), 126. See also Rivera, *Poetics of the Flesh*, 32, 40.

37. See Brittany E. Wilson, *Unmanly Men: Refigurations of Masculinity in Luke-Acts* (Oxford: Oxford University Press, 2015), 190–242.

they are tempted to lose themselves in unhealthy self-sacrifice according to the gendered trajectories of their own sexed bodies or to deny their bodies altogether and lose themselves in the identity of the other. Conversely, they might also be tempted to become puffed up by the way in which God chose to utilize their particular embodiment for the process of salvation and imagine they do not have need of the other. Were the imagery limited to one sex, either sonship or motherhood, the temptations would be imbalanced, but because the imagery includes both mothers and sons, the struggle to embrace the gospel picture is shared.

The best way to prevent this fall back into temptation is to grasp the hand of the other, so that the balance of the community is taut and secure. The temptations do not go away and so the precarity of leaning back remains, but the fall is prevented by not letting go of one's partner—by keeping a vision of their temptations and their contributions, partnering together to do the gospel work of rebirth in a fallen world. The sexed challenge of the good news—of the way in which God freely decided for salvation to manifest—becomes the very site at which the need for and the blessing of having differently sexed bodies actively contributing to the Christian community becomes most apparent.

Throughout the letter Paul is speaking about division, Jews over gentiles, masters over slaves, an opposition he demonstrates with his term *oude*, "or," in Galatians 3:28. However, with the final pair of male and female, he instead has an "and" (*kai*). As he is proclaiming the baptismal reality of new creation, he does not separate men from women, as he does in the other groups. He does not change the fact that God said "male *and* female" at the very beginning of the human story (Gen 1:27). As is true with the other pairings, the patterns of relationship are different in Christ than they are outside of him. In this instance, it seems that Paul's negation suggests that biological pregnancy is no longer necessary to the continuation of the faith.[38] The pairing itself, nevertheless, remains. Given the imagery throughout the letter, the "and" demonstrates the benefit of having both male and female members in the Christian community. A community need not, indeed should not, have slaves and free to demonstrate the grace of freedom because the time has changed and slavery has come to an end. A community could have either gentile or Jew to show how God redeems both. Conversely, it stands as an ideal (as Paul will say in 1 Corinthians

38. This aligns with Paul's statements that people are added to the family of God/the descendants of Abraham through faith (Gal 3:7, 29) as well as his preference for celibacy (1 Cor 7:7–8).

11:12) that the Christian community have both males and females to show the distinction of sex, a distinction that points to the way in which salvation happened according to the free divine will. Paul will not, even in his language, separate men from women.

One might imagine that the bodies of women are present to remind the congregation of pregnancy, Jesus's actual experience of pregnancy and the spiritual discipline of birthing Christ within oneself and for others. This is true. Clearly it is not the case that all females experience pregnancy, but bodily particularities and the ability to testify of them act as a signpost to the way God has chosen to work in the world. Women can share what it is like to have a body that can form life within it, the pain and the joy therein. It is also easy to see that men can share what it is like to be a son, the bodily realities of living into the privileges and responsibilities of being a male member of family and society.

Lest interpretation be limited to natural bodies, in Galatians the opposite is also true. Men are not only present to demonstrate what it is to be a son; women are not only present to point to the actual and metaphorical pregnancy of salvation. Women demonstrate in an embodied way the reality and metaphor of pregnancy, and women also demonstrate God's grace that allows them to be sons of God. Men embody sonship; men are also signs that demonstrate God's grace that allows them to experience spiritual labor pains. Women naturally image the bearer; men naturally image the one born, and also *by grace* women image the Son, and men *by grace* image the ones who bring him to the world. Both men and women contribute from their bodily and cultural existence, and both show the grace given by God for what their bodies alone cannot do. Just like Sarah, the mother of the free son, all the congregation shows that God does not dismiss our embodied realities but empowers them to do beyond what we think possible. While embracing the identity of a mother and a crucified Jewish man might be a demotion in the culture in which they live, in this new family, that which is not esteemed in the eyes of the world is honored in the economy of the community. Women are clothed with the honor of Christ, and men get to have the honor of being like the one God chose to bear him. We are all God's good creation, but in Christ we are also a new creation, who bodily communicate the divine good of nature with our given bodies and also the grace to do what our natural bodies could not without God's power. Our bodies communicate literally and figuratively, for we are all are invited to think and live as laboring sons.

That striking linguistic image of laboring sons is the place from which

I can argue that the church is at its best when the gathered body of Christ images and proclaims the process by which God elected to become the incarnate body of Christ. In freely sending the Son by being born of a woman and by inviting confessors of that Son to live as both mothers and sons, Galatians demonstrates God's free choice to include the embodied testimony of both males and females in the church. For those who are not either, whatever particular bodily configuration or sense of gendered identity they bear, the ecclesial imagery Paul utilizes could provide encouragement that the created good of male and female is not obliterated but retained, purged of the oppressive categories of sin in which they are known east of Eden and reimagined in the spiritually fruitful family of God so that all in Christ are unsettled as we receive meaning and purpose for our embodiment in the figurative reemployment of sexed and gendered categories in the new creation community.

God's free choice for the Son to be born becomes a model for Christian discipleship, revealing that we experience the most abundant life when we freely live in dependence upon one another. The very sex-specific way God chose to be for us, physically once, and then spiritually replicated thereafter, demonstrates that we, as embodied beings, should use our God-given freedom for one another, to serve and also to be served by each other, to acknowledge our need for the body, the testimony, the presence and activity of the other. The God who is for us is freely for all of us and invites us to utilize and depend upon our embodied testimonies so that many more members might be birthed and raised in the family of God.

CHAPTER 10

FOR US AND OUR TRAUMATIZATION

Toward a Modern Promeitic Christology

PRESTON MCDANIEL HILL AND JOHN SWINTON

The assertion that God is "for us" is one of the most basic affirmations of Christian faith. Billions of Christians across time and space have confessed belief in a God "who for us and our salvation came down from heaven and was incarnate," as the Nicene Creed states. This assertion of divine promeity—that God is "for us" (*pro nobis*)—is implicit in the narrative structure of all major Christian creeds and confessions that center affirmations of incarnation and atonement. The narrative of Christ crucified and risen demonstrates a divine will that is fundamentally benevolent and open toward the entire created order. In Christ, God has not simply come to us but has come "for us."

Since at least the time of the Reformation, a distinctive theme of Protestant theologians has been to accentuate and explore the outer limits of divine promeity. Just how much and in what specific ways can God be said to be "for us"? This is the essence of the question posed by Dietrich Bonhoeffer at the end of his life in a letter written from prison: "What keeps gnawing at me is the question, what is Christianity, or who is Christ actually for us today?"[1] As Phil Ziegler has noted, Bonhoeffer's emphasis on contemporary context as a place to explore divine promeity suggests the need for "subjective value judgments and contextual appropriations"[2] to illuminate Christology's relevance and practical authenticity. A possible

1. Dietrich Bonhoeffer, *Letters and Papers from Prison*, ed. J. DeGruchy, trans. C. Gremmels et al., DBWE 8 (Minneapolis: Fortress Press, 2010), 362.
2. Philip Ziegler, "Christ For Us Today—Promeity in the Christologies of Bonhoeffer and Kierkegaard," *International Journal of Systematic Theology* 15, no. 1 (2013): 26.

implication of this perspective is that knowledge of God in Christ is fundamentally "self-interested and self-involving, being decisively shaped by the present demands of our situation and our place within it."[3] Put slightly differently, divine promeity is not universal in shape and form and cannot be understood without reference to the specific "us" that God in Christ is being "for." The knowledge that God is "for us" requires knowledge of the self that God is for, meaning that knowledge of God and knowledge of self are mutually intertwined, as John Calvin memorably states.[4] If Christ is identified as the one who has come "for us and our salvation," then discerning Christ's identity requires ongoing reference to the context of "us and our salvation."

None of this is to say that promeity necessarily reduces Christology to a complete contextual wax nose.[5] For example, one could draw with Phil Ziegler on Søren Kierkegaard's philosophy of the "eternal contemporaneity" of Christ to show that since Christ is already "contemporary" with every human experience—and as such is already "for us" in whatever situation we happen to occupy—there is no need for promeity to be "made relevant" to any given human context.[6] Because Christ is already for us at all times, no one time is decisive for defining Christ's promeity. In this way, the epistemic priority for determining the context of promeity lies within divine promeity itself rather than with the decisiveness of any particular human context. Or as my (Preston's) exuberantly joyful *Doktorvater*

3. Ziegler, "For Us Today," 26.

4. John Calvin, *Institutes of the Christian Religion*, ed. J. T. McNeill, trans. Ford Lewis Battles (Louisville: Westminster, 1960), 1.1.1; hereafter, *Inst.* It is important to note that our paper is not committing to any one theory of the self or personhood. Some modern views of the self as an unchanging stable entity that can be held responsible for what it knows about the world may be problematic for certain circumstances where the self either changes very quickly into something quite different from before or is constantly changing through time, such as in cases of brain damage or dementia. Likewise, as will become clear in our paper, trauma changes the self in profound ways, and this requires flexibility for how one theorizes the self and personhood. For more on this, see John Swinton, *Dementia: Living in the Memories of God* (Grand Rapids: Eerdmans, 2012).

5. The subjective appropriations involved in promeity raise important questions. For example, world history is composed of billions of potential selves each inhabiting their own unique context such that any comprehensive account of divine promeity that is context-specific would be stuck in an endless regress of hypothetical context acquisition before God could ever actually be "for" any one of "us" in particular. Furthermore, a promeity that is context-dependent could "threaten to underwrite an entirely instrumental approach to Christology, perhaps even to encourage the proliferation of christologies of ever-shifting existential, political and sociological 'gaps'" (Ziegler, "For Us Today," 27). Simply put, constructing Christian theology in ways that are context-specific raises architectural complexities for the overall stability of Christian doctrine.

6. Søren Kierkegaard, *Practice in Christianity*, trans. and ed. Howard V. Hong and Edna H. Hong (Princeton: Princeton University Press, 1991), 62–66. See Ziegler, "For Us Today," 35–39. It is important to note that while promeity may not "need" to be made relevant, it does need to be made tangible and accessible in ordinary experience if it is to hold meaning for people in the real world, something that we attempt in this paper.

Alan Torrance is fond of saying, "The direction of the pressure of interpretation flows from God's self-disclosure, not toward it."[7]

Despite these qualifications, while specific contexts may not necessarily be epistemically decisive for the fact of promeity, they are not unimportant or inconsequential for understanding the God who is "for us." Since Christ has come not just "for us" but "for us and our salvation," it seems imperative to have an account of what we are saved *from*, what we are saved *for* and what we are saved *into* to have a full-orbed account of promeity. However, defining what it means to "be saved" may likely be a task not just of receiving an inherited tradition but of the ongoing development of the tradition in a progressive task of "faith seeking understanding." According to Bonhoeffer and others, this likely implies some level of contextual appropriation because identifying what constitutes "us and our salvation" involves an ongoing process of ecclesial, social, and political discernment.[8]

This essay explores psychological trauma as an emblematic modern context that is especially important for illuminating divine promeity today. A modern promeitic Christology, we think, may necessarily be posttraumatic since promeity in Christian dogmatics presumes human vulnerability to wounding in need of divine attunement. This is not to say that trauma is the "one context to rule them all"; nor is it to say that trauma is merely one among many equally possible points of departure. Rather, as we will suggest, psychological trauma presents unique challenges and opens unique possibilities for advancing a modern theology of God's being "for us" that may be timely for illuminating, in Bonhoeffer's words, who Christ is for us today.[9]

Drawing from Protestant traditions of promeity, we specifically identify Reformation interpretations of Christ's descent into hell as promising dogmatic terrain to cull a modern promeitic Christology for contexts of trauma and spiritual struggles. In particular, we explore Calvin's interpretation of Christ's cry of dereliction as an experience of traumatic disbelief in divine goodness to suggest a generative tension between faith and

7. Alan Torrance, communication with author, 2017. This same phrase occurs in varying form in multiple publications of Torrance.

8. For a classic outline of the meaning of *fides quarens intellectum* and its function as prolegomena in Christian theology, see Daniel L. Migliore, *Faith Seeking Understanding: An Introduction to Christian Theology* (Grand Rapids: Eerdmans, 1991). For a recent adventurous and compelling proposal that indicates our posture here toward the development of tradition, see David Bentley Hart, *Tradition and Apocalypse: An Essay on the Future of Christian Belief* (Grand Rapids: Baker, 2022).

9. For an outline of this approach to trauma theology, see Preston McDaniel Hill, *Holy Saturday and Trauma Theology* (New York: Cambridge University Press, forthcoming).

doubt that falls within the purview of normative human experience in the economy of salvation. If God is for us in Christ, and Christ experienced doubt in divine goodness (or even a sense of divine abandonment), then traumatic experiences of doubt or divine hiddenness are not necessarily evidence of an absence of faith in the lives of survivors. This has significant implications for reframing the possibilities of normative religious experience given the facts of divine promeity.

Protestant Promeities

While promeity is often associated with modern Protestant theologians such as Barth or Bonhoeffer in their discussions of election or Christology, the origins of this theme are far-reaching in the history of Christian thought and, in particular, took unique precedence in the theology of the Reformation. That is not to say that promeity did not exist before the early modern period, but simply that promeity, as it operates in theology today, owes much to the spirituality and doctrinal intuitions of Reformation theologians. While there is no space to comprehensively survey these intuitions here, a sample of promeity in Reformation writings will point us in that direction and illuminate the significance of this theme for Christian dogmatics today.

Consider Martin Luther's famous spiritual reflections in *The Freedom of a Christian.* In this breakout text at the brink of Luther's growing alienation from Rome, he outlines a dynamic understanding of promeity as central to proper Christology:

> I believe it has not become clear that it is not enough or in any sense Christian to preach the works, life, and words of Christ as historical facts, as if the knowledge of these would suffice for the conduct of life; yet this is the fashion among those today who must be regarded as our best preachers. . . .
>
> Rather ought Christ to be preached to the end that faith in him may be established that he may not only be Christ, but be Christ for you and me, and that what is said of him and is denoted in his name may be effectual in us. Such faith is produced and preserved in us by preaching why Christ came, what he brought and bestowed, what benefit it is to us to accept him. This is done when that Christian liberty which he bestows is rightly taught and we are told in what way we Christians are all kings and priests and therefore lords of all and may firmly believe

> that whatever we have done is pleasing and acceptable in the sight of God, as I have already said.[10]

This citation is indicative of some of Luther's most enduring spiritual convictions that emphasize the role of personal and experiential knowledge of the benefits of Christ for proper Christian teaching, preaching, and catechesis. Note that Luther names promeity ("that he not only be Christ, but Christ for you and me") as definitive for the proper object of faith and the subsequent "benefits" that Christians experience by faith in this object, namely, the royal priesthood of all believers. We might say that, for Luther, one is justified by faith alone, not just if Christ is the object of faith, but if and only if the object of faith is a specifically promeitic Christ, Christ "for you and me."

These convictions catalyzed similar emphases among second-generation Reformers. Consider Luther's protégé and friend Philip Melancthon, who has become famous in Christian theology for the Latin phrase *hoc est Christum cognoscere, beneficia eius cognoscere*, commonly translated "to know Christ is to know his benefits."[11] The context of this phrase is a passage in his famous *Loci Communes* (or "commonplaces" in theology) where he prioritizes promeity as fundamental to systematic Christian teaching:

> For through these topics Christ is properly known, if it is true that to know Christ is to know his benefits, and not, as they teach, to contemplate his natures and the modes of his incarnation. Unless you know why Christ took on flesh and was crucified, what is the profit of knowing historical facts about him? Or is it enough for a doctor to know the shapes, colors, and features of herbs, no matter that he does not know their inherent power? Just so, we must come to know Christ, who has been given to us as our remedy, and to use a scriptural word, our salvific remedy, in some way other than that which the Scholastics urge.

10. Martin Luther, *The Freedom of a Christian, 1520*. For the full text with background, see Timothy J. Wengert, *The Freedom of a Christian, 1520: Annotated Luther Study Edition* (Minneapolis: Fortress, 2016).

11. Much discussion has been devoted in Christian theology to the potentially problematic gap this dictum opens between the person and work of Christ. On the one side, Paul Tillich represents a kind of "functional" Christology that reduces the person of Christ to the work of salvation. Tillich, *Systematic Theology*, vol. 2, *Existence and the Christ* (Chicago: University of Chicago Press, 1957), 150. On the other side, Dietrich Bonhoeffer expresses a strong hesitation regarding this reduction, which he deems a form of "apostasy." Bonhoeffer, *Christ the Center* (New York: Harper & Row, 1966), 37, 48. For more on this, see Julie Canlis, *Calvin's Ladder* (Grand Rapids: Eerdmans, 2010), 153–59.

> This, finally is Christian knowledge—to know what the Law demands, where to find the power to fulfil the Law, where to claim grace for sins, how to strengthen a wavering soul against the devil, the flesh, and the world, and how to console the afflicted conscience.[12]

Like Luther, Melancthon here centers promeitic Christology as the cornerstone of Christian teaching and catechesis. Importantly, Melancthon expressly indicates in this passage the important pastoral benefits of centering promeity in dogmatics: it is precisely "how to strengthen a wavering soul against the devil, the flesh, and the world, and how to console the afflicted conscience."

Countless similar citations could be added to this list. Promeity became a ubiquitous intellectual reflex among Reformation theologians, pastors, and preachers. One can find multiple examples in Calvin,[13] Zwingli,[14] Bucer,[15] and other Reformation thinkers to show this theme was not incidental but central to the shared spiritual ethos of the period. Suffice it to say that promeity was a major "load-bearing structure"[16] in the self-understanding of Reformation theologians, an important point given the social splintering and tense diversity that quickly emerged among members of this dynamic group. While they differ sharply on other topics relating to sacramentology, ecclesiology, and political theology, there is something of an early consensus among magisterial Protestant theologians that Christ is only Christ if he is Christ "for us." A meaningful Christology is always a promeitic Christology.

---

12. Philip Melancthon, *Loci Communes, 1521.* For the full text, see *Commonplaces: Loci Communes 1521*, trans. Christian Preus (Saint Louis: Concordia, 2014).

13. A major expression of this theme in Calvin is his emphasis against theological speculation (God *in se*) in favor of restricting attention to revealed theological knowledge (God *quoad nos*). See Calvin, *Inst.* 1.2.2; 1.5.1, 9; 1.11.3; 3.2.6. For more on this theme in Calvin, see Paul Helm, *Calvin's Ideas* (New York: Oxford University Press, 2004), 11–34; Canlis, *Calvin's Ladder*, 110, 134. Calvin also connected this to atonement with expressions like "Christ is never to be separated from the sacrifice of his death," in his Commentary on Hebrews, found in *Calvin's Commentaries*, 22 vols. (Edinburgh: Calvin Translation Society, 1843–56; repr., Grand Rapids: Baker, 1998), vol. 22, 2:9. For more on this, see the classic study of Calvin's atonement in Paul van Buren, *Christ in Our Place* (Grand Rapids: Eerdmans, 1957).

14. For an introduction to this and other themes in Zwingli, see Bruce Gordon, *Zwingli: God's Armed Prophet* (New Haven, CT: Yale University Press, 2021).

15. For an introduction to this and other themes in Bucer, see Brian Lugioyo, *Martin Bucer's Doctrine of Justication* (New York: Oxford University Press, 2010); Donald K. McKim and Jim West, *Martin Bucer: An Introduction to His Life and Theology* (Eugene, OR: Cascade, 2022).

16. On the theme of conceptual "load-bearing structures" in systematic theology, see Oliver D. Crisp, *Analyzing Doctrine: Toward a Systematic Theology* (Waco: Baylor University Press, 2019).

Christ's Descent into Hell

While certainly not authoritative for all expressions of Christology, emphasizing promeity has become a central theme of modern theology, especially among Reformed and Lutheran theologians. For example, some recent lively discussions of Karl Barth's Christology demonstrate the importance of promeity for his central conviction that God freely elects from all eternity to be incarnate "for us and our salvation" (whatever metaphysical implications for divine life that claim may entail).[17] Another example is Bonhoeffer, who at the end of his life outlined a "religionless" ethic of "being there for others" grounded in the promeitic "for others" life of Jesus.[18]

More specifically, the theme of God's being "for us" in Christ has taken unique shape in the writings of Barth—as well as theologians like Jürgen Moltmann, Alan Lewis, and Hans Urs von Balthasar—each of whom draws special attention to Christ's descent into hell and the cry of dereliction from the cross as a kind of best possible (or at least, most ideal) expression of divine promeity.[19] In fact, using the descent into hell as a shorthand summary for what it means that God has come "for us and our salvation" is a doctrinal gesture common to many Reformation theologians and seems to be a key feature of how the theme operates in theology today. In this paper, we focus specifically on Christ's descent into hell in the theology of John Calvin as an exemplar for clarifying the role of the *descensus* in promeitic Christologies that can apply to modern contexts. This is not because Calvin's *descensus* interpretation is any more valuable than others but simply because his interpretation most succinctly captures the promeitic intuitions our paper explores.

Calvin devotes more space in his *Institutes* to discussing the descent into hell than to any other clause of the Apostles' Creed. His interpretation remained virtually unchanged throughout his life—from his first treatise, the *Psychopannychia*, written in his mid-twenties, through all his commentaries to the final edition of the *Institutes* near his death.[20] For Calvin, it is all

17. Karl Barth, *Church Dogmatics* IV/1, *The Doctrine of Reconciliation*, trans. Geoffrey W. Bromiley (Edinburgh: T&T Clark, 2009). For a very useful summary, see Rowan Williams, *Christ the Heart of Creation* (London: Bloomsbury, 2018), 174–81.

18. Dietrich Bonhoeffer, *Letters and Papers from Prison* (New York: Touchstone, 1997), 381. For a fuller expression of this, see Dietrich Bonhoeffer, *Ethics* (New York: Touchstone, 1995).

19. For a summary and comparison of these theologies, see David Lauber, *Barth on the Descent into Hell* (Farnham: Ashgate, 2004).

20. For a definitive and in-depth exposition of this theme and these points, see Preston McDaniel Hill, *Christ's Descent into Hell and Holy Saturday in the Theology of John Calvin* (London: T&T Clark, forthcoming).

about what he calls "the death of the soul," by which he means a psychological experience of feeling forsaken by God, cut off from flourishing in life, burdened with torment, grief, guilt, sorrow, spiritual anxiety, and the terrors of death itself. In general, the death of the soul is a catchall for any kind of psychological adversity regarding one's spiritual orientation. To call such experiences "hell" is patently not "metaphorical" or "figurative" for Calvin for the simple reason that hell is not ontological at all but completely psychological, as he expressly states in multiple passages. Hell is not a place and does not necessarily correspond to anything in the divine life but is simply the experience of perceiving oneself in an adverse spiritual condition. For Christ to descend into hell, then, is not for Christ to "go" anywhere but simply to have the kind of spiritual experience that humans have in a world that is oriented toward alienation from God. As Calvin memorably states:

> And surely no more terrible abyss can be conceived than to feel yourself forsaken and estranged from God; and when you call upon him, not to be heard. It is as if God himself had plotted your ruin. We see that Christ was so cast down as to be compelled to cry out in deep anguish: "My God, my God, why has thou forsaken me?" . . . His words clearly were drawn forth from anguish deep within his own heart.[21]

Calvin clarifies that Christ experienced this kind of spiritual alienation throughout his incarnate life, culminating in the anxieties of Gethsemane, succinctly expressed in the cry of dereliction from the cross, and even continuing through Holy Saturday until his resurrection from the dead. While this rendering of Calvin's interpretation may seem surprising, a careful reading of his writings makes it quite apparent, as I (Preston) have tried to show in multiple publications.[22]

Interpreted this way, the pastoral significance of the descent into hell was not lost on Calvin. Commenting on what it means that Christ descended into hell "for us and our salvation," Calvin states this of Christ:

---

21. Calvin, *Inst.* 2.16.11.

22. Preston McDaniel Hill, "'The Useful and Not-To-Be-Despised Mystery of a Most Important Matter': The Place of Christ's Descent into Hell in the Theology of John Calvin," in *Calvinus Frater in Domino: Papers of the Twelfth International Congress on Calvin Research*, ed. Arnold Huijgen and Karin Maag (Göttingen: Vandenhoeck & Ruprecht, 2020), 243–55; Preston McDaniel Hill, "The Death of the Soul: Christ's Descent into Hell in the Thought of Calvin, Lefèvre, and Cusa," *Reformation and Renaissance Review* 24, no. 3 (2022): 140–60; Preston McDaniel Hill, "Pastoral Care and Fear of Hell in the Reformed Tradition," in *Calvin, Exile, and Religious Refugees: Papers of the Thirteenth International Congress on Calvin Research*, ed. Karin Maag and Arnold Huijgen (Göttingen: Vandenhoeck & Ruprecht, 2024), 167–80.

> He had, therefore, to conquer that fear which by nature continually torments and oppresses all mortals. This he could only do by fighting it. . . . Therefore, by his wrestling hand to hand with the devil's power, with the dread of death, with the pains of hell, he was victorious and triumphed over them, that in death we may not now fear those things which our Prince has swallowed up.[23]

This passage shows the dual reference to the *status exinanitionis* (the "state of humiliation") and the *status exultationis* (the "state of exaltation") normally operative in Protestant promeities: In his descent into the lowest hell for us, Christ has procured the highest spiritual blessings for us. This brings profound spiritual comfort to those who contemplate the costliness of divine care manifest in Christ's willingness to descend into the same psychological hell as those farthest from God. As Calvin summarizes, "This is our wisdom: duly to consider how much our salvation cost the son of God."[24]

The pastoral significance of this promeitic *descensus* interpretation has trickled down into catechisms and liturgies that continue to define the Reformed tradition. Two examples will suffice. First, the Heidelberg catechism offers a useful summary of the issue:

> **Q 44. Why does the creed add, "He descended to hell"?**
>
> A. To assure me during my attacks of deepest dread and temptation [*Anfechtungen*] that Christ my Lord, by suffering unspeakable anguish, pain, and terror of soul, on the cross but also earlier, has delivered me from hellish anguish and torment.[25]

As this question makes clear, the clause is included in the Christian creed "to assure me" of what Christ has done for me (*pro me*). It is intentionally pastoral and expressly promeitic. A final beautiful expression of this pastoral import can be seen in the order of baptism for children from French reformed liturgies:

> Little child, for you Jesus Christ has come, he has fought, he has suffered. For you he entered the shadow of Gethsemane and the horror of

23. Calvin, *Inst.* 2.16.11.

24. Calvin, *Inst.* 2.16.12.

25. For the English text, see "The Heidelberg Catechism," in *Our Faith: Ecumenical Creeds, Reformed Confessions, and Other Resources* (Grand Rapids: Faith Alive, 2013), Q&A 44, 83; for the German text, see *Der Heidelberger Katechismus und vier verwandte Katechismen*, ed. August Lang (Leipzig: Deichert, 1907), 19.

> Calvary. For you he uttered the cry 'It is finished!' For you he rose from the dead and ascended into heaven and there he intercedes—for you, little child, even though you do not yet know it. But in this way the word of the Gospel becomes true. "We love him, because he first loved us."[26]

Posttraumatic Contexts

While the promeitic significance of the descent into hell may have been obvious to Protestants in the early modern period, using Christology and atonement to express divine promeity seems more tenuous in theology today. Of course, Christian dogmatics today still traditions the affirmation that God's being "for us" is supremely revealed in the death and resurrection of Jesus Christ. However, since at least the late twentieth century, theologians have increasingly recognized clear tensions that arise when classic affirmations about God such as this are set alongside the extremities of human experience.

Jürgen Moltmann, for example, is representative of many theologians who have tried to reformulate Christian doctrine in the aftermath of the atrocities of the past century, such as the Holocaust.[27] While theologians prior to Moltmann, such as Barth and Bonhoeffer, responded to modern violence with theologies of political resistance, womanist and feminist theologians after Moltmann have responded with theologies that deconstruct classic approaches to Christology and atonement. A standard example is the essay "For God So Loved the World?" by Joanne Carlson Brown and Rebecca Parker, in which they bluntly state that

> Christianity is an abusive theology that glorifies suffering. Is it any wonder that there is so much abuse in modern society when the predominant image or theology of the culture is "divine child abuse"—God the Father demanding and carrying out the suffering and death of his own son? If Christianity is to be liberating for the oppressed, it must be liberated from this theology.[28]

---

26. James B. Torrance, *Worship, Community and the Triune God of Grace* (Downers Grove, IL: InterVarsity, 1996), 76.

27. Jürgen Moltmann, *The Crucified God: The Cross of Christ as the Foundation and Criticism of Christian Theology*, trans. R. A. Wilson and John Bowden (New York: Harper & Row, 1974).

28. Joanne Carlson Brown and Rebecca Parker, "For God So Loved the World?," in *Christianity, Patriarchy, and Abuse: A Feminist Critique*, ed. Joanne Carlson Brown and Carole R. Bohn (New York: Pilgrim, 1989), 26.

While this assertion no doubt raises questions about the supposed causal relation between doctrine and social life, it is representative of what Oliver Crisp has called "the problem of atoning violence,"[29] which has been the subject of many well-known proposals in atonement theology.[30] The net result of such approaches to deconstruct dogmatics has been a shift away from dominant atonement narratives that are thought to problematically center either the death of Christ to glorify suffering or the resurrection of Christ to idealize triumph over suffering.[31]

Furthering these intuitions, a new set of voices has emerged in the field of "trauma theology," which draws special attention to the ways psychological trauma raises unique challenges and prospects for classic Christian doctrine.[32] Whereas traditional theologies tend to center Christ's death and resurrection as events that completely assume and heal the wounds of fallen human nature, trauma theologians tend to destabilize this approach by showing that traumatic experiences do not neatly fit this framework. Theologian Shelly Rambo has been especially influential in her approach to trauma:

> Suffering is what, in time, can be integrated into one's understanding of the world. Trauma is what is not integrated in time; it is the difference between a closed and an open wound. Trauma is an open wound. For those who survive trauma, the experience of trauma can be likened to death. But the reality is that death has not ended: instead, it persists.[33]

Following Rambo, we might clarify trauma with this definition: Trauma is any "inescapably stressful event that overwhelms one's coping mechanisms"

---

29. Oliver D. Crisp, *Approaching the Atonement: The Reconciling Work of Jesus Christ* (Downers Grove, IL: InterVarsity, 2020), 131ff.

30. For example, Hans Boersma, *Violence, Hospitality, and the Cross* (Grand Rapids: Baker, 2004); *Stricken by God? Nonviolent Identification and the Victory of Christ*, ed. Brad Jersak and Michael Hardin (Grand Rapids: Eerdmans, 2007); J. Denny Weaver, *The Nonviolent Atonement* (Grand Rapids: Eerdmans, 2011).

31. See this discussed in Preston M. Hill, "Christ's Body Keeps the Score: Trauma-Informed Theology and the Neuroscience of PTSD," *TheoLogica* 7, no. 1 (2023): 102–20.

32. Jennifer Beste, *God and the Victim: Traumatic Intrusions on Grace and Freedom* (New York: Oxford University Press, 2009); Serene Jones, *Trauma and Grace: Theology in a Ruptured World* (Louisville: Westminster John Knox, 2009); Flora Keshegian, *Redeeming Memories: A Theology of Healing and Transformation* (Nashville: Abingdon, 2000); Cynthia Hess, *Sites of Violence: Christian Nonviolence and the Traumatized Self* (Plymouth: Lexington, 2009); Shelly Rambo, *Spirit and Trauma: A Theology of Remaining* (Louisville: Westminster John Knox, 2010); Rambo, *Resurrecting Wounds: Living in the Afterlife of Trauma* (Waco: Baylor University Press, 2018); and Deanna A. Thompson, *Glimpsing Resurrection: Trauma, Cancer, and Ministry* (Louisville: Westminster John Knox, 2018).

33. Rambo, *Spirit and Trauma*, 7.

(such as wartime combat, domestic violence, and childhood sexual abuse) and disables normal human functioning through the classic symptom set of autonomic nervous system hyperarousal, dissociative symptoms, hypervigilant and avoidant behaviors, intrusive thoughts, and intense feelings of rage, terror, and powerlessness.[34] Importantly, these symptoms often persist even after years of treatment and are, therefore, more like a psychiatric disability than a curable disease.[35] However, while disabled individuals may eventually learn to suffer (i.e., to be "longsuffering," to bear with) their disability, posttraumatic life, by definition, is unbearable, intolerable, and insufferable.

Given the uniqueness of trauma, what new challenges or prospects does this experience open for Christian dogmatics? For one, there is an overtly spiritual symptom of the posttraumatic syndrome. Nearly all classical studies of trauma to date note that survivors ubiquitously struggle with finding a sense of meaning, purpose, and connection to God after trauma.[36] This is because the violence they have experienced has overwhelmed normal human biopsychosocial access to confidence in any benevolent divine order in the world. Trauma has "shattered" their assumptions that God can be trusted, or in many cases, that there even is a God to be trusted.[37]

What is worse, many survivors experience profoundly disorienting "spiritual struggles" after trauma, especially if this trauma is perpetrated by religious authorities, in which case they may find themselves burdened with intractable negative beliefs about their own spiritual worth. As Michael Rea and Michelle Panchuk have argued, religious trauma, in particular, may provide reasonable grounds for disbelief in divine goodness and the experience many survivors have of "divine hiddenness."[38] For many, this spiritual aspect of posttraumatic stress represents all that is

---

34. The first part of the definition is taken from *Traumatic Stress: The Effects of Overwhelming Experience on Mind, Body, and Society*, ed. Bessel van der Kolk, Alexander McFarlane, and Lars Weisaeth (New York: Guilford, 2007), 279. For the formal diagnosis, see *Diagnostic and Statistical Manual of Mental Disorders*, 5th ed. (Washington, DC: American Psychiatric Association, 2013).

35. On trauma as a disability, see *Disability and Eschatology: Essays on Hope, Justice, and Flourishing*, ed. Preston McDaniel Hill and Aaron Davis (Lanham, MD: Lexington, 2025).

36. For example, see this theme classically stated in Robert Jay Lifton, "Understanding the Traumatized Self," in *Human Adaptation to Extreme Stress: From the Holocaust to Vietnam*, ed. J. P. Wilson, Z. Harel, and B. Khana (New York: Plenum, 1988); Judith Herman, *Trauma and Recovery* (New York: Basic, 1992); Bessel van der Kolk, *The Body Keeps the Score: Mind, Brain, and Body in the Transformation of Trauma* (New York: Penguin, 2017).

37. R. Janoff-Bulman, *Shattered Assumptions: Toward a New Psychology of Trauma* (New York: Free, 1992).

38. Michael C. Rea, *The Hiddenness of God* (Oxford: Oxford University Press, 2018); Michelle Panchuk, *Religious Trauma* (New York: Cambridge University Press, forthcoming).

opposite to the idea of divine promeity. Instead of God being "for us and our salvation," trauma can cause many survivors not only to doubt divine goodness and promeity but to be acutely stuck in the experience that God is against them, what we could call "divine contrameity."[39] In sum, for traumatized people, God is not just *not* "for me"; God may feel or seem actively "against me." If we combine this with theologies that indicate that the sacrifice of Jesus was to appease an angry and vengeful God, then we can see just how difficult it might be for someone to feel that God is with them and for them in any kind of positive sense.

Toward a Promeitic Christology of Trauma

It is here that we return to Bonhoeffer's timely question: "Who is Christ actually for us, today?"[40] How can Christian dogmatics today develop answers to this question and the contextual appropriation it demands when presented with contexts of trauma and spiritual struggles? Who is Christ "for us and our salvation," and how is God "for me" when trauma intractably shatters my capacity to believe in divine promeity? In short, is it even possible to speak of divine promeity given the traumatic experience of divine contrameity?

While many answers could be provided, we sketch here an initial affirmative answer to this question drawing on and developing Protestant traditions of divine promeity. We think it is possible and plausible to affirm divine promeity even against the backdrop of traumatic doubt for the simple reason that these traditions open dogmatic access to affirmations of God's own experience of divine contrameity.[41]

To understand this, consider again Calvin's promeitic interpretation of the descent into hell: "And surely no more terrible abyss can be conceived than to feel yourself forsaken and estranged from God. . . . It is as if God himself had plotted your ruin."[42] Using our terminology in this paper, Calvin is affirming Christ's experience of divine contrameity. In his

39. *Contrameity* is a term we are coining in this paper. Just as *promeity* comes from the Latin meaning "for me" (*pro me*), so *contrameity* is constructed from the Latin meaning "against me" (*contra me*).

40. Bonhoeffer, *Letters and Papers*, 362.

41. It is important to note that for Calvin, as for majority Christian tradition, Christ's cry of dereliction does not signal any ontological rupture in the Trinity or actual alienation between Christ and the Father. Rather, the cry of dereliction signals the psychological experience of Christ's human nature and perception. Even though he genuinely feels forsaken by God, God has not forsaken him (*Inst.* 2.16.11). For more on this, see Thomas H. McCall, *Forsaken: The Trinity and the Cross, and Why It Matters* (Downers Grove: InterVarsity, 2012).

42. Calvin, *Inst.* 2.16.11.

descent into the psychological state of experiencing alienation from God and all manner of spiritual ills, Christ is having an experience of God's absence and, as such, is undergoing an experience not dissimilar from the spiritual experience of trauma survivors. Equivocating and anachronizing, we might say that Christ is experiencing traumatic spirituality.[43]

But note that, for Calvin as for the broader Protestant intuitions he represents, Christ's experience of divine contrameity is the atoning mechanism for communicating divine promeity. We cite again from the same passage in the *Institutes*:

> We must with assurance, therefore, confess Christ's sorrow, as Ambrose rightly teaches, unless we are ashamed of the cross. . . . His goodness—never sufficiently praised—shines in this: he did not shrink from taking our weakness upon himself. Hence, it nowise detracts from his heavenly glory. . . . There is no reason why Christ's weakness should alarm us. For he was not compelled by violence or necessity, but was induced purely by his love for us and by his mercy to submit to it.[44]

According to Calvin, Christ's experience of divine contrameity is the strongest possible evidence of divine promeity because Christ himself is God. We might say that, according to Protestant traditions of interpreting the *descensus* promeitically, in Jesus Christ God's coming for us and our salvation are supremely revealed by God's willingness to descend into our condition of experiencing what it is like to feel God against us. The divine willingness to experience divine contrameity with us is itself evidence of promeity, that God is for us. God has felt God's absence with us, and this can be a form of God's presence for us.

This insight has significant implications for reframing normative expectations for religious life today. If God is for us in Christ, and the manner of God's demonstrating such promeity is through Christ's experiences of spiritual struggle, doubt, disbelief, and even divine hiddenness, then what follows is that such experiences in themselves are not immediate

---

43. It is important to note that the term *contrameity* as we use it does not necessitate that someone feel that God is actively "against" them. It might be the case that they simply feel the absence of God and experience a sense of disconnection and dislocation in their relationship with the divine. Such experiences would also be a kind of contrameity as we are using the term. Our essay does not specify the exact "kind" of mental experience of contrameity in view since we do not have direct access to the mental life of Christ during his passion. But at the very least, our work is using the term *contrameity* to indicate the general disconnected orientation of Christ signified in his cry of dereliction.

44. Calvin, *Inst.* 2.16.12.

evidence of a lack of faith in the life of trauma survivors. This is because, as Calvin states, despite all his experience of divine hiddenness and contrameity, Christ was still morally perfect and free of any spiritual state of sin. Perhaps paradoxically—and profoundly comforting to survivors—God's manner of expressing promeity in Christ opens the possibility to affirm that doubting divine goodness under extreme spiritual stress is not immediate evidence that survivors are outside the range of normative religious experience. God can be for us even when God feels against us because in Christ God has assumed even that feeling itself.

This gesture toward a promeitic Christology of trauma does not answer all questions opened by traumatic experience. The applied and practical question still remains how survivors can actually access the fact of this promeity in their own lived experience. Furthermore, there are questions from classic dogmatics about the viability of attributing such experiences to Christ and whether Christ can doubt divine goodness and still be morally perfect. Nevertheless, as we have shown, there are resources at the very heart of Christian dogma that can be developed to address advancements in our understanding of human illness and flourishing. In particular, trauma presents unique challenges to Christian faith. But to answer Bonhoeffer's question, we might say that Christ today is the one who has come not only "for us and our salvation" but more specifically even "for us and our trauma."

Pastoral Implications: A God Who Knows Our Darkness

The theological exploration of Christ's descent into hell as an experience of divine contrameity offers profound pastoral implications for those grappling with trauma and spiritual struggles. It dismantles the harmful expectation that faith necessitates a constant and unwavering feeling of God's presence. Instead, it normalises doubt, fear, and the feeling of abandonment by God as legitimate experiences within the Christian life, even mirroring Christ's own journey.

In particular, the exploration of promeitic Christology through the lens of trauma offers profound pastoral implications that can significantly enhance pastoral care and ministry. By understanding Christ's descent into hell as an experience of psychological and spiritual anguish akin to trauma, pastors and caregivers are better equipped to offer empathetic and nuanced support to those grappling with traumatic experiences.

First, by emphasizing Calvin's interpretation of Christ's cry of dereliction as an experience of traumatic disbelief, pastors can help validate the spiritual struggles of trauma survivors. This perspective allows for a more compassionate approach to those experiencing doubt or feelings of divine abandonment, framing these experiences as part of the human condition that even Christ himself encountered. It normalizes doubt, fear, and the feeling of abandonment by God as legitimate experiences within the Christian life, mirroring Christ's journey. Second, the paper's suggestion that traumatic experiences of doubt or divine hiddenness are not necessarily evidence of an absence of faith provides a powerful tool for pastoral counseling. This reframing challenges the binary of "positive" and "negative" religious experiences, allowing for a more inclusive understanding of faith that acknowledges the complexities of human experience, particularly in the aftermath of trauma. It empowers survivors to engage their spiritual struggles authentically, finding meaning and connection with God within their pain.

Moreover, understanding trauma as potentially causing spiritual injury allows pastors to approach healing holistically. By recognizing that trauma can affect one's relationship with God and spiritual well-being, ministers can integrate spiritual care more effectively into trauma recovery processes. This understanding fosters a theology of radical empathy, enabling pastors and caregivers to approach survivors with compassionate understanding, acknowledging the depths of human suffering, including spiritual anguish, within the divine experience itself.

This essay's critique of theologies that glorify suffering or idealize triumph over suffering provides pastors with a framework to combat potentially harmful religious narratives. This can aid in developing more trauma-informed approaches to ministry and preaching, ensuring that theological reflections do not inadvertently perpetuate harm. Pastors can emphasize the ongoing nature of trauma recovery, encouraging the development of long-term support systems within faith communities, and shifting the focus from quick fixes to sustained, compassionate care. The promeitic understanding of Christ's descent into hell can also inform more meaningful liturgical and sacramental practices. For instance, baptismal liturgies could be crafted to emphasize God's presence even in the darkest human experiences. This enriched liturgical practice can help congregants experience a deeper sense of God's solidarity with human suffering.

Finally, the insights from this chapter could be integrated into pastoral education programs, equipping future religious leaders with a more nuanced understanding of trauma and its intersection with faith and spirituality. This approach allows for a theology that is deeply rooted in tradition and responsive to contemporary human experiences, offering hope and validation to those wrestling with the aftermath of traumatic events. This work invites a shift in pastoral care from a focus on fixing or resolving spiritual struggles to a posture of compassionate accompaniment. It encourages faith communities to journey alongside those experiencing trauma and doubt, creating spaces where vulnerability is met with understanding and where even the darkest experiences can become points of connection with a God who knows our suffering intimately.[45]

---

45. This research is made possible by a generous grant from the John Templeton Foundation (Grant ID: 62952, "Spiritual First Responders Project"), which explores avenues for spiritual flourishing and mental health among those experiencing a putative loss of religious commitment. Preston McDaniel Hill is the grant project leader, and John Swinton is the theological consultant.

CHAPTER 11

AULÉN'S ACCOMPLISHED AND ONGOING ATONEMENT AS A RESOURCE FOR CONSTRUCTIVE THEOLOGY

SARAH SHIN

Gustaf Aulén is most well-known for his articulation of the *Christus victor* idea of atonement, which understands Christ's work on the cross as God's triumph over the inimical forces of sin, death, and the devil that hold humankind in bondage.[1] His book *Christus Victor* brought to prominence the concept of three "main" types of atonement: satisfaction, moral exemplar, and *Christus victor.*[2] Both Aulén's tripartite typology and his *Christus victor* articulation have received warranted critique and rebuttal. However, Aulén offers an unusual and underattended view of atonement as both accomplished once and for all through Christ's work at the cross and also ongoing through the Spirit in this time and this place. I suggest that Aulén's conception of atonement, as both accomplished and ongoing, offers resources for speaking of God's activity in delivering us from evil and also for envisioning human participation in God's delivering action, towards an eschatological horizon and ethic that robustly resist evil in the present.

In this essay, I first briefly summarize Aulén's three-agent soteriology, known as *Christus victor.* Noting criticisms that have been raised about the *Christus victor* idea of atonement and also about Aulén's tripartite taxonomy,

1. Gustaf Aulén, *Christus Victor: An Historical Study of the Three Main Types of the Idea of the Atonement,* trans. A. G. Hebert (London: SPCK, 2010), 146.

2. When speaking of the book, I capitalize both words: *Christus Victor.* When speaking of the view of atonement, I use *Christus victor.*

I discuss where his later work fills in gaps and answers some, though not all, critiques. After observing that soteriology is also understood as a three-agent drama in apocalyptic Pauline studies and apocalyptic theology, I demonstrate how Aulén's account of accomplished and ongoing atonement offers valuable resources for speaking of God's activity for us today and also of human participation in God's delivering work. I close by suggesting some ways to thicken Aulén's account of human participation.

I. AULÉN'S *CHRISTUS VICTOR* AND THE "THREE TYPES"

Aulén's book was originally titled in Swedish as *Den Kristna Gudsbilden Genom Tiderna och i Nutiden* ("The Christian Image of God through the Ages and Today").[3] It was translated instead as *Christus Victor: A Historical Study of the Three Main Types of the Idea of the Atonement*—and this English title retains influence today. Aulén sought to bring renewed attention to the biblical theme of victory over the devil, which had not been addressed in discussions of atonement in Western theological discourse since the eighteenth century. His claim was that the image of God, particularly as rendered in interpretations of atonement, cannot be coherent without reference to the battle imagery and language of victory in Scripture. Aulén's goal was not to provide a complete account of atonement; instead, it was to point to this *idea*—that Christ's death on the cross must be understood as a climatic victory over evil in God's battle against inimical domination.

I briefly name some objections that have been raised about Aulén's taxonomy of atonement as well as about *Christus victor.* Oliver Crisp, Adam Johnson, and Bruce McCormack are among several who have rightly protested Aulén's tripartite typology. There exists a greater diversity and more interconnected themes than are represented in these three discrete types; furthermore, Aulén erroneously groups together certain thinkers and mischaracterizes Schleiermacher as a moral exemplarist.[4] Others have aptly pointed out that in the *Christus victor* idea of atonement, it is not always clear how victory over the devil is connected to sacrifice. The result

3. Gustaf Aulén, *The Drama and Symbols* (London, SPCK: 1970), ix.

4. See Oliver Crisp, *Approaching the Atonement: The Reconciling Work of Christ* (Downers Grove, IL: IVP Academic, 2020), 173; see also Adam Johnson, "Theories and Theoria of the Atonement: A Proposal," *International Journal of Systematic Theology* 23, no. 1 (2021): 98–100; see also Bruce McCormack, "Atonement," in *The Cambridge Dictionary of Christian Theology*, ed. Ian A. McFarland, David A. S. Fergusson, Karen Kilby, and Iain R. Torrance (Cambridge: Cambridge University Press, 2011), 43.

then is that it is also unclear how *Christus victor* deals with the problem of human sin and thereby leaves the sinner unreconciled to God.[5]

I demonstrate how Aulén's later work informs our understanding of how he might respond to the aforementioned warranted criticisms. As for the first critique about the problems in his taxonomy of atonement ideas, Aulén admits to the flaws in his characterizations of medieval and post-Reformation scholasticism; however, he stands behind his insistence that a dramatic outlook is critical to understanding atonement.[6] For Aulén, taking out the drama in which atonement is the climatic center distorts the image of God.

The second critique—about the lack of clarity in explaining how victory over the devil is linked to sacrifice—is appropriate to Aulén's earlier presentation of *Christus victor.* Though he later fills out his description of sacrifice and substitution as part of *Christus victor,* Aulén's initial presentation of *Christus victor* was, he admitted, not a complete account of atonement. His book *Christus Victor* erred on emphasizing victory over death at the expense of a more detailed account of why Christ's death is necessary for reconciliation. Such emphasis on victory over the devil is what has been carried forward in the reception of *Christus victor.* This emphasis on victory, without a stronger connection to the sacrifice that addresses the human sin that separates the human person from God, leaves *Christus victor* open to interpretation that departs from Aulén's original intention—including appropriation by those such as J. Denny Weaver who wish to focus on victory over the powers while rejecting sacrifice as part of atonement.[7]

As for Aulén's own account of *Christus victor,* what is important to emphasize is that Aulén is not opposed to the idea of the expiation of sin in his desire to emphasize and recover the idea of victory over the devil. In his description of divine love overcoming divine wrath through the sacrifice of Christ, Aulén demurs from trying to rationalize how Christ's death satisfies God's love, overcomes God's wrath, and realizes a victory. In the biblical witness, *it just is* that reconciliation through sacrifice and victory

5. See Crisp, *Approaching Atonement,* 54. See also Thomas Schreiner, "Penal Substitution Response," in *The Nature of the Atonement,* ed. James Beilby and Paul R. Eddy (Downers Grove, IL: IVP Academic, 2006), 52. See also Bruce R. Reichenbach, "Healing Response," in *Nature of the Atonement,* 54, 60.

6. Aulén, *Drama and Symbols,* ix.

7. J. Denny Weaver's rendering of atonement adopts the label *Christus victor* but rejects sacrifice and death as necessary for forgiveness of sin. Weaver also resists understanding the devil or Satan as a personified being—powers and principalities are for him spiritual dimensions of material structures. On all these counts, Weaver's account differs substantially from Aulén. See J. Denny Weaver, *Nonviolent Atonement* (Grand Rapids: Eerdmans, 2011), 306–9.

come together. In his effort to counter the preponderance of theology which excludes speech about victory over the devil and in his resistance to a rationalizing theory, Aulén provides little description of why death is necessary for forgiveness and reconciliation. This thinness in explanation is to some extent addressed in his later writings on sin as solidarity and on salvation as mediation offered by God through Christ's sacrifice and victory over the devil. However, even there, it is not always clear how *Christus victor* deals with individual human sin and accountability before God, and thus the relationship between victory and sacrifice remains to be explained further.[8]

Despite the gaps in Aulén's account of sacrifice and victory, he finds shared company with apocalyptic Pauline scholars who also envisage soteriology as a three-agent drama. Ernst Käsemann, J. Louis Martyn, and Beverly Gaventa are among many who have emphasized the apocalyptic gospel and Christ's contestation of the powers of sin, death, and the devil.[9] Noting that both Aulén and the apocalyptic Pauline school speak of soteriology as a three-agent drama, Philip Ziegler, who also conceives of soteriology as a three-agent drama, writes that Aulén "recommends the apocalyptic discourse of *Christus victor* in part because of its power to demythologize our all-too-human sense that sees us, wrongly and desperately, as the only agents on the field of history."[10]

Aulén's willingness to link victory to sacrifice also differs from a tendency that Grant Macaskill observes—and resists—in apocalyptic Pauline discourse: the positioning of forensic covenant language in Torah against the apocalyptic and mystical.[11] Jamie Davies likewise warns against the tendency in apocalyptic discourse to take what Martinus de Boer presented as two tracks, the "cosmological apocalyptic" (following Ernst Käsemann) and the "forensic apocalyptic" (following Rudolf Bultmann), and to present them as more antithetical to the other than de Boer ever

---

8. This deficit in Aulén's construction can also be seen indirectly in Fleming Rutledge's account of the crucifixion. Though Rutledge is largely in favor of Aulén's *Christus victor* idea, she reaches for Anselm's view of sin as debt in order to address what she appears to perceive as a gap in Aulén's *Christus victor*, as well as in certain apocalyptic Pauline accounts: the idea of sin as responsible guilt for which rectifying reparation must be made. See Fleming Rutledge, *The Crucifixion: Understanding the Death of Jesus Christ* (Grand Rapids: Eerdmans, 2015), 147, 152.

9. See Ernst Käsemann, *On Being a Disciple of the Crucified Nazarene*, ed. Rudolf Landau and Wolfgang Kraus, trans. Roy A. Harrisville (Grand Rapids: Eerdmans, 2010), 7–8; J. Louis Martyn, "The Apocalyptic Gospel in Galatians," *Interpretation* 54, no. 3 (2000): 246–64; Beverly Gaventa, *Our Mother St. Paul* (Louisville: Westminster John Knox, 2007), 81. See also Philip Ziegler, *Militant Grace* (Grand Rapids: Baker Academic, 2018), xv, 20.

10. Philip Ziegler, "Christ Must Reign: Ernst Käsemann and Soteriology in an Apocalyptic Key," in *Apocalyptic and the Future of Theology*, ed. Joshua B. Davis and Douglas Harink (Eugene [OR]: Cascade Books, 2012), 216.

11. Grant Macaskill, *Union with Christ in the New Testament* (Oxford: Oxford Academic, 2013), 305.

intended, resulting in reductionistic tendencies on "zero-sum" terms.[12] Davies instead commends approaching apocalyptic accounts of Christ's saving work in a noncompetitive "complex-multi-level manner" as recognizing both forensic and cosmological deliverance.[13]

Ziegler, Susan Eastman, and Macaskill are among several who, like Aulén, conceive of Christ's sacrifice and victory as both forensic forgiveness and cosmological deliverance, albeit each in their own manner.[14] They demonstrate that forensic forgiveness and cosmological deliverance need not be pitted against each other; instead, they can work together noncompetitively in a three-agent soteriology. These thinkers demonstrate the possibility of cohering sacrifice and victory in an account of atonement that emphasizes God's battle against and victory over the third agent. Insight from these scholars may help to address gaps in Aulén's account. While constructing that deeper connection between victory and sacrifice is beyond the scope of this essay, these scholars demonstrate the possibility of a way forward.

II. Accomplished and Ongoing Atonement

I now move to present a possible resource in Aulén's theology: his underattended claim that atonement is both accomplished and ongoing. Aulén contends that the biblical message is that "the Atonement is not only an act in the past, but also a *continuous* work."[15] To unpack its meaning, this distinctive assertion requires an explanation of how Aulén conceives of atonement, sin, and contemporaneity.

A. Aulén's Conception of Atonement

First, Aulén seems to use *atonement* in the widest possible sense of the word, "at-one-ment,"[16] to speak of God's reconciliation with human

12. Jamie Davies, "The Justice and Deliverance of God: Integrating Forensic and Cosmological in the 'Apocalyptic Paul,'" *Currents in Biblical Research* 21, no. 1 (2022): 78–88. See also Martinus de Boer, "Paul and Jewish Apocalyptic Eschatology," in *Apocalyptic and the New Testament: Essays in Honor of J. Louis Martyn*, ed. Martyn J. Marcus and M. Soards (Sheffield: JSOT, 1989), 169–90.

13. Davies, "Justice and Deliverance of God," 85.

14. Philip Ziegler, "'Bound Over to Satan's Tyranny': Sin and Satan in Contemporary Reformed Hamartiology," *Theology Today* 75, no. 1 (2018): 94. See also Davies, "The Justice and Deliverance of God," 85.

15. Gustaf Aulén, "Chaos and Cosmos: The Drama of the Atonement," *Interpretation* 4, no. 2 (1950): 166, emphasis mine.

16. The hyphenated "at-one-ment" is employed to speak of the larger meaning of atonement and discussions of the matter by scholars throughout the *T&T Clark Companion to Atonement*, whether with reference to thinkers such as Thomas Aquinas, Colin Gunton, and Oliver Crisp, or themes such as covenant and the question of evil. See *T&T Clark Companion to Atonement*, ed. Adam J. Johnson (London: Bloomsbury Academic, 2017).

persons, without letting go of the sacrificial act of Christ's death on the cross. Second, atonement, as a drama involving three agents, is an *ongoing* drama. Sin, death, and Satan, though judged, have not disappeared. God's redemptive work in Christ is both a once-and-for-all completed work—and also an ongoing work that will continue until the last battle is complete.[17] God's victory over the powers is not merely something that occurred and belongs to the past, but it is also something that happens "continuously, daily, and spiritually" in every Christian.[18]

Aulén's capacious conception of atonement, as inclusive of sacrifice but also continuing, shares common ground with Stephen B. Chapman's protest against the problematic conflation of "the terminology and procedures of priestly sacrifices" with the wider theme of reconciliation and redemption in Scripture.[19] Chapman argues that reconciliation cannot be understood without atonement, and the narrower sense of atonement should be recognized as "part and parcel of this larger sphere of reconciliation" that is the redemption of all things.[20] Chapman's presentation of atonement would comport well with that of Aulén and apocalyptic Pauline scholars who bring together forensic apocalyptic and cosmological apocalyptic themes.

B. Aulén's Conception of Sin

Second, it helps here to understand Aulén's account of sin. Following Luther, Aulén defines sin as the perversion of the will and the dominion which keeps the will in bondage. Sin is not finitude or imperfection.[21] Aulén contends that framing sin as finitude presents an unbridgeable gap between the finite and the infinite, rendering fellowship with God impossible.[22] He argues further that original sin is not about the transference of a discrete, tainted, or purely physical quality.[23] Original sin instead is about the interrelatedness of sin: Individual, specific actions are related to and rooted in the perversion of the human will, and this sinful will for

---

17. Gustaf Aulén, *Faith of the Christian Church*, trans. Eric H. Walhstrom (Philadelphia: Muhlenberg, 1960), 68.

18. Aulén, *Faith of the Christian Church*, 68.

19. Stephen B. Chapman, "Reconciling Work: Atonement in the Old Testament," in *T&T Clark Companion to Atonement*, 96.

20. Chapman, "Reconciling Work," 96–97.

21. Aulén, *Faith of the Christian Church*, 88.

22. Aulén, *Faith of the Christian Church*, 88.

23. Aulén, *Faith of the Christian Church*, 90. He writes, "Ever since the days of Augustine the concept of original sin has tended to relate sin to the purely physical and has thereby obscured the nature of sin as volition and as a corruption of the will. When this occurs, the concept no longer serves to deepen the perception of sin, but rather injects into it an element foreign to faith."

each person always exists in the "context of comprehensive human interrelationships."[24] As such, all sin is original sin; actual sin is the "external manifestation of original sin."[25] There exists a solidarity of humanity as a whole in sin, as all are in bondage to the dominion of sin as a power.[26] Thus, sin includes but extends beyond individual acts and individual will; sin is also about the interconnected relationships, the social conditions that "surround and determine" humans—as well as the demonic power that holds dominion over the individual.[27]

Aulén's realism about the devil is connected to a multilayered account of sin as personal, corporate, and cosmological. This is in contrast to commonplace practice in Reformed teaching, which acknowledges the devil but places emphasis upon the individual without engaging the corporate aspects of sin, and it is also in contrast to nonapocalyptic views which present accounts of social sin but reject speech about the devil.[28] Instead, Aulén creatively brings together the individual, corporate, and cosmological aspects of sin.

C. *Aulén's Deployment of Contemporaneity*

Third, Aulén utilizes the term *contemporaneity* to speak of the ongoing work of atonement—without mention of Søren Kierkegaard, who famously utilized the concept to speak of the Christian as a contemporary of Christ.[29] I will discuss how contemporaneity is deployed by Kierkegaard and some of his heirs before I explain Aulén's own creative use of contemporaneity in his discussion of the work of atonement.

Kierkegaard presents the Christian life as that which is contemporary with Christ's life on earth.[30] He writes, "But as long as there is a believer,

24. Aulén, *Faith of the Christian Church*, 89.

25. Aulén, *Faith of the Christian Church*, 89. He observes, "Sinfulness does not belong simply to separate individuals; it is characteristic of the whole human race. Individual man as a member of society participates in the sinfulness of the race. This brings to the fore the idea of the inevitability of sin. Man stands by inner necessity under the power of sin. The context of sin surrounds him and determines his life," *Faith of the Christian Church*, 89.

26. Aulén, *Faith of the Christian Church*, 89.

27. Aulén, *Faith of the Christian Church*, 89.

28. Schleiermacher is a prime example of a theologian whose account of social sin rejects discussion of the devil. See Friedrich Schleiermacher, *The Christian Faith* (London: Bloomsbury T&T Clark, 2016), trans. H. R. Mackintosh et al., §44.1, 161 and §71.2, 287–89.

29. Joshua Cockayne provides a helpful summary of Kierkegaard's view of Christian contemporaneity with Christ's life upon earth. See Joshua Cockayne, "Imitation and Contemporaneity: Kierkegaard and the Imitation of Christ," *British Journal for the History of Philosophy* 25, no. 1 (2017): 41.

30. Cockayne writes, "Kierkegaard tells us that this enigmatic concept is the 'decisive point' of his life's work, and he urges his reader to '[p]ay sharp attention to the matter of contemporaneity.'" Cockayne, "Imitation and Contemporaneity," 41.

this person . . . must be just as contemporary with Christ's presence as his contemporaries were. This contemporaneity is the condition of faith, and, more sharply defined, it is faith."[31] Without offering any detail on how this is possible, Kierkegaard asserts that the Christian, in her time and place, is connected to Christ's life.[32] This is not a historical contemporaneity but a genuine contemporaneity—and as such the contemporary disciple is at no greater distance from Christ than the disciples who saw Jesus face-to-face in the gospels.[33]

Discussions of contemporaneity that emerge after Kierkegaard are usually located within Christology.[34] As an example, Dietrich Bonhoeffer affirms that the presence of Jesus Christ in the church is possible "at a particular time and place," that Christ is contemporary with us, because as human, Jesus Christ is in time and space, and as God, he is eternally present.[35] Lea Weber demonstrates Kierkegaard's influence on Bonhoeffer's Christology, including the theme of contemporaneity, with the key difference that for Bonhoeffer, contemporaneity is possible through the resurrection.[36] Christopher Holmes presents how Paul Lehmann and Bonhoeffer both attend to contemporaneity and the ongoing activity of God in Jesus Christ in discussions of Christology.[37] Ziegler explains how the concept of promeity in Kierkegaard is closely tied to Kierkegaard's emphasis on contemporaneity—and how, in the christological accounts of both Kierkegaard and Bonhoeffer, the promeity of Christ offers "a powerful conceptual gloss on the identity" of the God who is for us and our salvation in the midst of our life today.[38]

---

31. Søren Kierkegaard, *Practice in Christianity*, ed. and trans. Howard V. Hong and Edna H. Hong, Kierkegaard's Writings 20 (Princeton, NJ: Princeton University Press, 1991), 9.

32. Cockayne notes that despite the prominence of contemporaneity in Kierkegaard's work, a clear definition is never offered on how the bridging of two thousand millennia is possible, "Imitation and Contemporaneity," 42.

33. Cockayne, "Imitation and Contemporaneity," 43.

34. Lea Weber writes, "Since the *Fragments*, contemporaneity has remained Kierkegaard's 'signature category' in Christological discourse, containing his existential objective in a nutshell." Weber, "Kierkegaard's and Bonhoeffer's Paradox Christology," in *Bonhoeffer and Christology: Revisiting Chalcedon*, ed. Matthias Grebe, Nadine Hamilton, and Christian Schlenker (London: Bloomsbury, 2024), 53.

35. See Dietrich Bonhoeffer, "Lectures on Christology," in *Berlin: 1932–1933*, ed. Larry Rasmussen, trans. Isabel Best and David Higgins (Minneapolis: Fortress, 2009), 334. See also M. Jenson, "Real Presence: Contemporaneity in Bonhoeffer's Christology," *Scottish Journal of Theology* 58, no. 2 (2005): 143–60.

36. Weber, "Kierkegaard's and Bonhoeffer's Paradox Christology," 53.

37. Christopher J. Holmes, "The Contemporaneity of God for Ethics Today: Paul Lehmann's Contribution to a Neglected Theme, in Dialogue with Dietrich Bonhoeffer," *Studies in Christian Ethics* 23, no. 3 (2010): 285.

38. Philip Ziegler, "Christ for us Today—Promeity in the Christologies of Bonhoeffer and Kierkegaard," *International Journal of Systematic Theology* 15, no. 1 (2013): 28, 40–41.

In a slight but significant alteration from Kierkegaard, Aulén's deployment of contemporaneity happens in his discussion of atonement—as both a once-and-for-all accomplished work in Christ and also an ongoing, continuous work of *Christus Kyrios* (the risen Christ) and the Spirit of the risen Christ.[39] Aulén writes:

> Christ is continually engaged in his work of revelation and reconciliation in the world. The victory over the forces hostile to God is won anew in a renewed struggle. Christian faith expresses this *contemporaneous* aspect of the work of Christ both by confessing him as Kyrios, the risen, living and active Victor; and by its proclamation of the work of the Holy Spirit who is also the Spirit of Christ.[40]

It is in this ongoing atonement, in the work of the risen Christ and the Spirit, that the Christian experiences contemporaneity.

D. Accomplished and Ongoing Atonement

In Aulén's account of atonement, which he describes as God's reconciling and making himself one with human persons, the continuing activity of God is essentially connected to the finished work: "It is precisely this finished act which in the present is continually realized anew."[41] The completed and once-and-for-all finished work of Christ does not merely establish "the condition for the coming of the Spirit"—it is also "a continuing work in 'the Spirit.'"[42] If Kierkegaardian contemporaneity conceives of the Christian as contemporary with *Christ's life* on earth, in contrast Aulén utilizes contemporaneity to speak of the believer as contemporary with Christ's victory through the ongoing work of the Spirit, in *our time* and *our place.*

Thus, Aulén makes the striking claim that not only is atonement the victory that Christ gained over the inimical powers once-and-for-all, but this victory is also continued and seen in the work of the Holy Spirit. The atonement is not only a once-and-for-all completed work but "also a work that is continued until the last judgment, the church of Christ being the instrument of this work."[43] He writes,

---

39. I offer here a brief distinction between the two connected themes: Christology focuses on the person of Christ, and atonement, while overlapping with Christology, discusses how the triune God offers reconciliation and redemption through the life, death, and resurrection of Jesus Christ.

40. Aulén, *Faith of the Christian Church*, 68, emphasis mine.

41. Aulén, *Faith of the Christian Church*, 69.

42. Aulén, *Faith of the Christian Church*, 83.

43. Aulén, "Chaos and Cosmos," 157.

> The drama is not ended. The conditions of the fight have been radically changed. But the fight is going on between the two dominions—God's fight against the powers of resistance and destruction. And thereby the Spirit of God has the same hard work to do with every new generation and every new [hu]man. The drama will continue until finally the last great act, the greatest, comes.[44]

Aulén's presentation of atonement as an ongoing work points to the Spirit as the agent who continues God's battle in every context. Aulén holds to the inimitable, one-time act of Christ's redemptive work through the cross and resurrection while also insisting upon the ongoing reality of inimical evil that resists the victory of God—but will one day be defeated in totality. Emphasizing the not-yet-ended drama acknowledges that evil still lingers despite the reality of the cross, as church and world history of the past two thousand years can confirm. The Spirit continues the fight in each time and place, as God's activity in the present, in the work that is ever new.[45]

For Aulén, faith, as understood in this three-agent drama, is always in the present tense.[46] He rejects viewing redemption as an event that happened "once and for all" because there is no place for the *now*, the present time, in such a conception.[47] Christian faith is involvement, a relationship of trust and obedience towards God, who is ever at work in his ongoing resistance against the powers that would enslave, and the Spirit continues this divine resistance against the enslaving powers.[48] This involvement takes place "in time and space, 'now and here'—in *this world* where the human lives, in *this time* which is now."[49]

III. Valuable Elements for Constructive Theology

With Aulén's understanding of accomplished and ongoing atonement thus summarized, I name two ways in which Aulén's account offers resources for

---

44. Aulén, "Chaos and Cosmos," 167.
45. Aulén, *Drama and Symbols*, 51.
46. Aulén, *Drama and Symbols*, 52.
47. Aulén, *Drama and Symbols*, 50.
48. Aulén, *Drama and Symbols*, 45.
49. Aulén, *Drama and Symbols*, 48–49, emphasis mine. However, Aulén specifies in the same breath that this God who is involved "is raised above the world of finitude and over the limits of time." To have faith is to have fellowship with God, to share in what belongs to God—"to be anchored in the world of eternity." Eschatology refers not only to future and coming promise but also to God's activity here and now. Aulén, *Drama and Symbols*, 49.

constructive theology today: an account of God's activity for us, here and now, and an account of human participation in God's delivering action.

A. First Resource: An Account of God's Activity for Us Today

First, by ascribing ongoing atonement, the continuing of battle and establishing of victory to the Spirit's work, Aulén provides an account of God's activity for us, here and now, as the believer faces particular suffering, evil, and challenges. This is anchored to Christ's inimitable accomplished work of redemption on the cross but continues through the Spirit. However, by locating the Spirit's work of ongoing atonement in the present and particular context of every Christian and church, Aulén is able to speak of God's activity confronting the ongoing reality of inimical evil that resists the victory of God but will one day be defeated in totality. In keeping with his desire to reflect Scripture's speech about the image of God and the New Testament witness to the reality of spiritual battle against a third agent, Aulén presents an account of God's activity that emphasizes the Spirit's work in that battle today.

I gesture here, through a number of brief sketches, at how Aulén might contrast with other figures in modern theology. Aulén's inflected response to Bonhoeffer's question "Who is Christ really for us today?"[50] might be somewhere along these lines: "The One who has delivered me from sin, death, and the devil, and the One who through his Spirit continues to deliver me."[51] For Aulén, God's being for us and Christ's being for us are real in the human present through the Spirit's continuing work of deliverance for us. Aulén's conception of the Spirit's active role in ongoing atonement differs from Bonhoeffer, whose emphasis is upon Christ "existing as church-community" and of Christ being visibly present in Word, sacrament, and church community.[52] While not inimical to Bonhoeffer's emphasis on Christ, Aulén seems to speak of God's activity in ways that do not always fit neatly into Bonhoeffer's presentation of the Christ reality.[53]

It is not Christology that drives Aulén's account of God's present

50. Dietrich Bonhoeffer to Eberhard Bethge, April 20, 1944, in *Letters and Papers from Prison*, ed. John W. De Gruchy, trans. Isabel Best, Lisa E. Dahill, Reinhard Krauss, and Nancy Lukens (Minneapolis: Fortress, 2010), 387.

51. Another way to say this would be: Jesus Christ is for me at the cross and also in the Spirit's work of establishing the victory over the powers of sin, death, and devil here today.

52. Dietrich Bonhoeffer, *Sanctorum Communio*, ed. Clifford J. Green, trans. Reinhard Krauss and Nancy Lukens (Minneapolis: Fortress, 1998), 305; Bonhoeffer, "Lectures on Christology," 339. See also Dietrich Bonhoeffer, *Discipleship*, ed. Geffrey B. Kelly and John D. Godsey, trans. Barbara Green and Reinhard Krauss (Minneapolis: Fortress, 2000), 201–20.

53. Bonhoeffer writes in "Christ, Reality and Good" that "I find the reality of the world always already borne, accepted, and reconciled in the reality of God. That is the mystery of the revelation

delivering action, but ongoing atonement through the Spirit. For Aulén, the Spirit is the one who makes the objective presence of the crucified and victorious Christ known to us; human subjective experiences do not establish the veracity of the Spirit's work. From within his view of ongoing atonement, Aulén insists on knowing Christ's being for us not only through the lens of Christ's past suffering for us but also in light of Christ's ongoing victory which is being fought and won in each generation. Here, Aulén eschews speaking of the Spirit's work as the "subjective realisation of objectively accomplished reconciliation" (to use Barth's language).[54] Instead, the Spirit's role extends beyond the subjective dimensions of faith, into the continuing work of Christ in this time and place, through the Spirit.[55] While Barth asserts, "To say atonement is to say Jesus Christ. To speak of it is to speak of His history,"[56] Aulén's inflection might say something more akin to this: "To say atonement is to say Jesus Christ and the Holy Spirit. To speak of it is to speak of His history and His present activity."

Aulén is not alone in seeking to broaden speech about the Spirit's work. Cornelis van der Kooi has observed the Reformed tradition's tendency to focus the work of the Spirit on conversion and personal holiness. He charges that Jürgen Moltmann and Wolfhart Pannenberg hesitate to speak of healing and that they "defend the idea that the future is already present here, but instead of becoming concrete, they remain stuck in generalities, if not obfuscations."[57] This is a striking critique given the criticisms of both Moltmann and Pannenberg that Barth's transcendental conception of God leads to issues in addressing eschatology.[58] Moving beyond this gap and in a manner consonant with Aulén's emphasis on the Spirit's delivering activity today, van der Kooi commends the Pentecostal

---

of God in the human being Jesus Christ." Bonhoeffer, *Ethics*, ed. Clifford J. Green, trans. Reinhard Krauss, Charles C. West, and Douglas W. Stott (Minneapolis: Fortress, 2005), 69.

54. Barth speaks of the Holy Spirit as the power which effects the "*subjective realisation* of the reconciliation" between God and humanity. See Karl Barth, *Church Dogmatics*, ed. G. W. Bromiley and T. F. Torrance, trans. G. W. Bromiley (Edinburgh: T&T Clark, 1956), IV/1, 719.

55. Aulén, *Faith of the Christian Church*, 83. Both Jürgen Moltmann and Frank Macchia reject limiting the Spirit's role to the subjective dimensions of faith. See Jürgen Moltmann, *The Spirit of Life: A Universal Affirmation*, trans. Margaret Kohl (Minneapolis: Fortress, 2001), 24–25; Frank Macchia, "Justification Through New Creation: The Holy Spirit and the Doctrine by Which the Church Stands or Falls," *Theology Today* 58, no. 2 (2001): 214.

56. Barth, *Church Dogmatics*, IV/1, 156.

57. Cornelius van der Kooi, *This Incredibly Benevolent Force: The Holy Spirit in Reformed Theology and Spirituality* (Grand Rapids: Eerdmans, 2018), 14–15.

58. See Jürgen Moltmann, *Theology of Hope: On the Ground and the Implications of a Christian Eschatology*, ed. James W. Leitch (Minneapolis: Fortress, 1993), 41; Jürgen Moltmann, *The Crucified God: The Cross of Christ as the Foundation and Criticism of Christian Theology*, trans. R. A. Wilson and John Bowden (Minneapolis: Fortress, 1993), 271. See also Wolfhart Pannenberg, *Problemgeschichte der Neueren Evangelischen Theologie in Deutschland* (Göttingen: Vandenhoeck & Ruprecht, 1997), 257.

and charismatic traditions' more holistic incorporation of the Spirit's liberative work in the social, economic, political, and physical aspects of life. Aulén's articulation of the Spirit's role in ongoing atonement would find much common ground with these presentations.

In addition, there is resonance between liberation theology's emphasis on God's liberative activity and Aulén's emphasis on the deliverance of God at the cross. However, unlike some liberation theologians who emphasize God's suffering, whether it is Moltmann's rubric of godforsakenness or James Cone's emphasis on God as Black, Aulén highlights also the victory of God that is being won anew in every generation through the Spirit. For Aulén, the cross is not "merely a cross of martyrdom."[59] It is not the suffering God that is the saving image, for such a lens "imprisons" the image of God in past events or deals with a "purely immanent image of God."[60] Interestingly, this critique would find some common ground with the critiques that Victor Anderson and Brian Bantum offer of James Cone: Centering and ontologizing the Black experience makes Blackness "defined by and coterminous with black resistance and black suffering" and only presses it further into "a perpetual space of self-preservation."[61] In short, defining Christology through the image of suffering alone *can* limit eschatological horizons. Aulén offers another way, through the lens of ongoing atonement and the work of the Spirit.

Aulén offers a qualified view of human suffering as it relates to redemption. Human suffering is neither inherently redemptive nor salvific; it can make life bitter, and there is no guarantee that suffering always makes life better. Instead, it is the way in which the human faces suffering that informs any gain.[62] Aulén and Cone offer contrasting readings of Christ's willingness in facing suffering at the cross. Aulén asserts that the suffering of Christ has saving power because Christ's suffering was a self-giving sacrifice where the power of God's love was involved—the death of Christ was God's victory, and the cross became changed into a sign of victory. The preaching of the disciples was not only a *theologia crucis,* but a *theologia gloriae crucis.*[63]

---

59. Aulén, *Drama and Symbols*, 187.
60. Aulén, *Drama and Symbols*, 187.
61. Victor Anderson, *Beyond Ontological Blackness* (London: Bloomsbury Academic, 2016), 104; Brian Bantum, *Redeeming Mulatto: A Theology of Race and Christian Hybridity* (Waco: Baylor University Press, 2010), 5, 4. J. Kameron Carter voices a similar critique in *Race: A Theological Account* (Oxford: Oxford University Press, 2008), 159–70.
62. Aulén, *Drama and Symbols*, 187.
63. Aulén, *Drama and Symbols*, 188.

Aulén's bringing together the terms *crucis* and *gloriae* warrants further investigation. The phrase *theologia gloriae* was first used by Luther to describe the theological model of speculation he attributed to scholastic theology, which he faulted for making the invisible nature of God the basis of theological reflection and method.[64] Against this, Luther distinguished his preferred theological method which centered on suffering and the cross, *theologia crucis*.

However, given Aulén's strong resistance to rationalization and speculative metaphysics, Aulén does not appear to be commending the speculative theological method that Luther associates with *theologia gloriae*.[65] Aulén seems to redeploy the terms towards a different meaning. For Aulén, a *theologia gloriae* is about the victory won in Christ's obedient death at the cross—victory is not about something that follows Christ's sacrifice of self-giving love, rather the sacrifice itself is the victory.[66] The resurrection reveals the humiliation as a victory.[67] For Christians, a *theologia crucis* is "at the same time a *theologia gloriae Christi*."[68] Aulén puts these terms together to speak of a *theologia crucis gloriae*.[69] He writes, "What links Christian faith to the cross is not that a martyr died there, but the assurance that Christ's death was his victory—and God's victory."[70] This *theologia gloriae crucis* carries with it both the victory of Christ at the cross and the continuing victory of God through the Spirit.

Aulén's locating the victory of God in the death of Christ at the cross finds resonance in Cone's thought. Despite his emphasis on suffering, Cone connects suffering and victory when he writes, "God took the evil of the cross and the lynching tree and transformed them both into the triumphant beauty of the divine."[71]

However, Cone's interpretation of Jesus's suffering as sacrificial victim differs from Aulén's understanding of Jesus's suffering as *willing* self-sacrifice. For Cone, Christ, in both his experience of oppression and

---

64. See Martin Luther, "Heidelberg Disputation," in *Martin Luther's Basic Theological Writings* (Minneapolis: Fortress, 1989), 43–46. Gaylon Barker offers a helpful overview of how Luther deployed and contrasted these two terms in *The Cross of Reality: Luther's Theologia Crucis and Bonhoeffer's Christology* (Minneapolis: Fortress, 2015), 26.

65. Aulén writes, "Speculation confuses the divine revelation of faith with rationalistic metaphysics," *Faith of the Christian Church*, 21.

66. Aulén, *Faith of the Christian Church*, 80.

67. Aulén, *Faith of the Christian Church*, 81.

68. Aulén, *Faith of the Christian Church*, 81.

69. Aulén, *Drama and Symbols*, 188.

70. Aulén, *Drama and Symbols*, 188.

71. James H. Cone, *The Cross and the Lynching Tree* (Maryknoll, NY: Orbis, 2011), 101.

his commitment to liberation, shows that Jesus is Black.[72] Though Cone's ethical protest against the evil of lynching and racial oppression should be taken seriously, his concluding assertion—that "black people are Christ figures" because they had no choice in suffering—is one that Aulén would likely question.[73] Jesus did have a choice; Black Americans suffering lynching and terror did not. To remove Jesus's agency, his decision to head to the crucifixion and the resurrection, seems to run against the witness of Scripture.[74]

In contrast, for Aulén the whole of Christ's life is marked by *willing sacrifice*. The Suffering Servant of the Lord in Isaiah 53 informs Aulén's view of the sacrifice of Christ as Messiah.[75] Sacrifice is not limited to Christ's death alone but spans the whole of incarnation and atonement. The sacrifice "begins already in his becoming [hu]man" and "reaches its culmination" at the cross, which completes the sacrifice that is to end all sacrifices.[76] Through his death, Christ makes the people of God "participants in the new age, the Kingdom of God, the new life, and the glory to come."[77] Thus God is intimately engaged in humankind's deliverance from bondage, which continues today in the Spirit's work of ongoing atonement.[78]

B. Second Resource: An Account of Human Participation

A second aspect of Aulén's account of accomplished and ongoing atonement that may be resourced for constructive theology is his account of human participation in God's delivering activity for us today. Aulén critically links the church to the Spirit's work of ongoing atonement and divine battle against the enslaving powers of sin, death, and the devil, here and now.[79] I summarize here how Aulén offers an account of human participation in the Spirit's work, names obstacles to that participation, and presents the church as a contending church in the battle that is the continuing three-agent drama.

---

72. James H. Cone, *God of the Oppressed* (Maryknoll, NY: Orbis, 1997), 145.

73. Cone, *Cross and the Lynching Tree*, 101.

74. Consider Matthew 16:21–23, where Jesus chastises Peter in the harshest terms for attempting to rebuke and dissuade Jesus from his journey to crucifixion—and resurrection.

75. Aulén, *Faith of the Christian Church*, 77.

76. Aulén, *Faith of the Christian Church*, 76.

77. Aulén, "Chaos and Cosmos," 161.

78. Interestingly, in *God of the Oppressed*, Cone points to the potential of Aulén's *Christus victor* idea: "If the classical theory is radicalized politically, then liberation and reconciliation can once again be grounded in history and related to God's fight against the powers of enslavement." Cone, *God of the Oppressed*, 236.

79. Aulén, *Drama and Symbols*, 45, 48–49.

First, Aulén clearly describes how the believer and the church participate in God's battle against the powers. Aulén writes, "The work of the Atonement continues in the preaching of the message of Christ; it continues in the sacraments, in baptism and the eucharist."[80] Aulén offers a capacious definition of preaching: It can take many forms, whether as a sermon, in personal encounter, in personal talks (whether in the form of confession or not), or in acts of service "that bear witness to, that proclaim the power of Christ."[81] Through both preaching and sacrament, the Spirit builds up the church, and "what happened in the past becomes a living reality in the present."[82]

With the manner of the church's participation in the Spirit's work described, Aulén thickens that account with a second aspect. He names the obstacles which hinder that participation. The church is both holy and sinful: holy because the Lord is present in his church and realizing the work of redemption which he accomplished once and for all at the cross, and sinful because at the same time the church is not free from sin, as its members are not free from sin.[83] In the church's failure to live up to this witness, preaching and even the sacraments can be compromised by human interpretation and administration.[84] Aulén is able to describe human participation in the Spirit's ongoing work with a critical realism that acknowledges the presence of sin and the reality of spiritual battle. The church is not "one, holy, and catholic" in a static manner but in the sense that it is being made that way, dramatically, through the work of the Spirit.[85] The church is thus an instrument of the Spirit, though it is flawed. Moreover, Aulén's rendering of sin as a state of bondage, as well as his account of accomplished and ongoing atonement which delivers human persons from bondage, offers the possibility of addressing the range of limitations in human agency that impact participation in sin.[86] For discussions of human reconciliation, such scope is important for acknowledging the diversity of sins related to commission of specific deeds, complicity, and social determination that accompany the history of race and colonization.

80. Aulén, "Chaos and Cosmos," 166.
81. Aulén, *Drama and Symbols*, 191.
82. Aulén, *Drama and Symbols*, 190.
83. Aulén, *Faith of the Christian Church*, 111.
84. Aulén, *Drama and Symbols*, 191.
85. Aulén, *Drama and Symbols*, 189.
86. See Katie Cannon's trenchant critique of Western theological ethics for failing to acknowledge the limited moral agency of Black persons, *Black Womanist Ethics* (Eugene, OR: Wipf and Stock, 1988), 3.

Third, in naming the church's participation in the Spirit's work and hindrances to that participation, Aulén provides a view of the church as engaged in active struggle, in this time and this place. The church, being in the world but not of it and living in the old age while belonging to the new, is a "contending church"—the *ecclesia militans*.[87] Its ministry of reconciliation is a ministry of struggle and conflict, "characterized by the unceasing struggle between the loving will of God and those destructive powers which in this age oppose God's will."[88] The believer is part of the church militant, part of the struggle against the destructive powers that seek to destroy her membership in the body of Christ.[89] The armor of God, as described in Ephesians 6:13, is necessary to participate in this struggle.

As a member of this contending church, the Christian is called to "become more and more a living member in the body of Christ," serving Christ by serving the neighbor.[90] For Aulén, the Christian life and Christian ethics are not about the egocentric ideal of the "ennobling and perfecting of one's personality."[91] Instead, Christian ethics is characterized by "service in love on behalf of the neighbor in the struggle against the destructive powers," obeying and following the commandments of God in various situations.[92] Aulén asserts that there is no sin against the neighbor that is not also sin against God, showing a concern for the horizontal, human-to-human aspects of reconciliation.[93] However, he also states that the church is not "merely a society for the promotion of better social conditions" or "a proponent of a future social utopia."[94] While urgent problems of the world are important for the church, the church participates in two worlds, the old age and the eschatological breakthrough of the new age, as an instrument in the struggle against the demonic powers.[95] The church "becomes an eschatological reality," its eyes focused on the consummation which will take place at the passing of the old aeon.[96]

In his presentation of the contending church, marked by fallibility but simultaneously engaged in spiritual battle as it is pulled between two

---

87. Aulén, *Faith of the Christian Church*, 134.
88. Aulén, *Faith of the Christian Church*, 133.
89. Aulén, *Faith of the Christian Church*, 134.
90. Aulén, *Faith of the Christian Church*, 134.
91. Aulén, *Faith of the Christian Church*, 135.
92. Aulén, *Faith of the Christian Church*, 135.
93. Aulén, *Faith of the Christian Church*, 86.
94. Aulén, *Faith of the Christian Church*, 111.
95. Aulén, *Faith of the Christian Church*, 107.
96. Aulén, *Faith of the Christian Church*, 107.

worlds, Aulén resists an idealist view of the church. He also resists a view that places the church at remote distance from the problems of the world.[97] Though fellowship with Christ is hidden, the communion of saints appears as a visible and tangible reality—"as a fellowship *in sacris*, in Word and in sacraments, in worship and prayer, as a fellowship in the service of Christ, in bearing one another's burdens, in 'the mutual conversation and consolation of brethren.'"[98] The ministry of the church rests upon the finished work of Christ, his victory won in atonement, and is carried out in new struggles in every age and generation.[99]

Overall, Aulén offers a clear account of human participation in God's ongoing deliverance, while acknowledging the church's fallibility in the midst of the battle against the inimical forces.

IV. Future Directions: Discernment, Repentance

However, more is needed to thicken Aulén's account of human participation in the Spirit's ongoing work of atonement and deliverance. Though Aulén states that there is no sin against the neighbor which is not sin against God, he does not offer a way to address broken relationships between believer and neighbor and between believers.[100] The ministry of reconciliation is presented primarily as how to speak up for the other in the world but not how to address the situation when things go awry within the church or when sin continues to impact a believer's relationship with her neighbor—despite Aulén's clear acknowledgement of the church's fallibility. If the church is to be an instrument and participant in the Spirit's work of ongoing atonement, a more substantive account of repentance, for particular human sin in this time, this place, and this history, is needed to address challenges in the church's response to the Spirit's work in ongoing atonement. This repentance should span addressing individual acts and sociostructural sin, as well as demonic and cosmological oppression.[101] In addition, a robust account of human discernment that responds to preaching is needed in order to form a stronger account of

97. Aulén, *Faith of the Christian Church*, 109–110.

98. Aulén, *Faith of the Christian Church*, 113.

99. Aulén, *Faith of the Christian Church*, 133.

100. Aulén, *Faith of the Christian Church*, 87.

101. Cone and Käsemann offer accounts of repentance that address a number of these realities. See Cone, *God of the Oppressed*, 221, and Ernst Käsemann, *Church Conflicts: The Cross, Apocalyptic, and Political Resistance* (Grand Rapids: Baker Academic, 2021), 50, 203.

human participation in the Spirit's work of ongoing atonement. Such an account is important for addressing matters of spiritual abuse, prescribing ecclesial repentance and reparations for complicity in historic injustices such as slavery, and resisting nationalistic and ideological corruption of church practice and belief.

In this essay, I presented an underattended aspect of Aulén's account of accomplished and ongoing atonement as a resource for constructive theology. To do so, I began by summarizing Aulén's *Christus victor* idea of atonement and noted the criticisms that have been raised about the *Christus victor* idea and also about Aulén's tripartite taxonomy of atonement. I demonstrated how his later work fills in gaps and answers some of those critiques. Contrasting Aulén with other modern theologians, I proposed that Aulén's creative rendering of atonement as accomplished and ongoing offers an account of God's activity for us, here and now through the work of the Spirit, and also a way of speaking of human participation in God's delivering activity for us today, in the midst of his continuing battle against sin, death, and the devil. I concluded by suggesting that a stronger account of repentance and discernment would strengthen Aulén's account of human participation in God's delivering action for us today.[102]

102. I am grateful for feedback given by Taido Chino, Rahel Siebald, Lea Weber, and Chris Whyte on drafts of this essay. All errors are mine.

CHAPTER 12

"THE GOD WHO IS FOR US IS ALSO FOR THEM"

MARK R. LINDSAY

In any serious consideration of the dogmatic theme that was addressed in Aberdeen in May 2024, "the God who is for us," natural and proper priority is placed on the questions that this theme raises for our understanding of God's ontology. These include questions of aseity, kenosis, and the intra-Trinitarian relations, among others. Each of these aspects entails certain consequences for how we conceive of God's manner of relating to the "us" that is indicated, but the starting point is clearly (and rightly) taken to be God, not us. While there is an entirely proper theo-logic to this direction, it does perhaps leave the "us"—howsoever they (we?) might be constituted—potentially occluded from view. To address such a possible occlusion, this paper seeks to enquire into the constitution of the "us" so named by considering a second occlusion—the "them" that is implied by the naming of any "us"—and the question whether that group of people, howsoever *they* may be constituted, is a group for whom God is consequently *not*. Thus, the objective of this paper does indeed bear upon how we understand God's being, but it does so by beginning with the potential and real occlusions identified in the theme rather than by beginning with the God who stands at its head. As a way of drawing out these ideas, the paper will employ the motif of the friend-enemy distinction, which occupies the centre of contemporary political theologies.

I

In 2004, in a provocative article entitled "Terror Right" for *The New Centennial Review*, comparative religionist Gil Anidjar noted, "We have not sufficiently thought of the enemy."[1] Outside the context of legal theory, he observed, all other disciplines—from "philosophy to poetry . . . ethics to politics, have affirmed their privileged relation to love and friendship—and [have] refrained from claiming or thinking the enemy."[2] Leveraging the political theorising of the German jurist Carl Schmitt, Anidjar went on to note the exteriorities that are both constituted by the enemy and by which the enemy is him- or herself also constituted. That is to say, the figuring of an enemy is the constituting of someone—some symbol—who thereby stands outside whatever geographical or ideological space is deemed normative.

In the two decades since Anidjar's article, much more thought *has* been given to a proper figuring of enmity outside the traditional disciplinary bounds of law and jurisprudence, with Anidjar's work itself being pivotal as both stimulus and content. Despite it not being one of those disciplines from which, according to Anidjar, an explicit theorising of enmity has historically been excised, theology has not been unaffected by these discursive developments. This is at least in part because of the enduring influence of Schmittian discourse, to which most contemporary political theologies, for good or ill, self-consciously refer, and which is at heart preoccupied with the aforementioned friend-enemy distinction.[3] But political theology is not dogmatic theology—indeed, it has not infrequently censured dogmatics for the latter's presumed disinterest in the dynamic that motivates political theology, namely the complex relations between "rival conceptions of power and authority, rival sources of sovereignty and legitimacy, and rival models of utopia and salvation."[4] As a consequence, the insights leading to a more robust conceptualisation of the enemy for which Anidjar was calling in 2004, despite their ubiquity within modern political theological discourse, have not yet significantly informed dogmatic theology.

How might one gesture towards some ways in which that (in)forming might be done? I argue in what follows that a consideration of the dogmatic concept of God's promeity, in conversation with the specific doctrinal locus of ecclesiology, may provide a way forward. Taking note at this point of William Cavanaugh's recent comment, that even the

1. Gil Anidjar, "Terror Right," *The New Centennial Review* 4, no. 3 (2004): 37.
2. Anidjar, "Terror Right," 39.
3. See in particular Carl Schmitt, *Der Begriff des Politischen* (Berlin: Duncker & Humblot, 1932).
4. Vassilios Paispais, "Political Theologies of the International—the Continued Relevance of Theology in International Relations," *Journal of International Relations and Development* 22 (2019): 270.

nonsecularised forms of political theology have "strangely neglected" the doctrine of the church, gives some permission to think that this is both a hitherto untested, but potentially promising, approach.[5] However, merely engaging with Gil Anidjar—despite his significance to the discursive question of enmity—is not sufficient for the purpose. Such a narrow focus would keep the conversation within the political-theological, without touching upon the truly dogmatic concerns towards which I wish to move, primarily in relation to the God, the us, and the them, as they are named or implied in the theme. Thus, the remainder of this paper will indeed attend to the possibilities of Gil Anidjar's political theologising but will do so in conversation with some ancient and some more modern interlocutors, namely: Augustine's *City of God*; the *Secunda Secundae* of Thomas Aquinas's *Summa*; and—perhaps most fruitfully—Dietrich Bonhoeffer's ecclesiological musings from the mid-1930s.

II

In the early fifth century, Augustine famously insisted upon what we might these days call the "mixed economy" of the spatiohistorical being of the church, the *ecclesia visibilis*.[6] Referencing Matthew 13, Augustine argued that this form of the church always and necessarily consists of both wheat and tares.

> Among those now professing, the City of God has in her company during her pilgrimage in the world, joined to her by sharing the sacraments, some who will not be with her to share eternally in the lot of the saints. Some secretly and some openly there are who even in company with our enemies do not hesitate to murmur against God under whose standards they serve, at one time with our enemies crowding the theatres, at another the churches with us.[7]

5. William T. Cavanaugh, "Church," in *Wiley Blackwell Companion to Political Theology*, ed. William T. Cavanaugh and Peter M. Scott (Chichester: Wiley & Sons, 2019), 431.

6. According to Sabrina Müller, the term *mixed economy* was first employed by Rowan Williams to refer to the blend of parochial and "fresh expressions" of church life within the Anglican Communion, especially within the Church of England. It neatly reflects, though, the diverse reality of the church militant's composition, as expressed by Augustine. See Sabrina Müller, "Towards the Acceptance of Diversity: A Brief History of the Mixed Economy of Church and Continental European Adaptations," *Ecclesial Futures* 1, no. 1 (2020): 37.

7. Augustine, *City of God*, vol. 1, books 1–3, trans. George E. McCracken, Loeb Classical Library 416 (Cambridge: Harvard University Press, 1957), 1.35, 137–39. As New Testament scholar Donald Hagner writes: "The present age is thus one in which human society (and thus even the Church) is a

Further Matthean support for Augustine's claim can be found in the First Evangelist's narration of Jesus's arrest in Gethsemane. At the very moment of betrayal, Jesus addresses Judas—the archetypal Christian enemy—and calls him "friend" (Matt 26:50). Thus it would seem that, even before the church existed *as* church, it consisted not only of enemies and friends but indeed of enemies *as* friends. Nevertheless, and notwithstanding the accuracy of Augustine's description of the church militant, it is also the case that the church has always *struggled* with and against the painful reality of its mixed economy. Thus, and rather than deferring with patience the determination of the tares to God's eschatological judgment, as Augustine seems to have wished, the church has instead preferred to find numerous ways of identifying *now* who might be "in" and who should be "out."[8] As David Congdon has noted recently, "The attempt to define 'true Christianity' and 'authentic faith' in self-serving ways is one of the oldest practices in Christian history."[9] Kathryn Tanner may optimistically claim that the church is these days largely content for our shared Christian identity to "no longer [be] a matter of unmixed purity, but a hybrid affair,"[10] but the *longue durée* of Christian history begs to differ. That is, the historic being of the church has for two millennia exercised itself with the determination of its own clearly demarcated boundaries, and thus the consideration of what might constitute boundary crossings, precisely so as to avoid such hybridity.[11] Andrew McGowan's comment that theological normativity has involved controversy and contest, such that it has not always been possible easily to determine "the most or only obvious way to be Christian," is true not only of the early centuries of ecclesial formation, about which McGowan was writing, but continues to be the case into the present.[12] Nevertheless, such boundary crossings have hardly been value neutral, nor has the difficulty in determining normativity been understood

---

mixture of those of the evil one and those of the kingdom." Donald A. Hagner, *Matthew 1–13*, Word Biblical Commentary 33A (Grand Rapids: Zondervan, 2015), 395.

8. In Augustine's day, of course, the presenting issue was Donatism, and the question whether the church's sacramental activity was and is dependent upon the purity of its clergy with respect to their self-distancing from the world of politics and empire. There is no doubt a continuing element of semi- or neo-Donatism within the church today. See, for example, John Thiel, "The New Donatism," *Commonweal* (5 July 2021). Nevertheless, the instinct to define clear boundaries around the church has historically been less concerned with sacramental efficacy, and more to do with doctrinal uniformity.

9. David W. Congdon, *Who Is a True Christian? Contesting Religious Identity in American Culture* (Cambridge: Cambridge University Press, 2024), xi.

10. Kathryn Tanner, *Theories of Culture: A New Agenda for Theology* (Minneapolis: Fortress, 1997), 42.

11. Howard Clark Kee, *Who Are the People of God? Early Christian Models of Community* (New Haven, CT: Yale University Press, 1995), 13–14.

12. Andrew B. McGowan, *Ancient Christian Worship* (Grand Rapids: Baker Academic, 2014), 14.

as adiaphoric. On the contrary, such contests have presented as the ecclesial expression of what Carl Schmitt calls the spatial partitioning of the world—or in this case, of the church—by "a global line that divide[s] . . . into two halves, one good and one bad, [and that describes] a *plus* and a *minus* line of moral evaluation." Such partitioning leads ineluctably to "a perpetual renunciation of the other side."[13] Taking Schmitt's observation of that perpetual renunciation as an unfortunate but self-evident truth of ecclesial formation, it is helpful to enquire, not so much into the inevitable reality (or identity) of the "tares" who live secretly within the church, as Augustine understood, but rather, first, into the manner in which the church nonetheless seeks to define sharp demarcations by which certain people and certain ideas are, *contra* Augustine, explicitly *and now* to be excluded, and second, into how we might reimagine such demarcations such that they do not bifurcate into fixed polarities of the "us" for whom we believe God *is* and the "them" for whom we (at least implicitly) believe God is *not*.

It is precisely this spatio-ideological dividing of the church that has characterised the many and various declarations of *anathema* against those individuals, as well as theological trends or novelties, deemed to be heterodox—the "outlawing," to use Anidjar's language, of those parts of the church that the church itself determines not to include. That is to say, theological aberrations (in whatever form they may take) are pronounced *hors la loi*, "excluded from the law by the law," which is as such the enactment of the sovereignty of the church.[14] Indeed, those moments of confessional and creedal decision have often been analogous to Schmitt's description of the "state of exception." By their very nature, creeds and confessions arise out of moments in which existing laws and certainties either cannot account for the presenting issue or simply do not yet exist to account for it. Thus, the church enacts its sovereignty not only by determining the outcome of the issue but more so by determining that an exception exists that must be handled in the first place. Of course, one might wish to leverage someone like Bonhoeffer (to whom we will attend in more detail shortly) as an ally in any attempt to render such ecclesial dividing ultimately impossible, by reference to the inherent graciousness of God's promeity in Christ. Such promeity, for Bonhoeffer, is ingredient to Christ's identity and is the "christological form of God's commitment to

13. Carl Schmitt, *The Nomos of the Earth in the International Law of the Jus Publicum Europaeum* (New York: Telos, 2003), 289, 295. Cited in Anidjar, "Terror Right," 57.

14. Anidjar, "Terror Right," 41.

humankind" *as such*.[15] There is, in other words, a divine binding (*Bindung*) to humanity that seemingly rules out of order any reestablishment of walls of hostility, not least within the church. That may indeed be true. But this is not as such an argument against ecclesial division but only against the suggestion that one might encounter Christ in any way *apart from* his promeity. That Christ is heard only where he allows himself to be heard is Bonhoeffer's shorthand for saying that *only* as *pro me* can Christ be met.[16] That is, the *pro me* structure of Bonhoeffer's Christology is not itself the antidote to ecclesial enmifying.

Indeed, this divine "being-for-me" has, as has been suggested above, historically occluded an implied divine "*not*-being-for-others," the "me" in the equation being presumptively restricted to those in whom we believe we can see the hallmarks of orthodox faith and praxis, with everyone else consigned to (or better, remaining within) the *massa damnata* to which (according to Augustine) we all, by nature, belong. Christopher Holmes has noted, on the very basis of Bonhoeffer's rendering of christological promeity, that "just as Christ does not 'accommodate himself to any self-chosen "us,"' so, too, the church must not think that it exhausts the 'us.'"[17] And yet this is precisely what the church has traditionally done. Theological justification for such consignment of the many is illustrated (though not, can I stress, *provided*) by D. A. Carson's rather grim assessment, that "the fundamental human problem is that God *is against us*."[18] Such a vision of God suggests an antipathy within God that is more proper to him than any gracious—but logically subsequent—pro nobity. That we believe that some of us have now escaped that fate, such that we are now the "us" for whom God graciously *is*, simply makes the "us" the exception proving the rule and allows us license to demarcate the "them." And this is no mere abstract speculation. On the contrary, it is reified ecclesiologically, insofar as we identify (and then exclude) the "them" who we

---

15. Philip Ziegler, "Christ for Us Today—Promeity in the Christologies of Bonhoeffer and Kierkegaard," *International Journal of Systematic Theology* 15, no. 1 (2013): 31, emphasis added. Ziegler is here referencing Bonhoeffer's Christology lectures of 1933. See Dietrich Bonhoeffer, "Lectures on Christology," in *Dietrich Bonhoeffer Works*, vol. 12, *Berlin: 1932–1933*, ed. Larry Rasmussen (Minneapolis: Fortress, 2009), 317. As Philip Ziegler has said, Christ's "'being Christ' is identical with his 'being-for-me,' such that 'I can never think of Jesus Christ in his being-in-himself, but only in his relatedness to me.'" Ziegler, "Christ for Us Today," 30.

16. Bonhoeffer, "Lectures on Christology," 315, 317.

17. Christopher Holmes, "Wholly Human and Wholly Divine, Humiliated and Exalted: Some Reformed Explorations in Bonhoeffer's Christology Lectures," *Scottish Bulletin of Evangelical Theology* 25, no. 2 (2007): 222.

18. D. A. Carson, "The Wrath of God," in *Engaging the Doctrine of God: Contemporary Protestant Perspectives*, ed. Bruce L. McCormack (Grand Rapids: Baker Academic, 2008), 53, emphasis added.

believe are within the "us." To return to David Congdon, when the church became the "guardian of orthodoxy," it established a "binary opposition between orthodoxy and heterodoxy, between saints and deceivers, between Christians and antichrists."[19] Or as we might put it in the terms of this paper, between the "them" and the "us." To cite just one example, and despite what Mark Smith has usefully described as the "conceptual plasticity" of Nicene orthodoxy, the insistence—by Athanasius of Alexandria and Basil of Caesarea, to name just two—on Nicaea's "unique role . . . as the guarantor of orthodoxy" has been sufficient to provide a catholic (that is, global) consensus on where theological and ecclesial partitioning may *and must* happen.[20] Creeds and confessional statements since Nicaea—one might think of the Athanasian Creed (Arts. 1, 2, 42) or even the "*wir verwerfen*" of the Barmen Declaration—have reified, and in some ways extended, the boundary that is, or is not, crossed, rendering those found to be on "the other side," as it were, "aliens from God . . . , from the benefits of the heavenly kingdom, and the hope of eternal salvation."[21] As Hermann Sasse put it in the febrile 1960s, "The truth cannot be confessed without rejecting error . . . such that [it] is the constant task of the Church" to do both.[22] Indeed, Sasse trembles at the thought of what might have happened "had the apostles been less orthodox, and more tolerant": "There would," he wrote, "be no Church today."[23]

But it is here that, at least according to Anidjar, the difficulty precisely lies. For "why is there a difference"—the positing of a boundary that can (but must not) be transgressed—"*precisely here*? Why is this difference deemed determining . . . ? [If] everything can be a site of difference," asks Anidjar, referencing Jacques Derrida, then "why is this particular site currently invested?"[24] With the benefit of hindsight, we might regard the norming of, for example, *homoousion* as self-evident, such that questioning the reasoning of its investment with inherent (and at least *pen*ultimately determinative) seriousness becomes redundant. But the necessary plasticity

19. David W. Congdon, *The God Who Saves: A Dogmatic Sketch* (Eugene: Cascade, 2016), 57.

20. Mark S. Smith, *The Idea of Nicaea in the Early Church Councils, AD 431–451*, Oxford Early Christian Studies (Oxford: Oxford University Press, 2018), 24–25.

21. Johann Gerhard, *Loci Theologici, cum pro adstruenda veritate, tum pro destruenda quorumvis contradicentium falsitate, per theses nervose, solide et copiose explicate*, 11.39. Cited in Heinrich Schmid, *The Doctrinal Theology of the Evangelical Lutheran Church*, trans. Charles A. Hay and Henry E. Jacobs (Eugene: Wipf & Stock, 2008), 589.

22. Hermann Sasse, "The Confession of Faith According to the New Testament," in *The Springfielder* 28, no. 3 (1964): 6.

23. Sasse, "The Confession of Faith," 6.

24. Gil Anidjar, interviewed by Nermeen Shaikh for The Asia Society, https://asiasociety.org/jew-arab-interview-gil-anidjar.

of Nicaea to which Smith refers speaks to the ways Nicene orthodoxy had, in the century after the Council, to be reinterpreted through creative "reading strategies" to include and make sense of a wider range of theological perspectives that were not *prima facie* coherent with Nicaea.[25] As Smith says, an "avowed fidelity to the simple wording of the Creed conveniently shrouded a multitude of doctrinal eccentricities."[26] We are faced, that is, with the question, why and how it is at this point and not any other that "the enemy"—the "outlaw," the "them"—is constituted?

We may well, and possibly should, ask that question. But the point, in fact, at least for the purposes of this paper, is not so much to enquire into the dogmatic necessity of this over that theological principle but to recognise that at whatever point the boundary is drawn, the church as such declares the transgressor to be the enemy, the outlaw, the "them" who stands apart from and opposed to the "us," the one who is determined *by* the law (of the church) to be *outside* the law (of the church).[27] In his controversial 1936 declaration, Dietrich Bonhoeffer sought to soften the institutional force of this judgment by declaring that it is the one who "*knowingly* separates [themselves] from the Confessing Church in Germany" who thereby separates themselves from salvation.[28] The self-consciousness of the separation is the key for Bonhoeffer because, he says, "the true church can never determine *from its own perspective* those who do not belong to it."[29] Rather, the claim that "here is the true church" is

25. As Smith puts it, "Athanasius's strategy offered a persuasive account of a contested and confusing past—it was a construal of 'Nicaea' intended to remedy the tensions that Nicaea had itself, at least in some degree, bequeathed." See Smith, *The Idea of Nicaea*, 22.

26. Smith, *The Idea of Nicaea*, 2.

27. I note that it is not simply from Gil Anidjar that we can take the language of ecclesial enmity. Such rhetoric is plentiful as far as back as the Church Fathers. For example, Cyril of Jerusalem writes: "Let us confidently say to God regarding all heretics, 'Did I not hate, O Lord, those who hated Thee, and did I not pine away because of Your enemies?' For there is an enmity that is laudable, as it is written, 'I will put enmity between you and the woman, between your seed and her seed.' Friendship with the serpent produces enmity with God, and death. Let us shun those from whom God turns away." See Cyril, Catechetical Lecture 16, "On the Holy Spirit," in *The Works of Saint Cyril of Jerusalem*, vol. 2, ed. Leo P. McCauley and Anthony A. Stephenson, Fathers of the Church 64 (Washington: Catholic University of America Press, 1970), 81. Similarly, Jerome observes: "And as for heretics, I have never spared them; on the contrary, I have seen to it in every possible way that the Church's enemies are also my enemies." See Jerome, "The Dialogue Against the Pelagians," in *Dogmatic and Polemical Works*, trans. John N. Hritzu, Fathers of the Church 53 (Washington: Catholic University of America Press, 1965), 232.

28. Dietrich Bonhoeffer, "On the Question of Church Communion," in *Dietrich Bonhoeffer Works*, vol. 14, *Theological Education at Finkenwalde, 1935–1937*, ed. H. Gaylon Barker and Mark S. Brocker, trans. Douglas W. Stott (Minneapolis: Fortress, 2013), 675, emphasis added.

29. Bonhoeffer, "On the Question of Church Communion," 659. In his response to Bonhoeffer's paper, Helmut Gollwitzer agreed that this "knowing-ness" is of critical importance. See Helmut Gollwitzer, "On the Question of Church Communion: Comments and Reservations," in *Dietrich Bonhoeffer Works*, 14:679.

heard either as law or as gospel, and how one hears it determines whether one stands in relation to the church so proclaimed in either judgment or salvation.[30] Bonhoeffer's formulation of ecclesial separation renders the outlawing a subjective act on the part of the outlaw—they outlaw themselves, as it were. Indeed, those who seek to demarcate the boundaries of the church are the very ones who have heard the claim "here is the church" *as* law and thus *as* judgment.[31] Or as David Bentley Hart memorably comments, "It is the soul . . . that lights hell's fires."[32] Yet this perhaps lets the church off the hook too lightly, for it is in truth the ecclesial community (or at least an authorised representative group within it) that decides both boundary and transgression. To quote from Karl Barth's explanation of the character of a confessional statement, "a confession"—which, as he had already recognised in late 1933, must include the possibility of the *damnamus*—"can only be an act of the *church*, and not of an individual professor"![33] To paraphrase Anidjar, the law establishes the law by which the outlaw is outlawed. Or, indeed, by which the enemy—the "them," in our formulation—is figured.

Thus, in contrast to a Bonhoefferian *subjective* alienation, we have an enemy, a "them," of *our own* making, whose existence is predicated upon the prior determination of the need for community boundaries, and the consequential assumption that such boundaries can and will be—but must *not* be—transgressed. Far from the "them," the enemy, being self-evident, they exist, insofar as they do, only in consequence of decisions made by others, the "us," that could have been made differently, thus rendering the identity of the "them" also different. The "us" is, as Holmes notes, "self-chosen."[34] Smith's acknowledgment of "doctrinal eccentricities," to which I referred earlier, at one level argues the opposite of what I am claiming here—the Nicene plasticity allowed for the toleration of a certain degree of difference. But at the same time, Smith also proves my point by acknowledging that demarcations and consequent anathemas are at least partially moveable feasts. This is not to say that the determinations of Nicaea, Barmen, or any other moment of confessional angst were wrong.

30. Bonhoeffer, "On the Question of Church Communion," 659.

31. Bonhoeffer, "On the Question of Church Communion," 659.

32. David Bentley Hart, *That All Shall Be Saved: Heaven, Hell, and Universal Salvation* (New Haven, CT: Yale University Press, 2019), 17.

33. Karl Barth, "Bekenntnis der freien Kirchensynode," in *Rheinische Bekentnissynoden im Kirchenkampf: Ein Dokumentation aus den Jahren 1933–1945*, ed. Joachim Beckmann (Neukirchen: Neukirchener, 1975), 34–46, emphasis added.

34. Holmes, "Wholly Human and Wholly Divine," 222.

It is simply to say that the enemy thus constituted—those who were (and are) deemed by those decisions to be *ex*-communicant, that is, outside of (and hence also against) the community—could have been constituted differently, had different decisions been made. If, then, we presume that those thus rendered enemies are separated from the promise of salvation—as indeed both the Athanasian Creed and Bonhoeffer's declaration both unequivocally state—and as a consequence must (or at least might reasonably) be understood (and have historically *been* understood) as amongst those for whom God is *not*, we are compelled to accept that that is neither an eternally generated determination of such people, nor is it an immutable status of them *coram Deo*.

III

But what has all this to do with contemporary ecclesiology? Simply this, that it is neither secret nor surprise that over the past thirty-odd years, the global church has been riven by deep enmities and divisions. Many of the rupturing controversies have concerned questions of race, gender, and sexuality rather than (or at least as well as) heterodoxies of belief. Ought women be ordained to the various forms and orders of ministry within the church? Can and should LGBTQI+ people be welcomed into the fullness of the church's life, in both its worshipping and its ministering activities? More recently, equally acrimonious fault lines within the church have emerged, particularly but not only in North America, around the issue of Christian nationalism. Does Christianity allow, or indeed mandate, the adoption of a particular attitude towards race and ethnicity or in favour of one form of political structuring over against all others?

Such contests have been fierce and in certain places have been enacted with the rhetorical force of enmity, schism, and damnation. That is, these battles have been waged as though they involve ultimate issues. The boundary transgressions that have been presumed to have occurred have thus made friends into enemies, and those who used to be "us" into those who are now reviled as "them." This should hardly be surprising. Gil Anidjar reminds us that both Cicero and Augustine recognised that "it is in the proximate (the human, the friend)" that the enemy is to be located.[35] As just one example, the Kigali Commitment, issued in April 2023

35. See Cicero, *In verrem*, ii.I.15; Augustine, *City of God*, volume VI: Books 18.36–20, trans. William Chase Greene, Loeb Classical Library 416 (Cambridge: Harvard University Press, 1960),

by the fourth Global Anglican Futures Conference (GAFCON), declared the right interpretation of legitimate sexual activity to be a salvation issue and that those—particularly within the Anglican Communion—who were advocating alternative interpretations (primarily around same-sex unions, and the blessing thereof) to be those who "walk in darkness," with whom no Christian fellowship was possible.[36] Or in a more overtly political register, one might think of Robert Jeffress, of First Baptist Dallas, who in September 2016, during the lead-up to the presidential election of that year, said this: 'This election is not a battle between Republicans and Democrats. It's a battle between good and evil, light and darkness, righteousness and unrighteousness."[37] In both sets of instances, sexual ethics and political allegiance have been figured as boundaries of ultimate theological concern, the transgression of which necessarily renders the transgressor not just mistaken, but "enmified." To quote Mahmood Mamdani, who comments on such issues in a different context, "Polarized identities [have been created] where you must be either one or the other. You cannot partake of both. . . . It sustains no ambiguity."[38]

What is at issue in these and other crises currently attending the church is less the rights and wrongs of any particular side and more the way the "polarized identities" of which Mamdani speaks have been parsed in salvifically ultimate ways to render the erstwhile friend, who used to be one of "us," into the irredeemable enemy, who can now only ever be part of the reprobated "them." Whereas Augustine, in his sermon on Matthew 13, allows that by the grace of God the tares in the field may tomorrow be wheat,[39] in far too many of our current debates the divisions that have been drawn between friends and enemies are presumed now to be irretrievably absolute. Importantly, such enemies are not only ours but are also—and primarily—God's. Indeed, they are only our enemies to the

---

19.5, 143. Gil Anidjar, *The Jew, The Arab: A History of the Enemy* (Stanford: Stanford University Press, 2003), 20.

36. https://www.gafcon.org/news/gafcon-iv-the-kigali-commitment. Note that the statement declares that 'Any refusal to follow the biblical teaching that the only appropriate context for sexual activity is the exclusive lifelong union of a man and a woman in marriage violates the created order (Genesis 2:24; Matthew 19:4–6) *and endangers salvation* (1 Corinthians 6:9),' emphasis added.

37. Robert Jeffress, cited in Alex Morris, "False Idol—Why the Christian Right Worships Donald Trump," in *Rolling Stone* (December 2019), https://www.rollingstone.com/politics/politics-features/christian-right-worships-donald-trump-915381/. John MacArthur made a similar comment to Donald Trump in 2020, to the effect that 'Any real, true believer is going to be on your side in this election,' quoted in Congdon, *Who is a True Christian?*, xi.

38. Mahmood Mamdani, *When Victims Become Killers: Colonialism, Nativism, and the Genocide in Rwanda* (Princeton: Princeton University Press, 2001), 23.

39. Augustine, Sermon 23, in *Nicene and Post-Nicene Fathers* I.6, ed. Philip Schaff (Edinburgh: T&T Clark, 1887), 335.

extent that we characterise them as being, in the first instance, opposed to God, who can thereby in justice also only oppose *them*. Having drawn the boundaries in *plastic* ways, the norming (and thus normative) community thus paradoxically defines the transgressors in a particularly immutable relation to God. Ecclesiologically, the consequences are disastrous. As Eugene Schlesinger notes in his recent book *Ruptured Bodies*, a divided church has no way of authentic discernment on any controversial question. We are, he says, "stymied . . . so long as the full complement of the *catholica* is not part of the deliberations."[40]

IV

It is here that Bonhoeffer's 1936 paper, "The Question of Church Communion," returns to relevance, for in that place—notwithstanding that it was here that he reiterated the Cyprianic *extra ecclesiam* in favour of the *Bekennende Kirche*—he accepted unreservedly the reality of heresy even within the true church. And he did so, not as a simple Augustinian recognition of the church's partially "tarish" composition but as an acknowledgment that, *precisely as* the true church, we exist in guilty solidarity with those with whom we would rather not be. In the context of the peculiar crisis that engulfed German Protestantism in the early to mid-1930s, Bonhoeffer noted that—remarkably—the Lutheran and Reformed churches had drawn closer together as a consequence of their mutual opposition to the *Deutsche Christen*. In forming a joint Confessing synod, the two traditions had "decisively left the Augsburg Confession behind." The differences between the Lutheran and Reformed churches, reified through their "formerly schismatic creedal antitheses," were now no longer sufficient, claimed Bonhoeffer, to prevent (an admittedly noneucharistic) unity.[41] The irony, Bonhoeffer observed, was that precisely the criterion that was, through its "rigorous application," compelling a break with the German Christians—what Bonhoeffer calls the "doctrinal principle"—was the very same principle that was being *neglected* (*Vernachlässigung*) so as to allow a communion between the Lutherans and the Reformed. There was nothing in principle, he noted, that might *a priori* prevent a similar neglect of that doctrinal principle so as to "create a common

40. Eugene Schlesinger, *Ruptured Bodies: A Theology of the Church Divided* (Minneapolis: Fortress, 2024), xix.

41. Bonhoeffer, "On the Question of Church Communion," 668–69, emphasis added.

foundation [even] for the German Christians."[42] To put it otherwise, insofar as this application and this neglect are consequent upon ecclesial *decisions* (*Entscheidung*) rather than being in any sense fixed, Bonhoeffer here acknowledges what we have referred to as the "plasticity" of ecclesial boundaries, such that what might be deemed an intolerable schismatic heresy when seen in one context is understood to be a tolerable nonschismatic difference when seen in another, even though the same doctrinal theological error is operative in both.[43]

What accounts for the difference? What, that is to say, outlaws a person or a group of people as enemy, as a "them," for and with whom both God and therefore the "us" *cannot be* in one context, but figures them as merely a mistaken part of the "us" with whom God and we *can still be* in another context? According to Bonhoeffer, the decisive matter is not doctrine but posture. Does the person, movement, or ideology in which error has been discerned stand with hostile intent towards the true church, wishing to fight and even destroy it? Or does the person, movement, or ideology in which error has been discerned stand with no such hostile posture, no such intent to declare itself the only location of ecclesial and salvific truth? In the first, says Bonhoeffer, there is occasioned "a struggle of life and death. Here there can be no talk of communion. Here the true church recognizes the Antichrist." In the second, however, there is simply a witness to the disunity that has been ever-present within the visible church, in which the true church stands side by side with its erring partner "in a shared confession of guilt."[44] In such an environment, there may be disagreement; there may even be the presence of both truth *and error*, orthodoxy *and heresy*. But there can also be, suggests Bonhoeffer, a toleration built on a mutually acknowledged love for the church, such that, even when doctrinal boundaries are transgressed, enemies are not made.[45]

---

42. Bonhoeffer, "On the Question of Church Communion," 670.
43. Bonhoeffer, "On the Question of Church Communion," 665.
44. Bonhoeffer, "On the Question of Church Communion," 666.
45. To be clear, I am not thereby wanting to suggest that those more conservative parts of the church that believe no communion can be had with those Christians who are more progressive on moral questions, are themselves representative of hostility to the true church by virtue of declaring themselves to be the only sites of salvation, and are thus to be identified with the Antichrist. It is clear that they have the weight of tradition, in both theological and ethical teaching, behind them. On the other hand, if the more progressive parts of the church—in which certain ethical and theological novelties have arisen—were to demand that only they represent the site of salvation, then and there it could be claimed that we see a posture of hostility, and thus a figure of the Antichrist. I have in mind here both Irenaeus and Tertullian, for whom *novelty* is an indication of error. See Irenaeus, *Against Heresies*, 1.10.1–3; Tertullian, *Prescription Against Heretics*, 30–33.

V

Taken together, this strange pairing of Dietrich Bonhoeffer and Gil Anidjar suggests for us that ecclesial "enmifying"—the figuring of a person, group, or ideological movement as an "outlaw" to the church, and thus both the subjective opponent of God and the objective target of God's opposition—is neither necessary nor static. Anidjar has demonstrated that the determination of the enemy, the "them," is, if not entirely arbitrary, at least such that the identification of the "them" could have been made differently.[46] Bonhoeffer, for his part, allows us to conceive of possibilities wherein even those with whom we vehemently disagree, even at decisive doctrinal moments, need not be figured as *extraecclesial* enemies, who stand outside the scope of salvation, but as errant members of the true church, with whom we can and should stand in solidarity—the one criterion being their posture of amity or hostility towards the true church. There remains, though, the question of what we ought to make of the inimical "them"—better, what we think *God* makes of them—and how that consideration informs our conception of the church. To answer this, let me speak briefly to the contributions made in this regard by Augustine and by Thomas Aquinas—both as mediated through Gil Anidjar.

Anidjar notes that for Augustine, that great rhetorician of war—for what else is *The City of God* but a treatise on and against those who oppose God?[47]—love of the enemy is subsumed, together with love of self and neighbour, under the one goal of love for God. Or as he writes in his *On Christian Doctrine* (which of course was written *before City of God*), "No sinner, *qua* sinner, should be loved; every human being, *qua* human being, should be loved on God's account. . . . All people should be loved equally."[48] Thus, distinctions between friends and enemies are affirmed but only in their inconsequentiality. The enemy is rendered ironically *absent*.[49] While this absenting of the enemy, the "them," has an attractiveness about it, it fails to account for the ecclesiological reality with which we now face and always have faced, and Augustine's constructive utility for

46. Church, and perhaps especially conciliar history, amply supports Anidjar's claim. One need only think, for example, of the multiple times that the hero of Nicaea, Athanasius of Alexandria, was deposed and exiled *subsequent* to Nicaea. That his depositions and exiles were largely politically motivated, or directed against his behaviours rather than his beliefs, does not alter the fact that he was routinely formally condemned by those who held opposing views.

47. "Burning with the zeal of God's house, I decided to write against [the pagans'] blasphemies and errors. . . . It is my purpose to defend the City of God against those who esteem their own gods above her Founder." Augustine, *City of God* 1, retractions, 3–5.

48. Augustine, *On Christian Teaching*, trans. R. P. H. Green (Oxford: Oxford University Press, 1997), 1.27–28, 21.

49. Anidjar, *The Jew, The Arab*, 19, 21–22.

this project is correspondingly reduced. The same, however, is not quite the case for Thomas Aquinas. In question 25 of the Secunda Secundae of the *Summa Theologica*, in which he discusses the question whether charity demands that Christians love their enemies (*inimicos*), Aquinas engages with Aristotle's conception of friendship, as set forth in the *Nicomachean Ethics*. There, he argues that charity is "friendship with God."[50] In an odd way, it is precisely because of this that our enemies are owed our love. Why? Aquinas says because our love for our friend—in this case, God—extends also to whatever belongs to him (for example, slaves, children), "even if they [the 'belongings'] offend us."[51] Thus, insofar as those who are the enemies of God (and are therefore also our own enemies) *belong to* God, we owe them our love, because of our love in friendship that we have with and for God.[52]

Naturally, Aquinas (like Augustine) repudiates the suggestion that our enemies should be loved in and for their enmity—this is "perverse" for it would imply "love of that which is evil."[53] Nevertheless, he does argue that our enemies should be loved "as to their nature, but in general," by which he means that it is only their enmity that renders them our contrary and not their essentiality as humans and thus as neighbours.[54] As Anidjar notes, Aquinas has here introduced the metaphysical distinction between accident and substance into the concept of the enemy. Unlike in Augustine, the enemy, the "them," is still noticeably present, but the quality that renders them "enmified" is accidental not substantial; the enemy's "themness" is not dissolved into inconsequentiality but is nevertheless not essential but contingent. For Aquinas, writes Anidjar, "The enemy may also be other than the enemy. . . . Being the enemy is therefore not natural, nor does it signal an essential difference between the one who loves and the enemy [who is loved]."[55] The distinctions between neighbour, enemy, and God that are dissolved in Augustine are thus "reactivated" by Aquinas. Anidjar argues that this reactivation of enmity renders the enemy someone it is impossible to love as such.[56] But in fact, Aquinas also recognises the contingency of the enmity, which is the very thing that

50. Guy Mansini, "Aristotle and Aquinas's Theology of Charity," in *Aristotle in Aquinas's Theology*, ed. Gilles Emery and Matthew Levering (Oxford: Oxford University Press, 2015), 125.

51. Thomas Aquinas, *Summa theologica*, trans. Fathers of the English Dominican Province (New York: Benziger Brothers, 1947), II-II.25.8.

52. Mansini, "Aristotle and Aquinas's Theology of Charity," 127, 131–32.

53. Aquinas, *Summa theologica*, II-II.25.8.

54. Aquinas, *Summa theologica*, II-II.25.8.

55. Anidjar, *The Jew, The Arab*, 24–25.

56. Anidjar, *The Jew, The Arab*, 26–28.

makes it possible to love them—not *as* enemy, not *as* the "them," but as someone who *exceeds* that determination.[57]

Aquinas's distinction accords with what we have observed of earlier Christian history—including but not least the Nicene debates—insofar as enmity is understood to be something that could have been different; the boundaries that are transgressed, and by which enmities are formed, are not as fixed as we have often been tempted to presume. It also aligns neatly with Bonhoeffer's recognition that a determination of the ultimacy of enmity can be deferred and is in any case not the church's determination to make. If both these things are the case, then we are able to return to the dogmatic question with which this paper is in fact concerned: Does God's being include a pro nobic or promeic aspect that implies also a separate group of people for whom God is in fact *not*? Is there, in other words, a *contra-tatem* within God's being with respect to a certain set of humankind that is as proper to him as his pro nobity? The argument of this paper is, at least from the perspective of ecclesiology, a resounding no. On the contrary, theologically the church has no basis on which to presume the fixity of God's opposition to any arbitrary "them" who may be conceived but must hold open the possibility that even those against whom—but, with Bonhoeffer, also *with* whom—we stand, are equally embraced by God's *for*. God's *promeity* is also his *illis*. To be for "us" means that God is also for the "them'" whom *we* produce.

57. Gregory of Nyssa makes much the same point, when he writes: "It is not that a human being is an enemy of other human beings, but that the evil movement of free will has set as enemy that wickedness which is joined to human nature." The enemy, that is to say, is the "evil movement" of the human will and not the human subject of that will as such who is thereby always separable from that which is the true location of enmity. See Gregory of Nyssa, "Discourse 1: The Nature of Prayer," trans. G. Stylianopoulos, https://www.orthodoxprayer.org/Articles_files/GregoryNyssa-Homily1 Lords Prayer.html.

SUBJECT INDEX

SCRIPTURE INDEX

2 Corinthians

Galatians

Ephesians

Philippians

Colossians

1 Thessalonians

1 Timothy

2 Timothy

Hebrews

1 John

Revelation

AUTHOR INDEX